Facebook®
for Grown-Ups

Michael Miller

Facebook® for Grown-Ups

Copyright © 2011 by Pearson Education, Inc.

ISBN-13: 978-0-7897-4712-9
ISBN-10: 0-7897-4712-X

Library of Congress Cataloging-in-Publication Data
Miller, Michael, 1958-
  Facebook for grown-ups / Michael Miller.
      p. cm.
  Includes index.
  ISBN 978-0-7897-4712-9
  1. Facebook (Electronic resource) 2. Online social networks. 3. Social networks--Computer network resources. I. Title.

  HM742.M55 2011
  006.7'54--dc22

                                    2010035622

Printed in the United States on America

First Printing: October 2010

Trademarks

Warning and Disclaimer

Bulk Sales

Que Publishing offers excellent discounts on this book when ordered in quantity for bulk purchases or special sales. For more information, please contact

> U.S. Corporate and Government Sales
> 1-800-382-3419
> corpsales@pearsontechgroup.com

For sales outside of the U.S., please contact

> International Sales
> international@pearsoned.com

Associate Publisher
Greg Wiegand

Acquisitions Editor
Michelle Newcomb

Development Editor
The Wordsmithery

Technical Editor
Vince Averello

Managing Editor
Kristy Hart

Project Editor
Andy Beaster

Indexer
Cheryl Lenser

Proofreader
Jennifer Gallant

Publishing Coordinator
Cindy Teeters

Cover Designer
Anne Jones

Compositor
Bronkella Publishing

Contents at a Glance

iv

Table of Contents

About the Author

Michael Miller has written more than 100 non-fiction how-to books in the past two decades, including Que's *Absolute Beginner's Guide to Computer Basics, Googlepedia: The Ultimate Google Resource,* and *Windows 7 Your Way*. He is also the author of Que's *Facebook Essentials* video and Pearson Higher Education's *Introduction to Social Networking* textbook.

Mr. Miller has established a reputation for clearly explaining technical topics to non-technical readers, and for offering useful real-world advice about complicated topics. More information can be found at the author's website, located at www.molehillgroup.com.

Dedication

To Sherry, we're not getting older—we're getting better.

Acknowledgments

Thanks to the usual suspects at Que Publishing, including but not limited to Greg Wiegand, Michelle Newcomb, Charlotte Kughen, Andy Beaster, and technical editor Vince Averello. And, of course, to all my Facebook friends—whether I actually know you or not.

We Want to Hear from You!

As the reader of this book, *you* are our most important critic and commentator. We value your opinion and want to know what we're doing right, what we could do better, what areas you'd like to see us publish in, and any other words of wisdom you're willing to pass our way.

As an associate publisher for Que Publishing, I welcome your comments. You can email or write me directly to let me know what you did or didn't like about this book—as well as what we can do to make our books better.

Please note that I cannot help you with technical problems related to the topic of this book. We do have a User Services group, however, where I will forward specific technical questions related to the book.

When you write, please be sure to include this book's title and author as well as your name, email address, and phone number. I will carefully review your comments and share them with the author and editors who worked on the book.

Email: feedback@quepublishing.com

Mail: Greg Wiegand
        Associate Publisher
        Que Publishing
        800 East 96th Street
        Indianapolis, IN 46240 USA

Reader Services

Visit our website and register this book at www.quepublishing.com/register for convenient access to any updates, downloads, or errata that might be available for this book.

Introduction

A confession:

I'm not as young as I used to be.

Back in the day, I used to be known as a young Turk, a whiz kid, a young man with potential. But I'm no longer Turkish, don't have a lot of whiz left, and long ago gave up on realizing that potential thing. I got older.

Somewhere along the line I acquired a big house and a bigger mortgage, got married (to my high school sweetheart), and inherited kids (well, stepkids) and grandkids (also stepped). I look at what all the younger people in my household are doing, and realize that I'm not doing anything remotely like that anymore. I'm an old guy kind of set in his ways—including the way I use technology.

Now, I write a lot of books about technology. To some degree, how a 50 year old person uses Windows is pretty much the same as how a 20 year-old person does; Windows is Windows, after all. I get by.

But there's this new thing called social networking. It's technology related, because you have to use your computer (or, in the case of the youngsters, your cell phone) to do it. And from what I've seen, how the young people use social networking is quite a bit different from how my wife and I do it. There's a definite generational difference here.

Which is where this book comes in. *Facebook for Grown-Ups* focuses on the biggest and most happening social networking site, Facebook, and how people of our generation are using it. Trust me, we don't use Facebook the same way our kids do. It's a different experience for us, and one that has to be learned.

Did you know, for example, that you can use Facebook to keep in touch with all your family members—including distant relatives? Or that you can find long-lost friends on the Facebook site—including that cute guy you had a crush on back in high school? Or that you can share your family photos with these friends and relatives? And keep them updated on what you're up to these days?

That's right, grown-ups use Facebook to get connected with the people we know today, as well as those we knew in years gone by. We also use Facebook to keep tabs on our kids, to drop them a note from time to time, and to see what mischief they're getting themselves into. (And they are getting themselves into mischief, trust me.)

The key is figuring out how to find all the people you want to find, and to share all the information you want to share—without sharing *too much* personal information about yourself. There's a bit of a trick to doing the social networking thing while still maintaining a semblance of privacy online.

I try to cover all that in this book. My focus is on using Facebook, yes, but as responsible adults—not as carefree kids. Because, let's face it, we haven't been carefree kids for quite some time now. Sad, I know, but true.

How This Book Is Organized

If I did my job right, *Facebook for Grown-Ups* should be a relatively quick but useful read. It contains a lot of information about Facebook's various and sundry features, with an emphasis on how us grown-ups use those features.

To make things a little easier to grasp, this book is organized into six main parts, each focused on a particular major topic:

- **Part I, "Getting Started with Facebook—and Social Networking,"** provides an introduction to this whole social networking thing, and helps you sign up for Facebook and find your way around the site.

- **Part II, "Facebook for Friends and Family,"** is all about finding and communicating with family members and friends on the Facebook site. You learn how to get back in touch with old friends (including that cute high school crush) and how make new ones online. You even learn how to use Facebook to keep tabs (or spy) on your kids. Really.

- **Part III, "Keeping in Touch with Facebook,"** is about the many ways to communicate with your friends and family. You learn how to post pubic status updates, exchange private messages, and even chat in real time— which may be the only way to get face time with your kids.

- **Part IV, "Sharing Your Life on Facebook,"** is about all the things you can share with your friends and family on Facebook. You learn how to share photos, home movies, even birthdays and other important events.

- **Part V, "Doing More with Facebook,"** covers some slightly more advanced things you might want to do, including personalizing your Profile page, becoming a "fan" of a performer or company, participating in topic-oriented groups, using Facebook for business networking and job hunting, using Facebook applications and games, accessing Facebook from your mobile phone, and buying and selling merchandise in the Facebook Marketplace.

- **Part VI, "Basic Facebook Housekeeping Chores,"** shows you how to manage your Facebook account—and configure all those privacy settings to keep your personal information private.

Although I recommend reading the book in consecutive order, you don't have to. Read it in chapter order if you want (I think it flows fairly well as written), or read just those chapters that interest you. It's okay either way.

Conventions Used in This Book

I hope that this book is easy enough to figure out on its own, without requiring its own instruction manual. As you read through the pages, however, it helps to know precisely how I've presented specific types of information.

As you read through this book you'll note several special elements, presented in what we in the publishing business call "margin notes." There are different types of margin notes for different types of information, as you see here.

Beyond the main text, I end each chapter with a kind of sidebar observation. These sections aren't necessarily factual, as the rest of the text is supposed to be; they're more opinion, looking at Facebook from my personal viewpoint. Take 'em or leave 'em; that's up to you.

One more thing. Facebook is a website, and websites seem to change the way they look and act on a fairly frequent yet unpredictable basis. (In Facebook's case, they changed their privacy features about a half-dozen times *while I was writing the chapter about privacy*. Thanks a lot, Facebook.) That means that what I describe in these pages might look or act a little different by the time you get around to reading it. So if I talk about a particular button that is now a link located somewhere else on the page, try to be understanding. You still should be able to figure things out.

Get Ready to Facebook

Now that you know how to use this book, it's time to get to the heart of the matter. But when you're ready to take a break from marveling at how old your friends look in their Facebook profiles, browse over to my personal website, located at www.molehillgroup.com. Here you can find more information on this book and other books I've written—including any necessary corrections and clarifications, in the inevitable event that an error or two creeps into this text. (Hey, nobody's perfect!)

In addition, know that I love to hear from readers of my books. If you want to contact me, feel free to email me at facebook4grownups@molehillgroup.com. I can't promise that I'll answer every message, but I do promise that I'll read each one!

But enough with the preliminaries. You want to find out what this Facebook thing is all about? Then turn the page, and start Facebooking!

Note

This is a note that presents some interesting information, even if it isn't wholly relevant to the discussion in the main text.

Tip

This is a tip that might prove useful for whatever it is you're in the process of doing.

! Caution

This is a warning that something you might accidentally do might have undesirable results—so take care!

Getting Started with Facebook—and Social Networking

Chapter 1

Welcome to Facebook: It's Not Just for Kids Anymore

Facebook is where all the young people hang out online.

Now, I know you're only as young as you feel, but if you're reading a book called *Facebook for Grown-Ups*, you're probably a tad past your school years. In other words, you're not that young anymore. So why should *you* care about Facebook?

There's a simple answer to that question. No matter what your age, Facebook and other social networks help you keep in touch with family, friends, and co-workers. Chances are you'll find lots of friends already on the site—including, it would be fair to wager, all of your children, nieces and nephews, and grandchildren, if you have them.

So if you want to keep in touch with (or keep tabs on) your kids, Facebook is the place to do it. Facebook is also a great place to catch up with old friends, even (and especially) those you haven't seen since you all were a lot younger than you are today. You see, Facebook isn't just for younger users; it's for anyone wanting to keep in touch with anyone else.

What Social Networking Is and How It Works

Let's not get ahead of ourselves. Before we get into what Facebook is and what it does, let's take a look at the whole social networking phenomenon. That's what Facebook is, after all—a *social network*. (And not just any old social network; Facebook is the world's largest social network. That's why everybody uses it.)

What Is a Social Network?

A social network is a large website that hosts a community of users, and makes it easy for those users to communicate with one another. Social networks enable users to share experiences and opinions with one another via *status updates,* short text messages that are posted for public viewing by all of that person's friends on the site.

There are lots of social networks out there on the Web. Some, such as LinkedIn or Flixster, are devoted to a particular topic or community. Others, such as Facebook and MySpace, are more broad-based. These general social networks make it easy for communities devoted to specific topics to develop within the overall site.

Why Do People Use Social Networks?

Okay, that's a fairly academic description of what a social network is. But what does a social network do—or, more concisely, why do people use a social network?

To my mind, social networks are all about communicating, staying in touch with one another. It's the 21st-century way to let people know what you're up to—and to find out what everyone else is up to, too.

In the old, old days, the only way you found out about what was going on was for someone to write you a letter. That probably sounds quaint today, as letter writing is somewhat out of fashion. But I'm guessing you're old enough to have written a few letters in your time, or at least to have seen your parents do so.

Ah, the joys of receiving a letter from an old friend! I miss seeing a friend's address in the top left corner, opening the envelope, and savoring the words within. Of course, most friends didn't write that often; writing was a lot of work, so you saved up your thoughts and experiences until you had a full letter's worth. But, man, it was great to read what your friends had been doing. It almost made the wait worthwhile.

That was then and this is now. Today, nobody has the time or the patience or the attention span to write or read long letters. At some point, a decade or so ago, email replaced the written letter as our primary means of correspondence. That wasn't necessarily a bad thing; emails were shorter than written letters, but you got them immediately—and you could respond to them immediately, too. With the Internet age came this faster and more direct form of communication, and we adapted to it.

For young people today, however, email is old hat. It's too slow and takes too much time. (They'd never have tolerated the age of the written letter...) Instead, our attention deprived youth prefer immediate communication, via text messages and instant messages and such.

The problem with all these forms of communication is that they're not centralized. If you're text messaging with a dozen friends, that's a dozen different "feeds" of information you have to keep track of. Same thing with instant messaging; there's no central repository where you can read all your friends' messages in one place.

This is where social networking comes in. Instead of writing a dozen (or a hundred) different letters or emails to each of your friends telling them that you just bought a new dress (or car or house or whatever), you make a single post that then those dozen (or hundred) different people can read. Something happens, you write about it, it gets posted on the social networking site, and everyone you know reads about it. It takes all the work out of keeping your friends up-to-date on what you're doing.

Of course, it works in the other direction, too. Instead of waiting for letters or emails or text messages from each of your friends, you just log onto the social networking site. There you find a feed of updates from everyone you know. Read the feed and you're instantly updated on what everyone is up to. That makes it really easy to keep in touch.

Now, social networking lets you do a lot more than just exchange status updates, but that's the most common activity and the reason most of us do the social networking thing. Communications to and from all your friends, all in one place, all done in your Web browser from your personal computer. (Or, if you're a mobile kind of person, from your cell phone.) It's like communications central for everyone you know—close friends or otherwise.

What Other Stuff Does a Social Network Do?

I just mentioned that social networking offers more than simple status updates. What is all that other stuff? Here's a short list:

- **Private communications.** This can take the form of a built-in email system (that is, the email is contained within the social networking site; you don't need separate software to use it) or live instant messaging.

- **Groups and forums.** These are like online clubs built around specific areas of interest. You can find groups for hobbies like woodworking or quilting, for topics like politics or sports, for just about anything you can think of. There are even groups devoted to specific companies, schools, and even entertainers—these last being more like fan clubs than anything else.

- **Photo and video sharing.** That's right, most social networks let you upload your pictures and movies and share them with all your friends on the network.

- **Games and applications.** If you have too much free time on your hands, most social networks include fun games you can play, as well as other applications and utilities that add functionality to the site. (For example, Facebook offers apps that help you track family members, organize your book and music libraries, and such.)

- **Marketplace.** Get enough people congregated on a single website, and there's a lot of things those people can do together—including buy and sell things. Many social networks offer online marketplaces, similar to Craigslist classifieds, so that you can find out what other members have for sale—or are interested in buying.

There's a bit more than even all this, including event scheduling and the like, but you get the general idea. A social network is an online community, and offers many of the same activities that you'd find in a real-world community.

Who Uses Social Networks?

With all that social networks have to offer, it's not surprising that so many people use them day in and day out. As with many new technologies, social networks started out as a thing used by college students. (That's how the Internet itself took off, after all.) But over time social networking spread from the young generation into the general public, including old farts like you and me.

Today, the audience for social networking is rapidly evolving. In fact, the fastest-growing demographic on the Facebook site are those of us 45 years or older. (Take that, you young whippersnappers!)

In practice, then, social networks are home to all sorts of users, including:

- Friends and family members who want to keep in touch
- People looking for long-lost friends
- Business colleagues who use the site for collaboration and networking
- Singles who want to meet and match up with other singles
- Hobbyists looking for others who share their interests
- Classmates who need study partners and homework advice
- Musicians, actors, and celebrities connecting with their fans

And, of course, college and high school students. (That's until they move onto the next big thing, of course.)

How Did Social Networks Develop?

Interestingly, today's social networks evolved from the earliest dial-up computer networks, bulletin board systems (BBSs), and other online discussion forums. That's right, Facebook and MySpace are only a few steps removed from CompuServe, Prodigy, and The WELL. (I assume you're old enough to remember some of these services—including the original America Online.)

These early proto-communities, most of which predated the formal Internet in the 1970s and 1980s, offered topic-based discussion forums and chat rooms, just like Facebook does today. What they didn't offer was a way to follow friends on the site, or to publicly share status updates. But the seeds of social networking were there.

Other components of social networking developed after the rise of the public Internet. For example, topic-based website communities, like iVillage, Epicurious, and Classmates.com, arose in the mid-1990s. Personal blogs, which let users post short articles of information and opinion, emerged around the year 2000. And photo-sharing sites, such as Flickr and Photobucket, became a part of the Internet landscape in the early 2000s.

The first site to combine all of these features was Friendster, in 2003. Friendster also introduced the concepts of "friends" and "friending" to the social Web; it all came from the name, not surprisingly.

Friendster enjoyed immediate popularity (more than 3 million users within the first few months of operations), but ran into technical problems associated with that growth and was soon surpassed by MySpace, which launched later the same year. MySpace became the most popular social networking site in June 2006, and remained the top social network for almost two years.

Say Hello to Facebook

The big dog in social networking was part of the second wave. It was 2004 when a site originally known as "Thefacebook" was introduced. What eventually became known as just "Facebook" was originally intended as a site where college students could socialize online. Sensing opportunity beyond the college market, however, Facebook opened its site to high school students in 2005, and to users of all ages (actually, users above the age of 13) in 2006.

This broadening in Facebook's user base led to a huge increase in both users and pageviews, with Facebook surpassing MySpace in April 2008. Facebook is currently the number-two site on the entire Internet, with more than 500 million users of all ages. That's a pretty big deal.

So if you want to social network today, Facebook is the place to do it. Facebook is a big honkin' Web community, a site that offers a lot of different ways to publicly and privately communicate with lots and lots of other people.

Chances are you already know a lot of folks who use Facebook. It goes without saying that your kids and their friends are all Facebook users; it's a rare youngster, indeed, who doesn't have Facebook as his or her browser

> ### Note
> The phrase "social network" can be either a noun or a verb. In practice, then, Facebook is a social network (noun) that lets you social network (verb) with your friends. Got it?

home page. But it's not just the younger generation. You'll also find neighbors, co-workers, friends, and older family members using the site.

What Facebook offers is a collection of user profile pages. Every user has his or own profile page, where they post their status updates, display their personal information, share photos and videos, and such. When you become a "friend" of a person, you get access to their profile page, and all that's on it. You have to ask people to be their friend; over time, you'll probably assemble a rather large list of such friends.

Figure 1.1.   *A typical Facebook personal profile page.*

Facebook also offers profile pages for groups. A group can be a charitable organization, a company, or just an online club revolving around a specific topic. Facebook has groups for cat lovers, chess players, gardeners, and the like. There are also groups (more like fan clubs) for musicians, comedians, actors, television shows, movies, and the like. As with personal profile pages, these group pages feature news about the topic at hand, photos, discussions, and such.

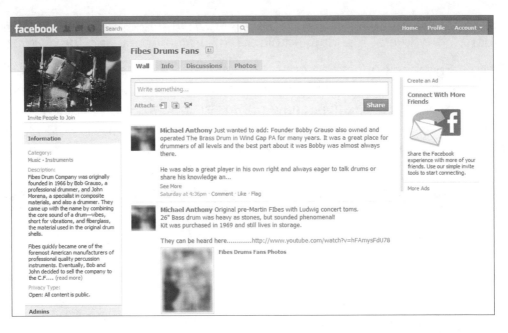

Figure 1.2. *A Facebook group page.*

News—called status updates—from your friends and the groups you join are displayed in a constantly flowing *news feed* that appears on your Facebook home page. Everything that everybody's doing is listed there; it's how you keep track of all you deem important.

As you'll learn in the next chapter, to use Facebook you have to join the site—become a member, as it were. Facebook membership and use is totally free; all you have to spend is your time.

Things You Can—and Can't—Do on Facebook

Okay, so Facebook is the most popular social network. What does that mean to you—and what can you use it for?

Things to Do

First off, you can use Facebook to let your friends and family know what you're up to. You do this in the form of status updates, short text messages that appear on both your home page and in the news feed that is displayed on your friends' home pages. It's easy to log on and post a short status update; you can even do it from your cell phone!

Next, you can use Facebook to view all your friends' status updates. As previously noted, all these updates are consolidated into a single news feed on your Facebook home page. Just open the www.facebook.com page, log in, and get updated on what all your friends are doing.

Figure 1.3. *The news feed on Facebook's home page—lots and lots of status updates from all your friends.*

You can also use Facebook to communicate privately with individual friends. Facebook offers a built-in email system for private messages, as well as real-time instant messaging (Facebook calls it "chat") with online friends. So not everything you do has to be public.

That said, you can also use Facebook to share photos and videos. Just upload the files you want to share and they're displayed on a tab on your profile page. New photos and videos you upload are also displayed as status updates, so your friends receive notice of them in their news feeds.

Facebook also offers a way to announce and track important events, such as parties and gatherings, as well as invite your friends to these events. Of course, you can join any group you find interesting on the site, as well as play games, buy and sell merchandise, and do all sorts of other fun and marginally useful stuff. It's a fairly robust website, after all—a real community online.

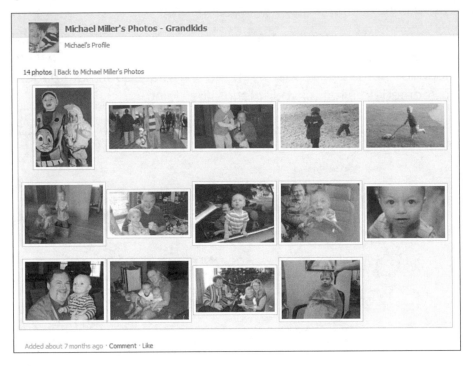

Figure 1.4. *A personal photo album, open for sharing on Facebook.*

Things *Not* to Do

With all the things you can do on Facebook, what sorts of things *shouldn't* you do? That is, what sorts of things is Facebook just not that suited for?

First off, you have to remember that communicating with people via Facebook is no substitute for face-to-face communication. Those short little status updates you make can't convey the same information as a longer letter, or the emotion of a telephone conversation. Facebook communication is, at best, a kind of shorthand. When you really want to discuss something in depth, you need to do it in person, not on Facebook.

Then there's the whole issue of what constitutes a friend. A person you call a "friend" on Facebook might not be someone you'd even recognize if you ran into them in the grocery store. It's easy to deceive yourself into thinking you're immensely popular because you have a long friends list, but these folks aren't really friends; they're just people you broadcast to online. They're more like an audience than anything else.

This leads to the issue of whether online social networking is an effective replacement for real-world communication. You may be "talking" to more so-called friends online, but you may actually be talking to fewer real friends in the real world. Physical relationships could suffer if you spend too much time communicating virtually on Facebook; it's a false sort of familiarity that results.

And when you have hundreds of people on your Facebook friends list, how well do you really know any of them? It's possible if not likely that some of the people you call "friends" really aren't the people they present themselves to be. For whatever reason, some people adopt different personas— including fake names and profile pictures—when they're online; it's possible that you're establishing relationships on Facebook that have no basis in reality—which could result in online stalking or worse.

Bottom line, you shouldn't let Facebook replace your real-world friendships. It can supplement your friendships, make some general communication easier, and even help you renew old acquaintances, but it can never replace a good conversation with an old friend. That sort of connection is—and will always be—priceless.

Why Grown-Ups Use Facebook

Many people use social networks such as Facebook as a kind of container for all their online activities. I like to think of Facebook as an operating system. This is particularly the case with teenagers and college kids, who have Facebook open in their browsers all day long. They do almost everything from within Facebook—read status updates, send and receive emails, instant message with other users, share photos and videos, you name it. They never exit the site; it's as constant for them as is Windows.

Older users, however, tend not to be as Facebook-centric as the young'uns are. I don't know of too many people my age who are on Facebook 24/7, like their kids. We might check into Facebook a few times a day, but it doesn't monopolize our lives. Or at least it shouldn't.

Instead, grown-ups use Facebook on a more occasional basis to keep tabs on what friends and family members are up to. We tend not to be as addicted to Facebook as our kids are; we don't have to know what everyone is doing on a minute-by-minute basis. Instead, we can log in once or maybe twice a day and get the general drift of everyone's activities. That's enough information for most of us.

Grown-ups also use Facebook to reconnect with people we haven't seen in a while. A long while, sometimes. Personally, I use Facebook to hook up with old friends from high school and college, and to reconnect with former colleagues and those I might want to work with again. I guarantee you'll find people on Facebook that you haven't thought about for a long time. (Which may not always be a good thing, I suppose…)

Facebook is also a great place for family members—especially extended families—to keep abreast of comings and goings. It might take a lot of effort to write your cousins and aunts and uncles and nieces and nephews and stepchildren and in-laws and all the rest, but a single Facebook status update will do the job of multiple letters and emails. You can also use Facebook to share family photos with the rest of your family, which is tons easier than printing and mailing photos manually.

Speaking of family members, Facebook is a great way to spy on your kids. I don't mean that in a bad way, of course (or do I?); I mean that Facebook lets you see what your children are up to without them actually having to have a conversation with you about it. All you have to do is add your kids to your friends list, and you'll see all their status updates in your Facebook news feed. (That's unless they adjust their privacy settings to exclude you from their most private thoughts, which if they're smart they'll do.)

Of course, there are plenty of ways for adult users to waste time on Facebook, just as our kids do. I know a fair number of supposed grown-ups who get addicted to Farmville and Mafia Wars and other social games, and spend way too much time playing them. So useless Facebook activity isn't the sole province of the young; us oldsters can also spend hours doing essentially nothing useful online.

Bottom line, grown-ups use Facebook for many of the same reasons as younger folks do, but in a smarter and less intrusive fashion. Or so we'd like to think, anyway.

Social Networking Do's and Don'ts

When it comes to using Facebook and other social networks, there are some general guidelines you should adhere to. These guidelines will help you better fit into the community—and protect yourself from any inherent dangers.

Do These Things

In general, a social network like Facebook requires your active participation. Logging in once a month won't do it; that's not near social enough.

If you want to become a Facebook member in good standing, then, follow these tips:

- **Post frequently—but not too frequently.** A social network is a community, and to be a member of that community you have to actively participate in that community. If you wait too long between posts, people will forget that you're there. Conversely, if you post too frequently, that might be perceived as overbearing or annoying. The best frequency is somewhere between once a week and a few times per day—for grown-ups, once every day or two is probably good.

- **Keep your posts short and sweet.** People don't want or expect to read overly long musings on Facebook. Instead, they tend to graze, absorbing the gist of what's posted rather than reading entire missives. On a site like Facebook, that means keeping your posts to no more than a few sentences. If you want to pontificate in more detail, get yourself a blog.

- **Use proper spelling.** While you don't have to use complete and proper grammar and punctuation (see the next tip), blatant misspellings can mark you as less informed than you might actually be. Take the time to spell things correctly; it's literally the least you can do.

- **Take shortcuts.** While you should always use proper spelling, you don't have to use full sentences when posting to a social network. In fact, it's okay to use common abbreviations and acronyms, such as BTW (by the way) and LOL (laughing out loud). Casual is good.

- **Link to additional information.** You don't always have space to provide a lot of background information in a status update. Instead, you can link to Web pages or blog posts that offer more details.

- **Be discrete.** Remember, Facebook status updates are public, for all to read. Post only that information that you'd want your friends (or spouse or employer or children) to read.

- **Be cautious.** You don't have to be paranoid about it, but it helps to assume that there are some dangerous people out there. Don't do anything that would put you in harm's way.

Don't Do These Things

Building on that last tip, you should, in general, avoid posting personal information in any public forum, including Facebook. Here are some specific things you should *avoid* when using Facebook:

- **Don't accept every friend request you receive.** You don't have to have a thousand friends. It's better to have a smaller number of true friends than a larger number of people you really don't know.

- **Don't post if you don't have anything interesting to say.** Some of the most annoying people on Facebook are those that post their every action and movement. ("I just woke up." "I'm reading my mail." "I'm thinking about having lunch." "That coffee was delicious.") Post if there's something interesting happening, but avoid posting just to be posting. Think about what you like to read about other people, and post in a similar fashion.

- **Don't assume that everyone online will agree with you.** Some people use social networks like Facebook as a platform for their opinions. While it may be okay to share your opinions with close (i.e., non-Facebook) friends, spouting off in a public forum is not only bad form, it's a way to incite a flame war—an unnecessary online war of words.

- **Don't post anything that could possibly be used against you.** Want to put your job in jeopardy? Then by all means, you should post negative comments about your workplace or employer. And future employment may be denied if a potential employer doesn't like what he or she sees in your Facebook posts. (And they will be looking...) As in most things, with social networking it's better to be safe than sorry; avoid posting overly negative comments that are better kept private.

- **Don't post overly personal information.** Along the same lines, think twice before sharing the intimate details of your private life—including embarrassing photographs. Discretion is a value us older folks should maintain; there's no reason for posting pictures of you falling down drunk at the holiday office party, or baring it all on the beach during your last vacation. Leave some of the details to imagination.

- **Don't gripe.** Building on that last tip, the last thing I and lots of others want to find in our news feeds are your private gripes. Oh, it's okay to grouse and be grumpy from time to time, but don't use Facebook as your personal forum for petty grievances. If you have a personal problem, deal with it. You don't have to share *everything*, you know. Whining gets old really fast.

- **Don't post personal contact information.** As nice as Facebook is for renewing old acquaintances, it can also put you in contact with people you really don't want to be in contact with. So don't make it easy for disreputable people or unwanted old boyfriends to find you offline; avoid posting your phone number, email address, and home address.

- **Don't post your constant whereabouts.** You don't need to broadcast your every movement; thieves don't need to know when your house is empty. It's okay to post where you were after the fact, but keep your current whereabouts private.

In other words, don't post every little detail and thought about everything you do. Keep your private life private. And make public only the most general information that those distant acquaintances you call Facebook friends want or need to know.

Other Social Media

Social networking is just one form of what the digerati call *social media*. (Who are these digerati, by the way?) Social media encompasses all websites, services, and platforms that people use to share experiences and opinions with each other.

In practice, that covers everything from social networks like Facebook to social bookmarking services, where users share the sites and articles they like. It also includes blogs, microblogs, and other forms of online communities.

Okay, that's a lot of jargon to just throw out there, so I'll give you a bit of background.

A *social bookmarking service*, like Digg or Delicious, lets users share their favorite Web pages with friends and colleagues online. When you join one of these social bookmarking services, you visit a website, Web page, news article, or blog post that you like, then click a button or link to *bookmark* that site. This bookmark then appears in your master list of bookmarks on the social bookmarking service site; you can share any or all bookmarks with anyone you like.

A *blog* (short for "web log") is a shared online journal consisting of entries from the site's owner or creator. Bloggers create posts of varying length; some posts are just a sentence or two, others several paragraphs long; blog posts can include text, photos, and videos. Most blogs are focused on a specific topic, and some are almost journalistic in their execution. (Others read like personal diaries, so there's a bit of variety out there.)

A *microblogging service* essentially separates the status updates from everything else offered on a social network. Microblogs exist solely to distribute short text posts from individual users to groups of followers. These posts are similar to traditional blog posts but much shorter. The most popular microblogging service is Twitter, which lets you make posts (called *tweets*) of 140 characters or less—but that's all. No groups, no communities, no nothing else, just tweets.

Then we come to social networks, which offer pretty much everything you find in other social media, but all in one site. So while you can keep a separate blog, create social bookmarks, and microblog to your heart's content on Twitter, if you want to do it all in one place, a general social networking site, like Facebook, is the better deal.

Chapter 2

Signing Up and Getting Started

If you've gotten this far in the book I assume you think Facebook sounds like a pretty good deal. Now you just have to sign up to start using the site. What does that entail?

Before You Sign Up

Here are two nice things about using Facebook: It's easy and it's free. That's right, even though you have to create an account, it's a free account; you never pay Facebook anything to use the site. That's because Facebook, like most websites these days, is totally advertiser supported. So you'll see some ads after you get on the site, but won't be out a single penny.

What do you need to sign up? Not much, really. You need a working email address, a first and last name, and a birthdate. You'll also need to know your gender (I hope you already do) and come up with some sort of password you want to use. That's about it, really. Pretty simple.

Now, after you create your account, Facebook will prompt you to enter all sorts of personal information. This includes everything from your street address and phone number to which books and movies you like. Fortunately, none of this info is mandatory; you don't have to enter any of this if you don't want to. (In fact, I recommend you *don't* enter a lot of the overly personal information; it's best not to publicize your contact information, for example.)

So you don't need to do a lot of prep work before you sign up. Assuming that you have a name and an email address, you're now ready to go.

Creating a Facebook Account

As I said, just about anyone can create a free Facebook account. All you have to do is follow these steps:

1. Go to the Facebook home page at www.facebook.com, shown in Figure 2.1.

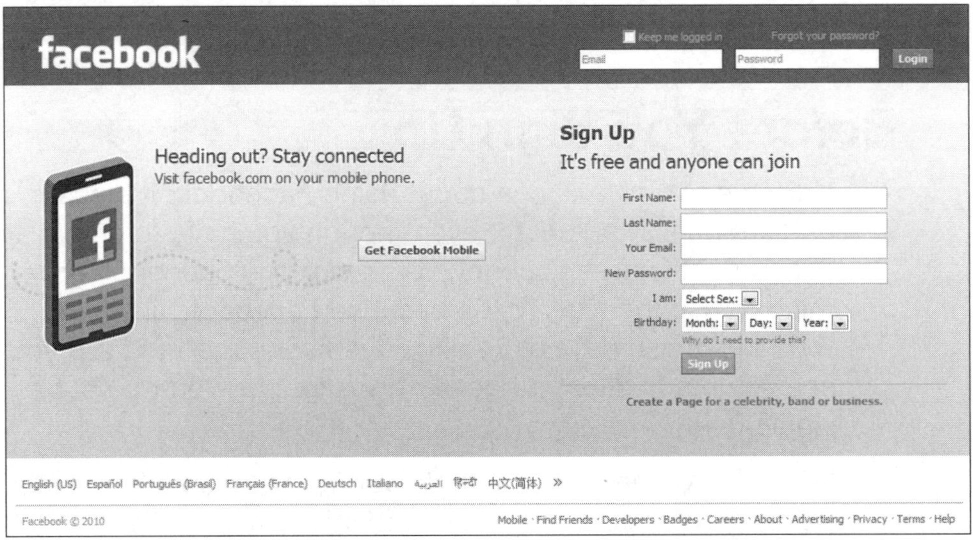

facebook

Keep me logged in   Forgot your password?

Email   Password   Login

Heading out? Stay connected
Visit facebook.com on your mobile phone.

Get Facebook Mobile

Sign Up
It's free and anyone can join

First Name:
Last Name:
Your Email:
New Password:
I am: Select Sex:
Birthday: Month: Day: Year:
Why do I need to provide this?

Sign Up

Create a Page for a celebrity, band or business.

English (US) Español Português (Brasil) Français (France) Deutsch Italiano العربية हिन्दी 中文(简体) »

Facebook © 2010   Mobile · Find Friends · Developers · Badges · Careers · About · Advertising · Privacy · Terms · Help

Figure 2.1. *Getting ready to create a new account from the Facebook home page.*

2. Enter your first name into the First Name box.

3. Enter your last name into the Last Name box.

4. Enter your email address into the Your Email box.

5. Enter your desired password into the New Password box. Your password should be at least six characters long.

Note

You'll use your email address to sign into Facebook each time you enter the site.

6. Select your gender from the I Am (Select Sex) list.

7. Select your date of birth from the Birthday (Month/Day/Year) list.

8. Click the Sign Up button.

9. When prompted to complete the Security Check page, enter the "secret words" from the *captcha* into the Text in the Box box, then click the Sign Up button on this page.

10. When you receive an email message asking you to confirm your new Facebook account, click the link in this email.

That's it—you now have a Facebook account. But Facebook isn't done with you quite yet. Read on to learn more.

Find Friends and Complete Your Profile

When you confirm your new Facebook account, Facebook prompts you to find friends and family who are already on Facebook. You're also prompted to add more information to your Facebook profile.

Now, you don't have to do any of these things; you can skip any or all of these next steps, by clicking the Skip or Skip This Step link on any given page. But if you have a few free moments, you might as well get this stuff out of the way.

Here's how it works:

1. The first page you see is shown in Figure 2.2. This page suggests one or more people

Tip

To make your password more secure (harder for someone else to guess, that is), include a mix of alphabetic, numeric, and special characters (punctuation marks). Longer passwords are also more secure.

Note

A *captcha* is a type of challenge-response test to ensure that you're actually a human being, rather than a computer program. You've seen lots of these things on the Web already; they typically consist of warped or otherwise distorted text that cannot be read by a machine or software program. Websites use captchas to cut down on the amount of computer-generated spam they receive.

Note

Learn more about the friend-finding process in Chapter 4, "How to Find Old Friends—and Make New Ones."

you might want to be friends with. Click the Add Friend button next to add that person as a friend and then click Continue, or just click the Skip link to move to the next step.

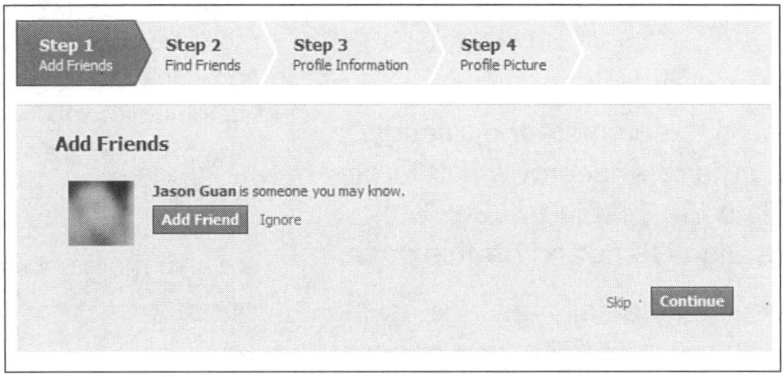

Figure 2.2. *Viewing Facebook's friend suggestions.*

2. Next, Facebook lets you find friends who are in your web-based email contact list who are also Facebook members, as shown in Figure 2.3. Enter the email address and password for your email account into the Your Email and Email Password boxes, then click the Find Friends button.

Figure 2.3. *Searching for email contacts to add as friends.*

3. Facebook lists people in your email contacts list who are also members of Facebook. To add one or more of these people to your Facebook friends list, check the box next to that person's name and then click the Add Friend or Add as Friends button. If you do not want to add any of these people, click Skip.

4. Next, Facebook displays a list of your email contacts who are not yet members of Facebook. To invite any of these people to join Facebook, check the box next to that person's name and then click the Invite to Join button.

Note

Step 2 is for web-based email only, such as Hotmail, Gmail, or Yahoo! Mail.

5. Facebook now displays the Step 3: Profile Information page, shown in Figure 2.4. This is where you start filling in your personal information to be displayed in your Facebook profile. If you want to do this, start by typing the name of your high school into the High School box, then select the year of your graduation from the Class Year list.

Step 1	Step 2	Step 3	Step 4
Add Friends	Find Friends	Profile Information	Profile Picture

Fill out your Profile Info
This information will help you find your friends on Facebook.

High School:
College/University:
Employer:

◄ Back   Skip · **Save & Continue**

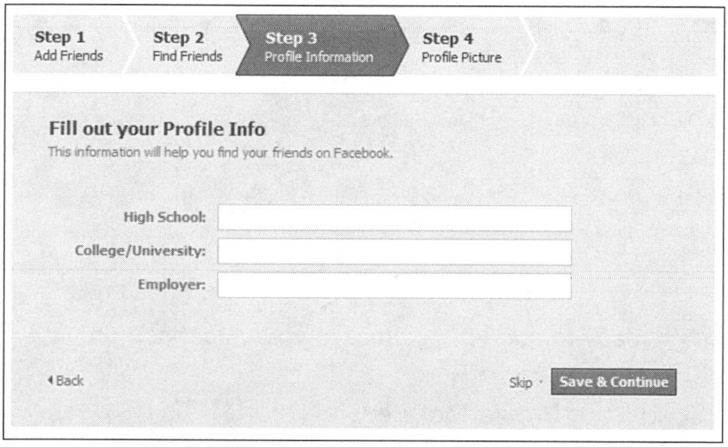

Figure 2.4. *Entering school and work information.*

6. If you graduated from or are attending a college or university, type the name of your college into the College/University box and select the year of your graduation from the Class Year list.

7. If you are currently employed, type the name of your employer into the Company box.

8. Click the Save & Continue button.

9. If you entered any school or work information, you will be prompted to add as friends

Tip

As you type into many boxes in the Facebook site, items that match what you're typing automatically appear in a list beneath the box. You can select the appropriate item from the list, if it's listed there, or just finish typing the complete name.

people you might know from those schools or businesses. (Facebook is a bear about adding friends.) If you so wish, click the names of any people you know and want as friends, then click the Save & Continue button.

10. Facebook now displays the Step 4: Profile Picture page, shown in Figure 2.5, where you're be prompted to set your Profile picture. Assuming you want to do this now, and that you want to use an existing photo stored on your computer, click the Upload a Photo link.

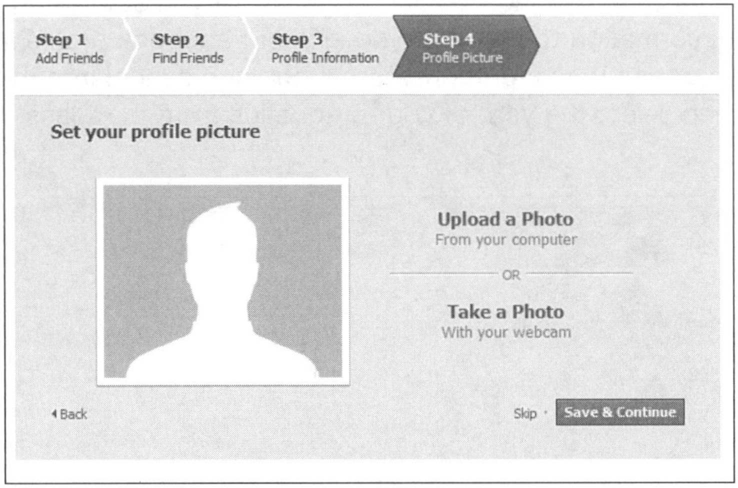

Figure 2.5. *Getting ready to add your picture to your Facebook profile.*

11. When the Upload Your Profile Picture window appears, click the Choose File button.

12. When the Open dialog box appears, navigate to and select the photo you wish to use. Then click the Open button.

13. When your picture appears on the page, click the Save & Continue button.

That's it, finally. You're now taken to a special Welcome page on the Facebook site, where you can start filling in your profile information.

> **Note**
>
> If your computer has a webcam built in or connected, you can use your webcam to shoot a new photo for your Facebook Profile. From the Step 4: Profile Picture page, click the Take a Photo link. When the Take a Profile Picture window appears, smile and click the camera icon. After the countdown has been completed, click the Save Picture button.

Filling Out Your Profile

> **Note**
> You can upload pictures in the JPG, GIF, or PNG formats, up to 4MB in size.

The next thing you want to do is fill out the personal information that will appear in your Facebook profile. There's a lot about yourself you can enter, although most of it is optional—so you don't have to divulge too much, if you don't want.

You start this process on the Facebook Welcome page that was displayed at the end of the sign-up process, as shown in Figure 2.6. (You can redisplay this page by going to the Home page and clicking Welcome in the sidebar.) Just follow these steps:

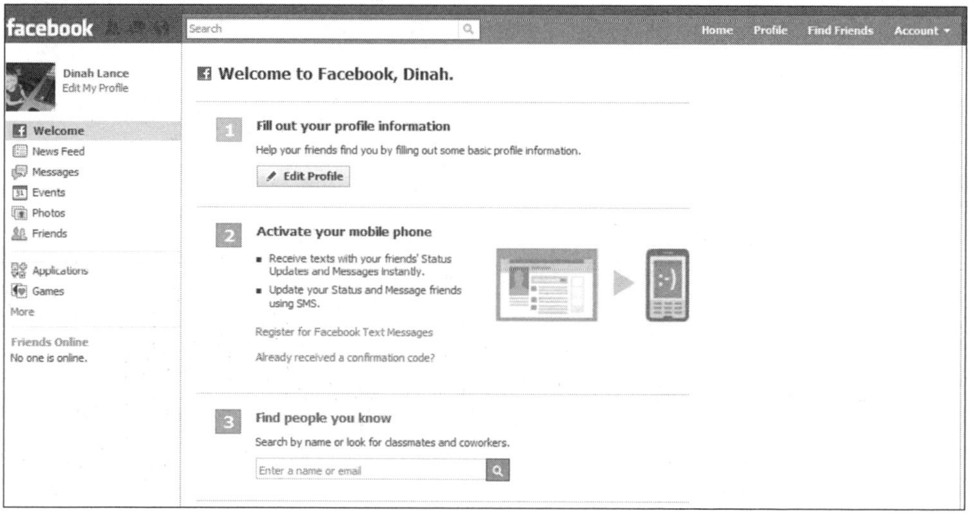

Figure 2.6. *Getting ready to enter profile information from the Welcome page.*

1. From the Welcome page, click the Edit Profile button.
2. When the Basic Information page appears, as shown in Figure 2.7, enter where you live into the Current City box.
3. Enter the place you grew up into the Hometown box.
4. Look at the Sex list and make sure it has the correct gender selected. If not, pull down the list and select your gender. If you prefer not to display your gender in your profile, uncheck the Show My Sex in My Profile option.

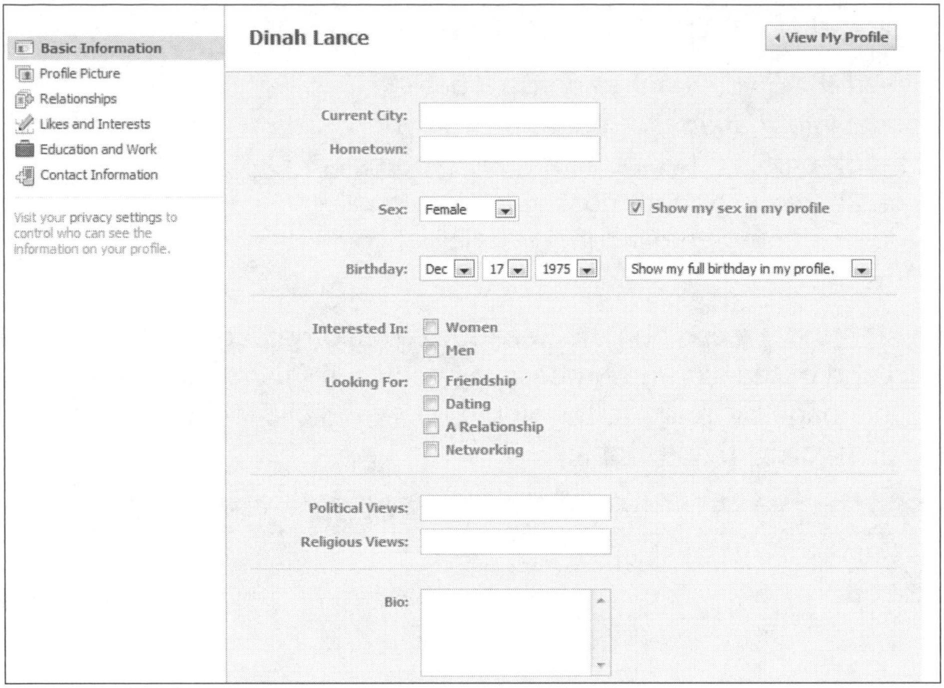

Basic Information
Profile Picture
Relationships
Likes and Interests
Education and Work
Contact Information

Visit your privacy settings to control who can see the information on your profile.

Dinah Lance

◄ View My Profile

Current City:

Hometown:

Sex: Female ▼ ☑ Show my sex in my profile

Birthday: Dec ▼ 17 ▼ 1975 ▼ Show my full birthday in my profile. ▼

Interested In: ☐ Women
☐ Men

Looking For: ☐ Friendship
☐ Dating
☐ A Relationship
☐ Networking

Political Views:

Religious Views:

Bio:

Figure 2.7. *Entering basic profile information.*

5. Confirm that the birthday listed is correct, or make any necessary adjustments. If you prefer not to display your birthday in your profile (if you're a little vain, perhaps), pull down the adjoining list and select Don't Show My Birthday in My Profile.

6. If you're so inclined, select which gender in which you're interested (Men or Women) in the Interested In section.

Tip

If you want your friends to be reminded of your birthday, but not necessarily know how old you are, select Show Only Month & Day in My Profile.

7. In the Looking For section, check which activities you're looking for: Friendship, Dating, A Relationship, or Networking. (Remember, you don't have to select any of these.)

8. Enter your political views (or the party you support) into the Political Views box.

9. Enter your religious views or affiliation into the Religious Views box.

10. Enter a short biography (a few sentences long) into the Bio box.

11. If you have any favorite quotations, enter them into the Quotations box.

12. Click the Save Changes button.

This gives you a good start on completing your profile—but you're not done yet. To access other parts of your profile, click one of the other links in the sidebar on the Welcome page. These links include:

- Profile Picture, shown in Figure 2.8, to add or change the picture that appears on your Profile page

- Relationships, shown in Figure 2.9, where you can define your current relationship status (single, married, in a relationship, it's complicated, and such) and enter the names of selected family members.

- Likes and Interests, shown in Figure 2.10, where you can add your favorite activities, interests, music, books, movies, and television shows.

- Education and Work, shown in Figure 2.11, where you can edit your current school and employer info, as well as enter past employers.

- Contact Information, shown in Figure 2.12, where you can edit or add additional contact information—email address, IM screen name, mobile or land phone, street address, and website URL.

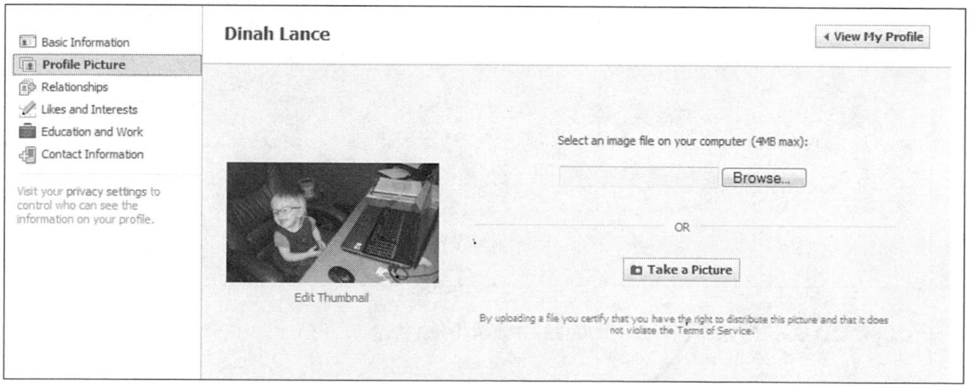

Figure 2.8. *Editing your profile photo.*

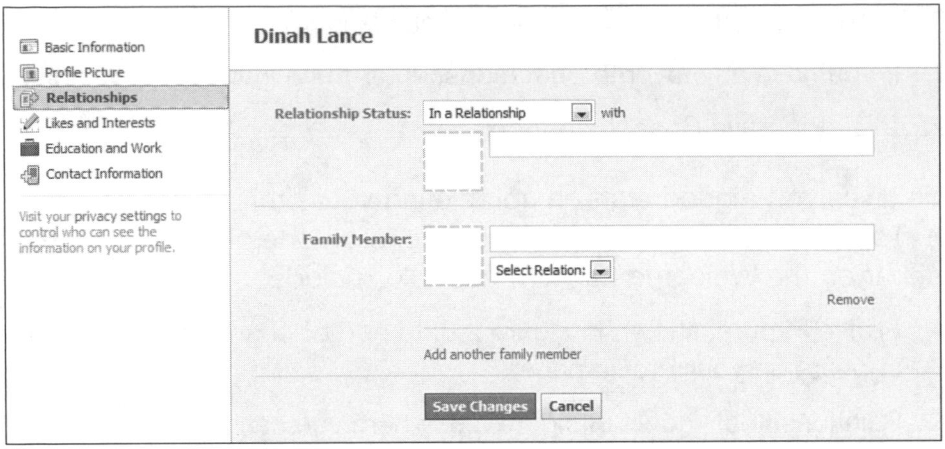

Figure 2.9. *Entering relationship and family information.*

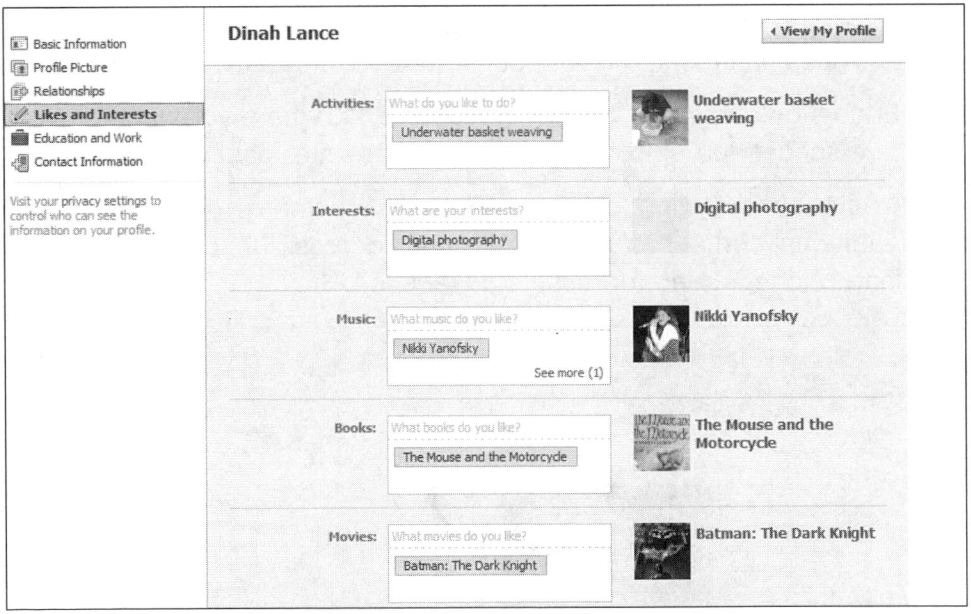

Figure 2.10. *Entering your likes and interests.*

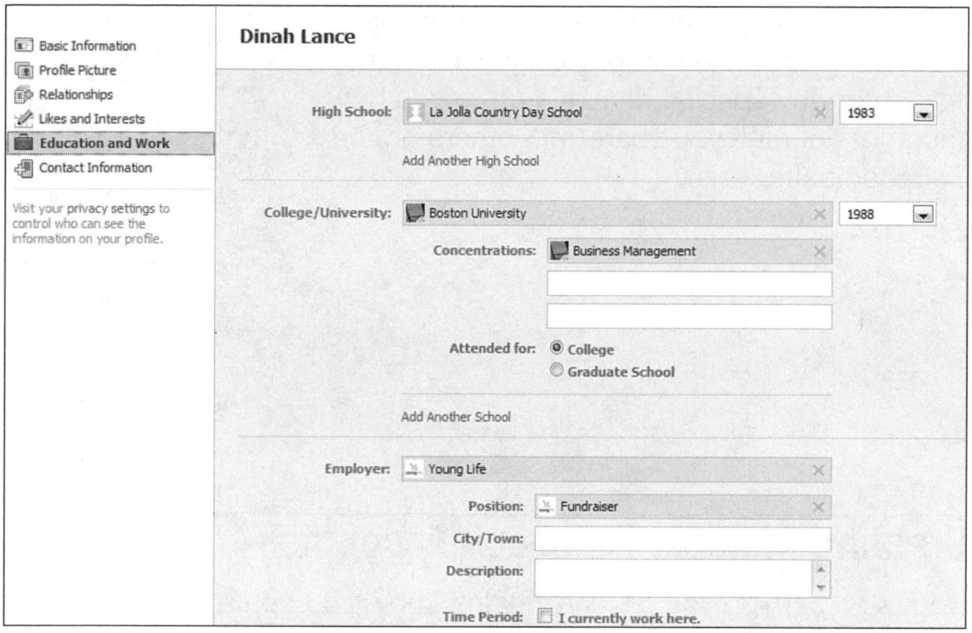

Dinah Lance

Basic Information
Profile Picture
Relationships
Likes and Interests
Education and Work
Contact Information

Visit your privacy settings to control who can see the information on your profile.

High School: La Jolla Country Day School   ✕   1983 ▾

Add Another High School

College/University: Boston University   ✕   1988 ▾

Concentrations: Business Management   ✕

Attended for: ◉ College
　　　　　　　　○ Graduate School

Add Another School

Employer: Young Life   ✕

Position: Fundraiser   ✕

City/Town:

Description:

Time Period: ☐ I currently work here.

Figure 2.11. *Editing school and work information.*

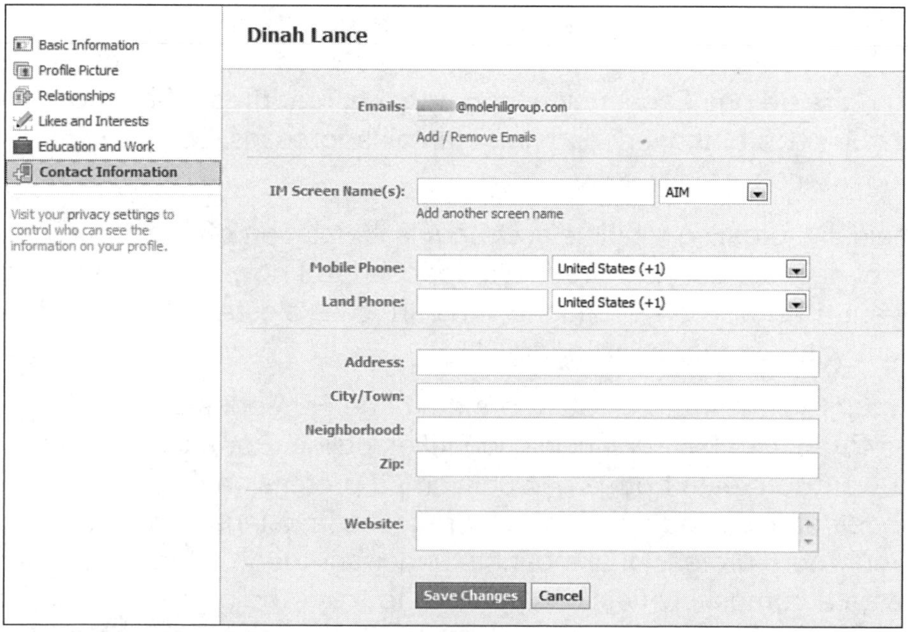

Dinah Lance

Basic Information
Profile Picture
Relationships
Likes and Interests
Education and Work
Contact Information

Visit your privacy settings to control who can see the information on your profile.

Emails: ████@molehillgroup.com
Add / Remove Emails

IM Screen Name(s): 　　　　　　　　 AIM ▾
Add another screen name

Mobile Phone: 　　　 United States (+1) ▾
Land Phone: 　　　 United States (+1) ▾

Address:
City/Town:
Neighborhood:
Zip:

Website:

Save Changes   **Cancel**

Figure 2.12. *Entering contact information.*

Remember, all of this information is optional. You don't have to—and probably don't want to—enter any specific item. It's up to you how much of yourself you share with others on the Facebook site.

Note

You don't have to enter all your profile information at this time. You can go back at any time and enter more information, or change the information you've already added. Learn more in Chapter 22, "Managing Your Facebook Account."

Creating Multiple Facebook Accounts

Here's something you probably didn't know you could do. For whatever reason you might have (and there are a few), you can actually create multiple Facebook accounts. All you need is multiple email addresses.

You see, Facebook bases each individual account on a unique email address. If you have more than one email address (and most of us do), you can create one Facebook account for each address. So, for example, if you have both work and home email addresses, you can create Facebook accounts for each.

(Technically, creating multiple accounts is a violation of Facebook's terms of service, but how are they supposed to know? I say go for it if you want; even if you get caught, you can always establish yet another account with another email address.)

Why might you want to create more than one Facebook account? It all has to do with having multiple identities online. For example, you might want to create both a personal and a professional persona on the Facebook site, so you can post your personal musings under one ID and your more professional thoughts under another. Or you might want to create a completely fictitious persona to track the online activities of your children. (More about that in Chapter 6, "Keeping Tabs on Your Kids.") Or, if you're really creepy, you can just create multiple identities to play around with. Whatever floats your boat.

In any case, as long as you have distinct email addresses, there's no rule against creating multiple Facebook accounts. So have at it, if you wish.

Chapter 3

Getting Around the Facebook Site

After you've signed up for Facebook, it's time to get to know the Facebook site. There's a lot there, if you know where to find it—which is what we discuss in this chapter.

What's What and What's Where on Facebook

When it comes to getting around the Facebook site, where do you start? Well, the logical place to start is the sign in page, and then what you see afterward—Facebook's home page.

Signing In

Point your Web browser to www.facebook.com and you see the Facebook sign in page, shown in Figure 3.1. (This is also the page you used to register for Facebook, in case you forgot.) Signing in is as easy as entering your email address and password into the two boxes in the top right of the page and then clicking the Login button.

 Tip

If you don't want to be prompted to enter your login information every time you access the site, check the Keep Me Logged In option.

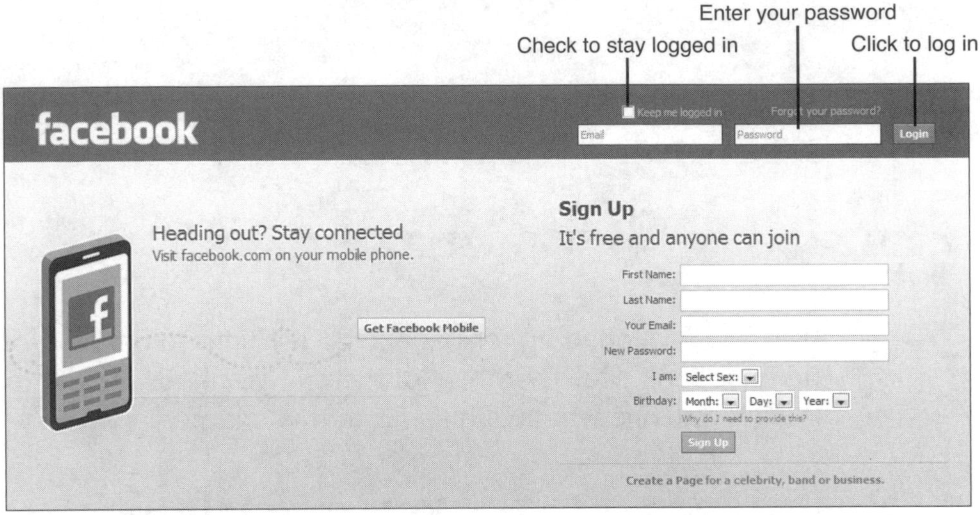

Enter your password

Check to stay logged in   Click to log in

Figure 3.1. *Signing into Facebook—enter your email address and password.*

Welcome to the Home Page

After you've signed in, Facebook drops you right onto the Home page. This is as good a place as any to start your exploration of the Facebook site. It's also where you keep up-to-date on what your friends are up to.

As you can see in Figure 3.2, the Home page consists of three columns, a big one in the middle and two smaller ones on either side. We'll focus our attention on the center column first, which contains something called the *News Feed*.

The News Feed is, in essence, a scrolling list of status updates from your Facebook friends. The most recent updates are on the top, with older updates scrolling to the bottom and then off the page. (To view even older updates, click the Older Posts link at the bottom of the page.)

By default, the News Feed displays only those status updates from friends that Facebook thinks are most important to you. Don't ask me how Facebook determines this, as they don't always get it right; that is, the default News Feed—dubbed Top News—often excludes posts from people you do want to read about.

Useful navigation column   News Feed   Click to display posts from all your friends   Fairly useless right-hand column   Facebook toolbar

Figure 3.2. *The Facebook Home page—complete with News Feed of your friends' status updates.*

Fortunately, you can display updates from *all* your friends instead of just these so-called top posts. All you have to do is click the Most Recent link at the top of the News Feed column, and everybody gets his or her say.

The right column of the Home page contains, to be honest, mostly useless information. Here is where Facebook places its advertisements (in the "Sponsored" section), suggestions for things you might like to do or people you might like to add to your friends list, notice of pending friend requests, upcoming friends' birthdays, and the like. Myself, I could do without this entire column, but there it is and there's not much you can do about it.

The left column of the Home page, however, is a lot more useful. This is one of your primary navigation aids to content on the Facebook site. Click a link here and you either display different information on the Home page (in place of the News Feed) or navigate to a different section of the site.

What do you find in the navigation column? Here's the list:

- **Welcome**: This handy page is for new users that helps you enter profile information, find new friends, and the like.

- **News Feed**: This is the default view on the Home page and where you view all your friends' status updates.

- **Messages**: All the private messages (also known as email) you've received from other Facebook members are displayed in this area. It's also the place you go to send new emails to other users.

- **Events**: This area displays any Facebook events you've signed up for, as well as upcoming birthdays of your Facebook friends. You can also click here to create new events.

- **Photos**: You can find the most recent photos and (with another click) videos posted by your friends.

- **Friends**: This area is where you go to find new friends on the Facebook site.

- **Applications:** All the applications you and your friends are using are displayed in this area. These are little widget-like utilities that add more functionality to the Facebook site.

- **Games**: All the social games you and your friends are playing on Facebook are listed in this area.

- **Ads and pages**: From this area, which displays the Facebook Advertising page, you can create a Facebook ad (nice if you want to promote a business) or fan page.

Learn more about Facebook's built-in email in Chapter 9, "Exchanging Private Messages."

Learn more about Facebook events in Chapter 13, "Sharing Birthdays and Events."

Learn more about finding Facebook friends in Chapter 4, "How to Find Old Friends—and Make New Ones."

Learn more about Facebook applications and games in Chapter 18, "Finding Fun Games and Applications."

- **Groups**: This area is displayed if you've joined a topic-oriented group and it lists all the topic-oriented groups to which you subscribe—and lets you create your own groups.

- **Friends Online**: This area is simply a list of all your Facebook friends who are currently online and logged into the site. Click a friend's name to start an instant messaging-like chat with that person.

And that, in a nutshell, is the Facebook Home page. It's more than just a gateway into the Facebook site; it's where you go to keep informed of your friend's activities. As such, it's the one page that most users always go to. I'd recommend bookmarking this page (which resides at www.facebook.com—after you've logged in, that is) in your Web browser.

Note

Learn more about fan pages in Chapter 15, "Becoming a Fan."

Note

Learn more about Facebook groups in Chapter 16, "Meeting Others in Groups."

Profile Pages

Past the Home page, most other important pages on the Facebook site are individual users' Profile pages. A Profile page, like the one shown in Figure 3.3, is where each user's status updates are listed, along with that person's personal information, uploaded photos and videos, upcoming events, and the like.

In essence, a Profile page is that person's home on the Facebook site. You have your own Profile page, of course, as does everyone else who's a Facebook member. You go to a friend's Profile page to learn more about that person, or to view his or her information, photos, and such.

Note

Learn more about viewing a friend's Profile page in Chapter 5, "Visiting Friends and Family on Facebook." Learn more about customizing your own Profile page in Chapter 14, "Personalizing Your Profile Page."

Figure 3.3.   *A typical Facebook Profile page.*

Navigating the Facebook Toolbar

As we just discussed, you can access many parts of the Facebook site from the navigation sidebar on the Facebook Home page. The other primary means of navigating the Facebook site is via the Facebook toolbar, shown in Figure 3.4, that you find at the top of every Facebook page. It's a key way to get around the site.

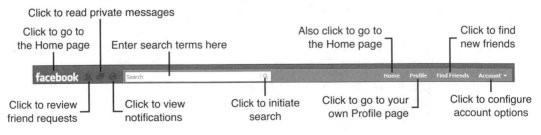

Figure 3.4.   *The Facebook toolbar.*

What can you do from the Facebook toolbar? Here's a list, from left to right:

- Click the Facebook logo to go to the Facebook Home page, complete with News Feed.

- View any friend requests you've received. If you have any pending friend requests, you'll see a red number—for the number of requests—on top of the icon. Click the icon to view a drop-down list of these requests.

- View your most recent private messages. As with the friend requests icon, a red number on top displays if you have unread messages. Click the icon to view a drop-down list of messages.

- View notifications from Facebook, such as someone commenting on your status or accepting your friend request. Click the icon to view the most recent notifications.

- Search the Facebook site for people and things. Just enter your query into the Search box and then either click the Search (magnifying glass) button or press Enter on your computer keyboard. (More on searching in just a sec.)

- Another way to go home, by clicking the Home button on the right side of the toolbar. (Yes, this does exactly the same thing as clicking the Facebook logo; this button was requested by Facebook's Department of Redundancy Department.)

- Display your Profile page by clicking the Profile button.

- Click the Find Friends button (not displayed on all accounts) to add new people to your Facebook Friends list.

- Access all sorts of account settings, including important privacy settings, by clicking the Account button and then selecting an option from the drop-down menu. Options are Edit Friends, Account Settings, Privacy Settings, Application Settings, Help Center, and Logout. (If you use Facebook's built-in currency to buy anything on the site, there may also be a Credits Balance option.)

Note

Learn more about Facebook's privacy settings in Chapter 21, "Keeping Some Things Private." Learn more about Facebook's account settings in Chapter 22, "Managing Your Facebook Account."

As I said, the Facebook toolbar appears at the top of each and every Facebook page. I use it primarily to jump back and forth between my Home and Profile pages. It's also useful to access your private email messages and to search the site—and of course, to access your privacy settings.

Searching Facebook

Let's talk a bit about searching Facebook. The Search box found in the Facebook toolbar can be used to search for virtually anything on the Facebook site.

That's right, Facebook uses a single Search box to search for all types of items. You can't fine-tune the search from the Search box; instead, you fine-tune the results when the results page appears.

How does it work, then? Well, all you have to do is enter your query into the Search box. As you type, a list of items that match your query are displayed in a drop down menu under the box, as shown in Figure 3.5.

Figure 3.5. *A list of suggestions appears as you enter a search query.*

If what you want is displayed in this list, great; click the item and go there. Otherwise, keep typing and then press Enter or click the Search button.

Facebook now displays a search results page, like the one shown in Figure 3.6. By default, all items that match your query are displayed—people, groups, pages, events, you name it. You can, however, narrow down the results by type of item. Just click the type of item in the left column, and the search results of that type are displayed.

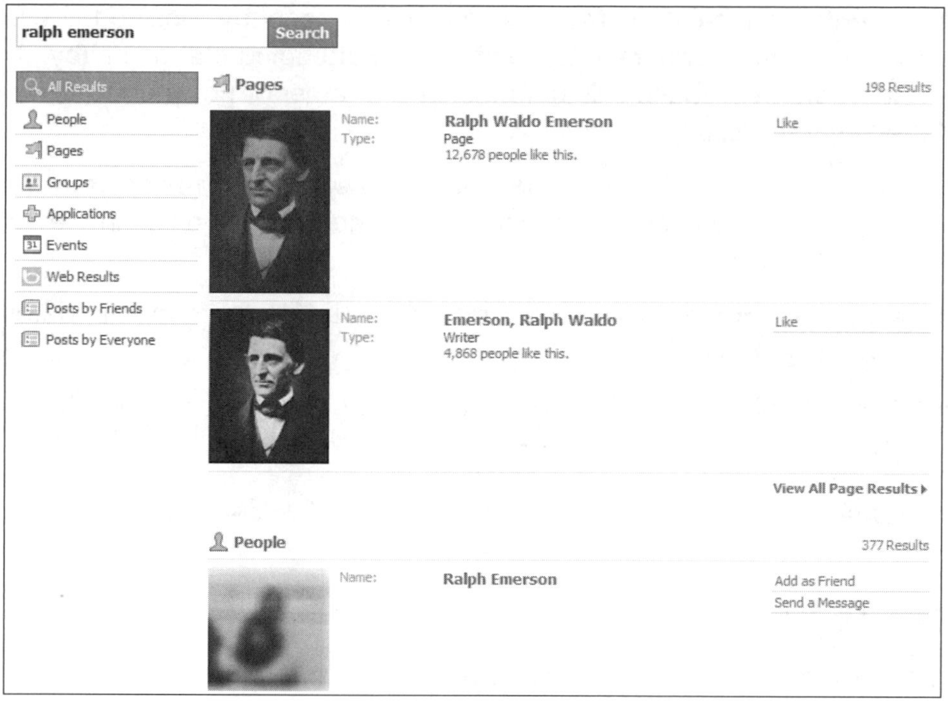

Figure 3.6.   *A typical search results page.*

For example, if you want to display only people that match your query (that is, if you're searching for a person), click People in the left column. If you want to display Facebook groups, click Groups. In this fashion, then, you can search for:

- **People**: You can then choose to visit a person's Profile page (by clicking their name on the search results page), add that person as a friend (Add as Friend), or send that person a private email message (Send a Message).

- **Pages, or what I like to call "fan pages"**: You can then visit a given page (by clicking the page's name in the search results), or choose to become a fan of that page (by clicking the Like link).

- **Groups**: You can then visit a given group page (by clicking the group's name in the search results), or choose to become a member of that group (by clicking the Join Group or Request to Join links).

- **Applications**: You can visit that application's Facebook page, and from there join the group, by clicking the View Application link.

- **Events**: You can then then visit an event's page (by clicking the event name in the search results), view people attending that event (by clicking the Confirmed Guests link), or indicate whether or not you're attending the event (by clicking the RSVP link).

- **Web results**: That's right, these are Web pages that match your query, as determined by Microsoft's Bing search engine. Click a link in the results to view that Web page.

- **Posts by Friends**: This search displays your friends' status updates that match your query.

- **Posts by Everyone**: To see all the status updates on Facebook that match your query—friends and otherwise—use this search.

Of course, to display all these items at once, click View All Page Results.

Signing Off

When you're done using Facebook and want to sign off from the site, all you have to do is click the Account button on the Facebook toolbar and then click Logout. When you do this, you then have to log back in the next time you visit www.facebook.com.

You don't have to sign off, however. If you just navigate to a different website, and you checked the Keep Me Logged In option when you last signed on, you'll display the Facebook Home page when you next visit www.facebook.com. It's your choice.

Getting Help

There's one option on the Facebook toolbar we kind of glossed over. That's the Help Center option you see when you click the Account button. (You can also access the Help Center by scrolling to the bottom of any Facebook page and clicking the Help link.)

The Facebook Help Center is your gateway to information about every Facebook feature. There are guides to Using Facebook, Facebook Applications and Features, and Ads and Business solutions. Click the links in the Help Center sidebar to view guides to Games and Apps, Help Discussions, Getting Started, and Safety.

Even more useful, if you have a question about using Facebook, just enter it into the Search box on the Help Center page. This will display a list of FAQs (articles) and discussions that have something to do with what you're asking about.

And about these Help Discussions. These are questions asked by other users, answered by members of the Facebook community. I find these useful if "official" information about a given topic doesn't exist, or is less than helpful. Just click the Help Discussion link in the Help Center sidebar, then click a given topic listed.

As you'll see, there's a bevy of information available in the Help Center. Look here if you're having trouble finding something on the site, or just don't know how to do something.

Facebook for Friends and Family

Chapter 4

How to Find Old Friends— and Make New Ones

Facebook is all about connecting with friends. In fact, the connections you make on Facebook are officially called "friends." You invite someone to be your friend, you add that person to your friends list, you manage your list of friends, your news feed displays the status updates of all your friends. Friends are part and parcel of the Facebook community.

Of course, before you can make someone your Facebook friend, you have to find that person on Facebook. That isn't always as easy as you might think, especially when you're looking for people you went to school with several decades ago. People move, women change their names when they get married (or divorced, or remarried, or some combination of the above), it's just darned difficult to track down some folks. Doesn't mean it can't be done, however. And if they're on Facebook, you can probably find them.

How Facebook Helps You Reconnect

When it comes to finding lost friends and family members, size is everything. That is, the more people there are in the community, the more likely it is that the person you're looking for will be there.

And when it comes to size, Facebook is the biggest online community out there. Five hundred million users makes for a pretty big pond; it's the one website that just about everybody signs onto, sooner or later.

The size of the Facebook community is both a good and a bad thing, of course. It's good in that it's so big that just about anyone you're looking for is probably a member. It's bad in that there are so many people to browse through, it's difficult to find any one individual. The person you're looking for is probably there, somewhere, if you only knew how to find him.

Fortunately, Facebook offers several tools for finding people on the site. First, Facebook can cross-tabulate your email and instant message contact lists with its own membership database, identifying your contacts who are also Facebook members. Second, you can search the site by name, although that can be somewhat frustrating when you're searching for someone with a fairly common name (try looking for "John Brown"—or "Michael Miller," for that matter). Finally, you can search for people by location (city or state), the school they went to, or the company they work or worked for; this is a good way to find former neighbors, classmates, and co-workers.

The end result is that you can create a Facebook network that consists of a fairly large number of people you used to know but haven't necessarily been in contact with for a while.

Personally, I've used Facebook to connect with several old high school and college friends, some of whom I hadn't talked to in more than twenty years. It took a bit of work, but once I made a few initial contacts, the others started to pour in. It's a matter of working through the connections, literally finding friends of friends.

That is, someone you know might be friends with someone else you know; this is particularly common when you're dealing with old school friends. After you connect with one friend, you can view their friends and find a lot of people you know in common. Knock down one domino and they all start tumbling.

As a result, I now have more than 150 friends on Facebook, and I'm making more by the day. Some of these friends are newer,—people I know in the publishing and marketing communities— but many are my old schoolmates. I can't say they all look familiar, not

Note

As far as Facebook is concerned, everyone you know is a "friend"—even family members. So when I talk about Facebook friends, these could be your siblings or children, people you work with, faint acquaintances, or even real friends. It's just a name.

after so many years (we all get older, don't we?), but I remember them all. Or most of them, anyway; the old memory isn't quite what it used to be.

Why Friends Are Important

Why are friends important? Well, I can't speak to the value of friends in real life (actually, I could, but this isn't the place for that), but I can tell you why friends are important on Facebook.

It's simple, really, and all about access. For a person to have full access to your Facebook Profile page and status updates, they must be added to your friends list. It's the same in reverse; you must be on that person's friends list to view his or her full Profile page and status updates.

In addition, when you add someone to your friends list, all of his or her status updates automatically appear on the News Feed on your Facebook Home page. Likewise, when you're added to someone else's friends list, all of your status updates appears in that person's News Feed. It's a great way of keeping tabs on what your friends are doing.

Fortunately, there is no practical limit to the number of friends you can have on Facebook (okay, you can have up to 5,000 friends—a number you're never going to reach), so you don't have to pick and choose; you can make anybody a friend if you so wish. Some people have hundreds of Facebook friends, while others have just a few. It's all up to you.

That said, there is no expectation that you will dutifully read all the posts from all of your Facebook friends. In fact, when you add a person to your Facebook friends list, that doesn't even imply that the person is a "friend" in the traditional use of the word. You might not even know that person; Facebook friends can be total strangers in real life. On Facebook, they're just people you follow—and who follow you.

Note

The process of finding new Facebook friends is called *friending*. When you remove someone from your friends list, you *unfriend* them.

Making Friends with People You're Already in Contact With

Let's start with the easiest way to find friends on Facebook—by letting Facebook do the work. If you recall, when you first signed up for your Facebook account, Facebook asked to look through your email contacts list for potential friends. You might have done this or you might not have; I typically ignore this step when I'm first getting started. In any case, there's a lot more looking that can be done, at any time you feel like it.

Finding Friends You Email

Even though today's college and high school generations seem to have abandoned email as being too slow and old fashioned (Email? Old fashioned already?), us oldsters still rely on email as a primary means of communicating online—especially for work and with family members. As such, it's a fair assumption that if you email someone on a regular basis, you might want to become Facebook friends with him or her.

To that end, Facebook can look through your email contact lists for people who are also Facebook members, and then invite those people to be your friends. Here's how it works.

1. Go to the Facebook Home page and click Friends in the sidebar. (Alternatively, click Find Friends on the toolbar, if you have that option.)

2. On the Friends page, shown in Figure 4.1, scroll to the Find People You Email section.

3. If you use a web-based email service, such as Yahoo! Mail or Gmail, type your email address into the Your Email box. Then type your password into the Email Password box. Click the Find Friends button to display a list of email contacts who are also Facebook members.

4. If you use Microsoft Outlook to check your email, click the Upload Contact File link. When the page changes to that shown in Figure 4.2, check the Automatically Import My Contacts from Outlook option and click the Find Friends button to display a list of Outlook contacts who are also Facebook members.

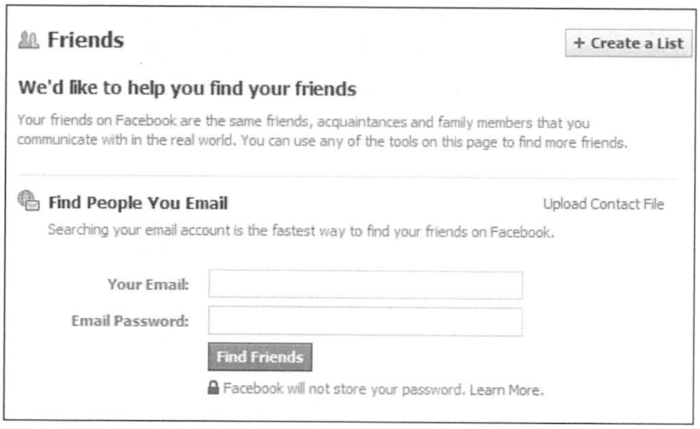

Figure 4.1. *Finding people you email.*

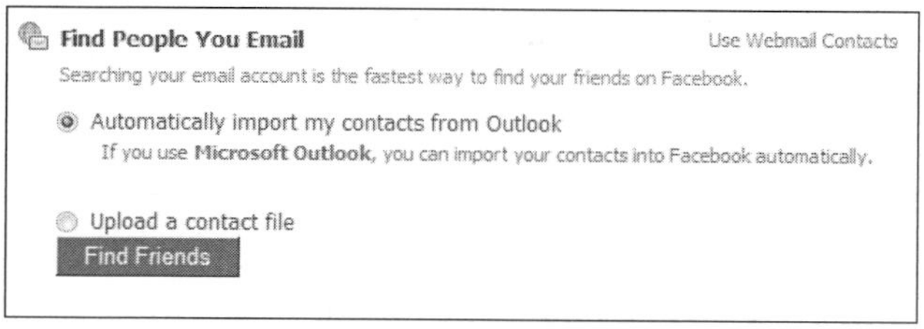

Figure 4.2. *Finding friends in your Outlook or other email client contact lists.*

5. If you use another software program to manage your email, such as Outlook Express, Eudora, or Mozilla Thunderbird, you should also click the Upload Contact File link. When the page changes, check the Upload a Contact File option and then click the Browse or Choose File button. When the Choose File to Upload dialog box appears, navigate to and select your email contacts file. When you return to the Friends page, click the Find Friends button to upload your email contacts list to Facebook and display a list of email contacts who are also Facebook members.

6. When the list of email contacts appears, as shown in Figure 4.3, check the box next to each person to whom you'd like to be friends.

7. Click the Add as Friends button to send friend requests to these contacts.

Facebook now sends friend requests to the people you selected. When a person accepts your request, you become friends with that person. If a person does not accept your request, you don't become friends.

Friends   + Create a List

You have 39 Gmail contacts on Facebook that you can add as your friends.

You are already Facebook friends with a person from your Gmail contact list.

Select which contacts to add as friends from the list below. You can also try another email account to find more friends.

☐ Select All Friends

☐   David F. Leopold

☐   Darlene Shepard

☐   Val Zamulin

☐   Stephanie Smith Miller

☐   Scott Clark

Add as Friends | Skip

Figure 4.3. *Identifying people you'd like to be friends with.*

Finding Friends You Instant Message

Just as email contacts are likely to be potential Facebook friends, the people you instant message (IM) with might also be people you want to add to your Facebook friends list. To that end, Facebook can look through your IM contacts and find those who are also Facebook members.

Follow these steps:

1. Go to the Facebook Home page and click Friends in the sidebar. (Alternatively, click Find Friends on the toolbar, if you have that option.)

2. When the Friends page appears, scroll to the Find People You IM section, shown in Figure 4.4.

Note

At the present time, Facebook can import friends' lists from AOL Instant Messenger (AIM), ICQ, and Windows Live Messenger. It is not yet compatible with Yahoo! Messenger or Google Talk.

Figure 4.4. *Finding friends you instant message.*

3. Click the link for the IM service you use: AOL Instant Messenger, ICQ Chat, or Windows Live Messenger.

4. When prompted, enter your IM screen name, number, or ID, along with your password.

5. Click the Find Friends button.

6. Facebook now displays a list of your IM friends who are also members of Facebook. Check the box next to each person to whom you'd like to send a friend request.

7. Click the Add as Friends button.

Facebook now does the whole friends request thing.

Finding Co-Workers

Here's another place to look for current friends—among the people you work with. Facebook makes it quite easy to find other employees of the company you work for, and then invite them to become friends. Here's how it works:

1. Go to the Facebook Home page and click Friends in the sidebar. (Alternatively, click Find Friends on the toolbar, if you have that option.)

2. When the Friends page appears, scroll to the Search for People section, shown in Figure 4.5.

3. Somewhere in this section should be a link for the business you currently work for—assuming that you specified your employer when you entered your personal information. Look for a link that says Find Coworkers From *Business,* then click that link.

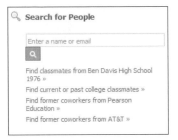

Figure 4.5. *Finding friends you work with.*

4. Facebook now displays a list of members who are also employed by this business. Check the box next to each person to whom you'd like to send a friend request.

5. Click the Add as Friends button.

Searching for Long Lost Friends

Note

If you work for a very large company, you're likely to see a long list of co-workers—even those who work in different locations. It might take some time to scroll through the list and find the people you physically work with.

The previous steps help you find people you currently associate with who are also members of Facebook. But what about those people who you haven't seen in a while—sometimes a very, very long while? This entails a bit more effort on your part.

Finding Former Co-Workers

Let's start by looking for people you used to work with—that is, co-workers at a former employer. Assuming you provided the name of your former employers when you filled in your personal information, Facebook should be able to list current and former employees of that business. You can then pick through the list and find those folks you want to reconnect with.

Just follow these steps:

1. Go to the Facebook Home page and click Friends in the sidebar. (Alternatively, click Find Friends on the toolbar, if you have that option.)

2. When the Friends page appears, scroll to the Search for People section.

3. Somewhere in this section should be a link for the business you used to work for. Look for a link that says Find Former Coworkers from *Business,* then click that link.

4. Facebook now displays a list of members who have also been employed by this business. Check the box next to each person to whom you'd like to send a friend request.

5. Click the Add as Friends button.

Finding Former Classmates

Finding people you used to go to school with is equally easy—assuming that both you and they entered your school as part of your personal information. You should find lists of Facebook members who went to your high school and your college, or even multiple colleges if you went that route. These will be lists of classmates who graduated the same year you did.

Here's how to find these folks:

1. Go to the Facebook Home page and click Friends in the sidebar. (Alternatively, click Find Friends on the toolbar, if you have that option.)

2. When the Friends page appears, scroll to the Search for People section.

3. Somewhere in this section should be a link for the school you went to. Look for a link that says Find Classmates from *School Year,* then click that link. (For example, I graduated from Indiana University in 1980, so I had a link for Find Classmates from Indiana University Bloomington 1980.)

4. Facebook now displays a list of members who also graduated from this school when you did, as shown in Figure 4.6. If you want to display classmates who graduated in a different class, pull down the list at the top of the page and select a different year.

5. Check the box next to each person to whom you'd like to send a friend request.

6. Click the Add as Friends button.

Searching for 🔍 _____ from people in Ben Davis High School 1976 ▼   More Search Options

Displaying 1 - 10 of 308 people.   **1** 2 3 Next

Name: **Aggie Newby Bastin**   Add as Friend
                                                    Send a Message
                                                    View Friends

Name: **Alicia Bryant Harper**   Add as Friend
                                                    Send a Message

Name: **Amanda Farlow-Davis**   Add as Friend
Friends: 1 mutual friend   Send a Message
                                                    View Friends

Figure 4.6. *Finding former classmates on Facebook.*

Searching by Name or Email Address

That's all well and good, but what about finding people you knew back then but didn't go to your school? Or long lost family members? Or just people you met along the way?

Fortunately, Facebook lets you search for people by either name or email address. (Although it's unlikely that you know the email address of someone you haven't seen in twenty years…) You can search for people from the search box on the Facebook toolbar or the one on the Friends page, although I prefer doing all my friend searching from the Friends page.

Follow these steps:

1. Go to the Facebook Home page and click Friends in the sidebar. (Alternatively, click Find Friends on the toolbar, if you have that option.)

2. From the Friends page, scroll to the Search for People section, shown in Figure 4.7.

3. Type a name or email address into the search box, then click the Search button (the magnifying glass) or press Enter on your keyboard.

Search for People

Enter a name or email

Figure 4.7. *Searching for friends on Facebook.*

4. When the search results page appears, as shown in Figure 4.8, make sure that People is selected in the sidebar.

Sam Spade   Search

All Results		
People	Filter By: Location / School / Workplace / Refine Search	
Pages	Name: -Sam Spade	Add as Friend / Send a Message
Groups		
Applications		
Events	Name: Sam Spade	Add as Friend / Send a Message
Web Results		
Posts by Friends		
Posts by Everyone	Name: Sam Spade	Add as Friend / Send a Message

Figure 4.8. *The results of a friends search.*

5. Click the Add as Friend link next to the person to whom you wish to send a friend request.

Accepting Friend Requests

Sometimes potential friends find you before you find them. When this happens, they will send you a friend request, which you can then accept or decline. You might receive a friend request via email, or you can view friend requests within Facebook.

Tip

If the friend you're looking for has a relatively common name, such as John Smith, there might be too many people with that name on Facebook to find the correct one. It may be easier to search for that person by entering his or her email address, if you know it.

Here's how it all works:

1. To view pending friend requests, click the Friend Requests icon in the Facebook toolbar, shown in Figure 4.9.

Figure 4.9. *Viewing pending friend requests.*

2. To view the Profile of a person requesting to be your friend, click his or her name.

3. To accept this friend request, click the Confirm button.

4. To refuse this request, click the Ignore button.

Now, here's the deal. You don't have to accept a friend request, even if you know that person in the real world. Remember, once you've accepted a friend request, that person can view all your personal information and status updates. (That's unless you alter your privacy settings to hide information from that person, as we'll discuss in Chapter 21, "Keeping Some Things Private.") You might not want to accept all the friend requests you receive; that's your prerogative.

Exploring Facebook's Friend Suggestions

Here's something else that Facebook does: Recommend people to be new friends. That sounds kind of odd and maybe a little intrusive, but that's the way Facebook works; it wants everybody to be friends with everybody else.

Facebook's friend recommendations typically come from mutual associations. That is, they're usually friends of existing friends, or they go to your school or are employed by the same company, or something similar. You can go along with these recommendations or just ignore them.

Remember, though, that these are just recommendations. If you agree that you'd like to be a friend with one of these folks, you still have to send them a friend request.

So here's how to view these recommendations—and how to deal with them:

1. Go to the Facebook Home page and click Friends in the sidebar. (Alternatively, click Find Friends on the toolbar, if you have that option.)

2. When the Friends page appears, scroll to the Suggestions section, shown in Figure 4.10.

Figure 4.10. *Viewing Facebook's friend suggestions.*

3. To send a friend request to a person, click the Add as Friend link.

4. To ignore a friend suggestion, click the X next to that person's name.

Finding Friends of Friends

Another way to find old friends is to look for people who are friends of your current friends. That is, when you make someone your friend on Facebook, you can browse through the list of people who are on their friends list. Chances are you'll find mutual friends on this list—people that both of you know but you haven't found otherwise.

You find friends of your friends on your friends' Profile pages. Look on the left side of the Profile page for a box labeled Friends, like the one shown in Figure 4.11; these are the people on this person's friends list. Click the See All link to view all these people.

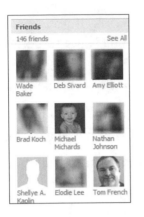

Figure 4.11. *The Friends box on a person's Profile page.*

Facebook now displays that person's Friends page, like the one shown in Figure 4.12. To view a person's Profile page, just click his or her name. To send a friend request to a person, click the Add as Friend button. You'd be surprised how many old friends you can turn up this way!

> **Note**
>
> There's also a box for Mutual Friends. These are people on both your friends list and your friend's friends list; you already know these folks.

Figure 4.12. *Viewing all of a person's Facebook friends.*

Finding Hard-to-Find Friends

When it comes to tracking down old friends on Facebook, sometimes a little detective work is in order. It's especially tough to find women you used to know, as names get changed along with marital status. Some women have enough forethought to enter their maiden name as their middle name on Facebook, so the Cathy Coolidge you used to know might be listed as Cathy Coolidge Smith, which means their maiden name will actually show up in a Facebook search. Others, however, don't do this—and thus become harder to find.

You can, of course, search for a partial name—searching just for "Cathy," for example. What happens next is a little interesting. Facebook returns a list of people named Cathy, of course, but puts at the top of this list people who have mutual friends in common with you. That's a nice touch, as it's likely that your old friend has already made a connection with another one of your Facebook friends.

Past that point, you can then display everyone on Facebook with that single name. But that's going to be a bit unwieldy, unless your friend has a very, very unique name.

One approach to narrowing down the results is to specify a location in your search. For example, if you're looking for a John Smith and think he currently lives in Minnesota, you would search for **john smith minnesota**. It's even better if you think you know a city; searching for **john smith minneapolis** will narrow the results even further.

Other information added to your query can also help you better find people. For example, if you know where that person works, add the name of the company to the query. So if you think John Smith works at IBM, search for **john smith ibm**.

Beyond these tips, finding long-lost friends on Facebook is a trial-and-error process. The best advice is to keep plugging—if they're on Facebook, you'll find them sooner or later.

Visiting Friends and Family on Facebook

After you've found family members and old friends and made them part of your Facebook friends list, now what?

Actually, there's a lot that can happen next. First, you can keep up-to-date on your friends' daily comings and goings via the News Feed on your Facebook Home page. You can pore over your friends' personal information, photographs, and the like on their individual Profile pages. You can even leave comments on your friends' postings and leave your own messages.

It's all part of the community aspect of the Facebook community—and how you can get closer to your friends online.

Catching Up with the Facebook News Feed

Let's start by going home—to the Facebook Home page, that is. This is where you find a constant feed of status updates from everyone on your friends list. It's how you keep abreast of the latest developments regarding your friends.

Viewing the News Feed

When you sign into Facebook and open your Home page (www.facebook.com—or click the Home button on the Facebook toolbar), you see something called the News Feed. As you can see in Figure 5.1, this is a feed of the most recent status updates from people on your friends' list.

Figure 5.1. *The News Feed on Facebook's Home page.*

These status updates are displayed more or less in reverse chronological order. This means that the most recent updates are at the top and the older ones are at the bottom. To view even older updates, scroll to the bottom of the page and click the Older Posts button.

What are you likely to find in a typical status update? Most updates are short text messages, although updates can also include photos, videos, notices of upcoming events, and links to other Web pages. If there's a photo in a status update, like the one in Figure 5.2, click the photo to view it at a larger size—and within the context of the photo album in which it resides. If there's a video in the status update, like the one in Figure 5.3, click the video to begin playback. If there's an event listed in the status update, like the one in Figure 5.4, click it to read more details and RSVP, if you're invited. If there's a link in the status update, like the one in Figure 5.5, click it to leave Facebook and visit the linked-to page. Pretty straightforward, really.

Figure 5.2. *A status update with a photo attached.*

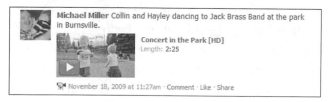

Figure 5.3. *A status update with a video attached.*

Figure 5.4. *A status update with an event attached.*

Figure 5.5. *A status update with a link to another Web page.*

By the way, if a friend posts from somewhere other than the Facebook page on his or her personal computer, you see this underneath the post. For example, Figure 5.6 shows a post made from a friend's iPhone. Posts can also be made from cell phones via text messaging and via third-party applications, such as TweetDeck and Foursquare, that automate posting to Facebook and other social networking sites.

Figure 5.6.   *A status update made via iPhone.*

Your friends are likely to post about what they're doing and what they're thinking. Some people post once a day, some post once a week, some post several times a day, some don't post much at all. There are no rules or guidelines as to how often someone should post, or what they should post about. To me, the best posts keep me updated on the most imortant events in my friends' lives—what activities they're participating in, what their kids are up to, when they're sick or well, that sort of thing. But you never know what your friends will post, which is what makes it interesting.

Viewing More Updates from More Friends

I said earlier that the News Feed contains status updates from your friends. That's true, but by default it doesn't include updates from *all* your friends. There are actually two levels of settings for what you see in the News Feed, and the default Top News setting filters out a lot of the people on your friends list.

That's right, by default Facebook doesn't show you updates from all your friends. The Top News setting only displays updates from whom Facebook determines are your most "interesting" friends. Don't ask me what this means. All I know is that only about a quarter of my friends show up in the Top News feed, which is a bit annoying.

If you want to view updates from *all* your friends, you have to switch the News Feed to the Most Recent setting. You do this by clicking Most Recent at the top right of the News Feed list, as shown in Figure 5.7.

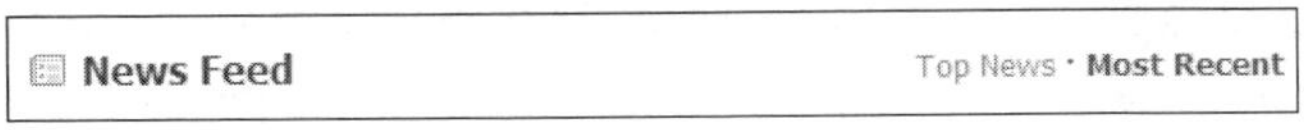

News Feed	Top News · **Most Recent**

Figure 5.7.   *Switching from Top News to the Most Recent News Feed.*

If you find the Most Recent list to be overwhelming, you can switch back to the Top News display by clicking the Top News link.

Viewing Only Status Updates from Your Friends

I said before that the News Feed displays status updates from your friends. That's true, but that's not the only thing displayed in the News Feed. Any posts or uploads that your friends make, such as pictures uploaded to their photo albums, are also listed in the News Feed, as are updates from the games and applications they use.

Some people feel this makes the News Feed a bit cluttered. If you'd prefer to view *only* status updates, from all your friends, you can display the Status Updates feed, shown in Figure 5.8. This is a somewhat hidden option on the Facebook site, but it's one you might want to check out.

Figure 5.8.   *The Status Update feed—lean and clean.*

To display the Status Updates feed, go to the Facebook Home page and click Friends in the sidebar. When the Friends page appears the Friends section in the sidebar also expands; click Status Updates in the Friends section to display the Status Updates feed.

The Status Update feed displays status updates only, no other notices or alerts. It's a pretty clean feed (there's not even a status update box at the top of the page), and one that many people wish was the Facebook default.

Hiding Friends You Don't Like

If you're like me, you'll find that some of your friends post a lot. No, I mean it, *really* a lot. Not just once or twice a day, but seemingly hourly.

Posting more frequently isn't always a good thing, of course; some of my more annoying "friends" post about when they got up in the morning, what they had for breakfast, when they're fixing coffee, when they're feeling sleepy, and when they're going to bed—way too much information, if you ask me.

Then there are those friends that really aren't friends sharing personal information, but rather are using Facebook to promote themselves or their businesses. Fine and dandy, but at some point I just don't care.

Of course, there are also those businesses and entertainers that you've said you "like" on Facebook. Posts from these entities also show up in your News Feed, and some of these can be really annoying.

The point is, you may not always want to view status updates from everyone or everything that shows up in your News Feed. Fortunately, there's a way to filter whose updates appear in the News Feed, by hiding updates from selected friends.

Hiding updates from a given person or entity is fairly easy. All you have to do is point to an update from that person to display the Hide button to the right of the post, as shown in Figure 5.9. This displays a box underneath the post, as shown in Figure 5.10. Click the Hide *Friend* button and no more status updates from this person will appear in your News Feed. Nice!

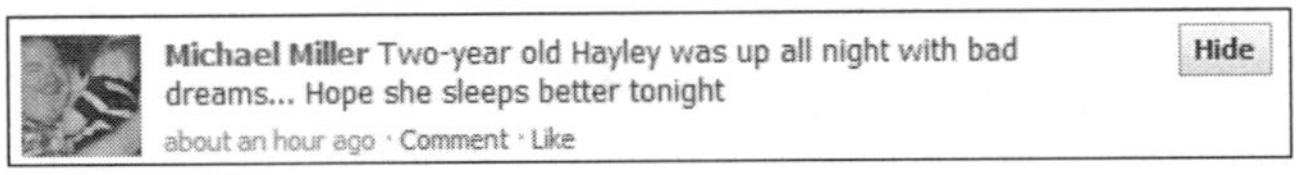

Michael Miller Two-year old Hayley was up all night with bad dreams... Hope she sleeps better tonight

about an hour ago · Comment · Like

[Hide]

Figure 5.9. *Point to a status update to display the Hide button.*

[Hide Michael] [Cancel]

Figure 5.10. *Hiding status updates from a given friend.*

Hiding Updates from Applications and Games

Some status updates aren't really updates from that person, but rather updates from an application or game that the person is using or playing. For example, you might see status updates alerting you that a friend has achieved a certain level on Farmville, or killed someone in Mafia Wars, or read a new book in their Goodreads library.

I find these automatically generated updates extremely intrusive—especially from people who incessantly play these social games. It's possible to see update after update after update from a person playing a game, which just takes up valuable space in your News Feed.

Learn more about Facebook applications and games in Chapter 18, "Finding Fun Games and Applications."

Now, you could decide to hide all posts from your game-addicted friend, but that would be throwing the proverbial baby out with the bath water; you'd also hide any important posts they might make. A better option is to hide posts from that game or application, so that you're never bothered by Farmville or Mafia Wars again.

Hiding posts from an application or game is similar to hiding posts from a person. Start by finding one of these annoying application-generated posts, then point to the post to display the Hide button. This displays a box underneath the post, as shown in Figure 5.11. This box contains three buttons: Hide *Friend*, Hide *Application*, and Cancel.

Figure 5.11. *Click the Hide* Application *button to hide all automatic posts from this application.*

This time you want to click the Hide *Application* button. This will hide all future posts from this application regarding *all* your friends. You can banish Farmville forever!

Commenting on Friends' Posts

Sometimes you read a friend's post and you want to say something about it. To this end, Facebook enables you to comment on just about any post your friends make. These comments then appear under the post in your News Feed, as shown in Figure 5.12.

Figure 5.12. *Comments under a friend's status update.*

To comment on a friend's status update, simply click the Comment link under that post. A Write a Comment box displays, like the one shown in Figure 5.13. Enter your comment then click the Share button; your comment will now appear underneath the original post, along with comments from any other people.

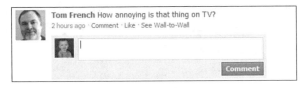

Figure 5.13. *Adding a comment under a friend's status update.*

Liking What You See

Sometimes you want to voice your approval for a post but don't necessarily want to take the time to type out a comment. In this instance, you can simply click the Like link under a status update. This puts a little "thumbs up" icon under the post, along with a message that you "like this."

By the way, if you later decide you *don't* like that post, can go back and remove your approval. Just click the Unlike link, and you won't be listed as liking it any more.

> **Note**
>
> You can both like and comment on a post; they're not mutually exclusive.

Sharing a Posted Attachment

When friends post an attachment to a status update—a photo, video, event, or Web page link—you can share that attachment with your friends on Facebook. You can share the attachment as a public post of your own, or via a private email message.

To share an attachment as a status update, follow these steps:

1. Click the Share link under your friend's status update. (This link only appears when an attachment is present; it isn't there for a standard text-only post.)

2. When the Post to Profile dialog box appears, as shown in Figure 5.14, enter the text of your accompanying status update into the text box.

Figure 5.14. *Sharing a friend's attachment as a new status update.*

3. Click the Share button, and you create a new status update with your friend's original post and attachment attached.

To share an attachment privately with another friend, follow these steps:

1. Click the Share link under your friend's status update.

2. When the Post to Profile dialog box appears, click the Send as a Message Instead link.

3. When the Send as a Message dialog box appears, as shown in Figure 5.15, enter the name of the recipient into the To: box. If you're sending to multiple friends, use commas to separate their names.

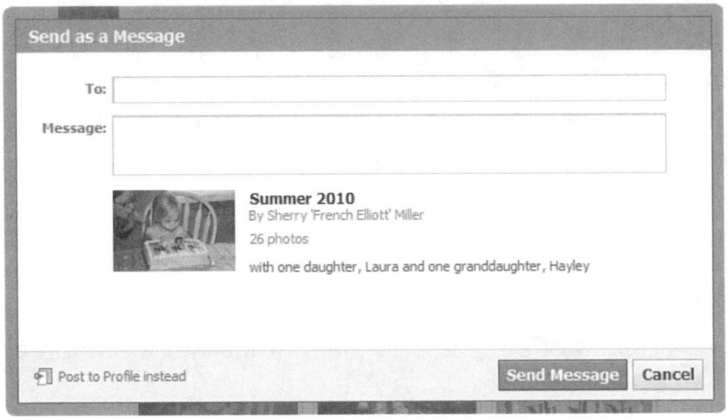

Figure 5.15. *Sharing a friend's attachment as a private message.*

4. Enter an accompanying message into the Message: box.

5. Click the Send Message button.

Your friend(s) will now receive a Facebook message with the original status update and its attachment attached.

Getting to and Getting to Know Your Friends' Profile Pages

Reading status updates in your News Feed keeps you up-to-date on your friend's latest activities. But what about older activities? Or if you want to look at any photos or videos they've uploaded? Of if you just want to view his or her personal information?

Everything you'd want to know about a Facebook friend is located on his or her individual Profile page.

Displaying a Profile Page

How do you display a friend's Profile page? It's easy: All you have to do is click that person's name anywhere on the Facebook site.

Where can you find a person's name to click? There are lots of places:

- In a status update in the News Feed on your Home page

- In the From: field of a private message sent to you

- In a chat window when you're using Facebook's chat (instant messaging) feature

- In the Friends section of your own Profile page

- In the Friends section of another friend's Profile page

You can also find your friends in your all-inclusive friends list. To display a list of all your friends, like the one shown in Figure 5.16, click Account in the Facebook toolbar and then select Edit Friends. When the next page appears, go to the Lists section of the sidebar and click Friends. What you see next is your friends list, alphabetized (by first name, unfortunately) from A to Z. Click any friend's name to display that person's Profile page.

Figure 5.16. *Your friends list.*

Navigating a Profile Page

What do you see when you display a friend's Profile page? As you can see in Figure 5.17, a typical Profile page consists of a sidebar on the left side of the page, a series of tabs in the middle of the page, and another sidebar on the right.

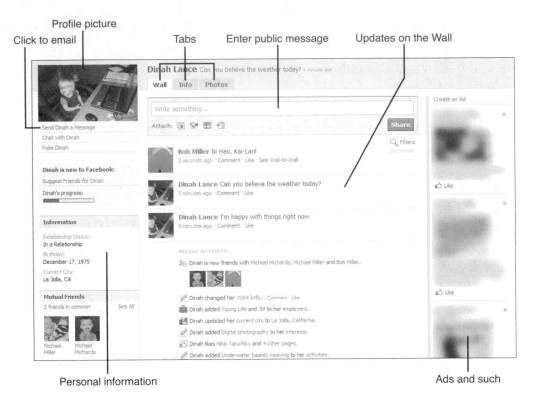

Figure 5.17. *A typical Profile page.*

The sidebar on the left is the most important one of the two. It contains your friend's Profile picture, a link to send this person a private message (via Facebook email), all manner of personal information (relationship status; spouse, children, and siblings; birthday; current city; and such), a list of mutual friends, a list of all that person's friends, links to your friend's photos, and assorted other information and links. It's a nice and concise introduction to this person.

The sidebar on the right is much less useful. Basically, it contains advertisements. You can ignore it.

The tabs in the middle of the page display more specific information. While some of the tabs might differ from person to person, everyone has the same three tabs on their Profile pages: Wall, Info, and Photos. You might also find tabs for Videos or Events, a Boxes tab with information about the applications that person uses, or even tabs for specific applications. It all depends on what that person does on Facebook and the configuration options chosen.

We'll look at the three most important tabs next.

Reading the Wall—and Leaving Your Own Comments

The first tab on a person's page is always the Wall, shown in Figure 5.18. The Wall is kind of like a News Feed of just that person's activities—status updates, photo postings, event subscriptions, and the like. Like a News Feed page, updates and postings are displayed in reverse chronological order, with the newest at the top.

Figure 5.18. *The Wall tab.*

You can comment on and "like" status updates on a friend's Wall. Obviously, other people's comments are also displayed.

You can also leave your own public messages on a friend's wall. Just type your message into the Write Something box at the top of the tab, then click the Share button. Your message to your friend will now be displayed on her Wall, for your friend and all of her friends to see.

You can attach a photo, video, link to another website, or a virtual "gift" to your posting; just click the appropriate button beneath the Write Something box and make the necessary choices. We talk more about these message attachments in Chapter 8, "Updating Your Friends on What You're Doing," as they're also available when you're making your own status updates.

Viewing Your Friends' Personal Information

The second tab on a friend's Profile page is the Info tab, shown in Figure 5.19. This tab consists of several sections of personal information, as follows:

- About Me, complete with Basic Info (gender, birthday, relatives on Facebook, current city, home town, and the like), Bio (a short biography entered by the person him- or herself), and Favorite Quotations.

- Work and Education, which functions as a mini-resume, complete with current and past employers, high schools and colleges attended, and such.

- Likes and Interests, including Activities, Music, Books, Movies, Television, and the like.

- Contact Information, if displayed, which can include a person's email address, postal address, website, and such.

Scattered amongst all these pieces of information are lots and lots of blue links. Clicking these links take you to other pages on Facebook. These can be other people's Profile pages, or pages for groups, locations, companies, entertainers, books, movies, you name it. Click around to see what you find.

Now, not every person opts to enter or display every piece of information. That's a personal choice, and understandable. Still, you can find out a lot about what a friend has been up to by perusing their Info tab.

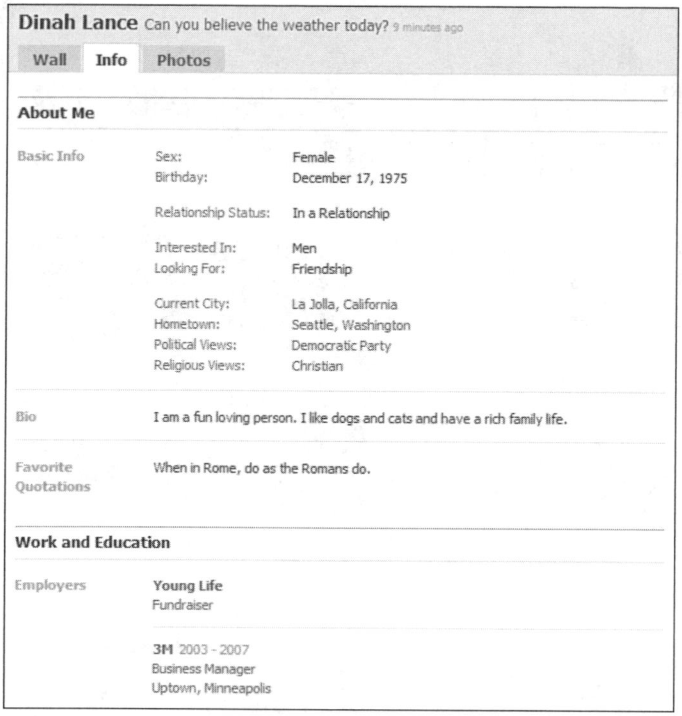

> **Dinah Lance** Can you believe the weather today? 9 minutes ago
>
> | Wall | **Info** | Photos |
>
> **About Me**
>
> | Basic Info | Sex: | Female |
> | | Birthday: | December 17, 1975 |
> | | Relationship Status: | In a Relationship |
> | | Interested In: | Men |
> | | Looking For: | Friendship |
> | | Current City: | La Jolla, California |
> | | Hometown: | Seattle, Washington |
> | | Political Views: | Democratic Party |
> | | Religious Views: | Christian |
>
> | Bio | I am a fun loving person. I like dogs and cats and have a rich family life. |
>
> | Favorite Quotations | When in Rome, do as the Romans do. |
>
> **Work and Education**
>
> | Employers | **Young Life** |
> | | Fundraiser |
> | | **3M** 2003 - 2007 |
> | | Business Manager |
> | | Uptown, Minneapolis |

Figure 5.19. *The Info tab.*

Looking at Photos

Many Facebookers use the site for sharing photos with friends and family. These uploaded photos are typically organized into photo albums and displayed on a person's Profile page, on the Photos tab.

As you can see in Figure 5.20, a typical Photos tab starts with photos of that person arranged at the top. Scroll down and you see the photo albums that this person has uploaded. Click the thumbnail for a photo album to see the photos inside. Click any photo thumbnail to view a larger version of that photo.

> **Note**
>
> Learn more about Facebook's photo features in Chapter 11, "Sharing Family Pictures."

Figure 5.20. *The Photos tab.*

Viewing Other Tabs

As I said before, some people will have more tabs than these displayed on their Profile pages. For example, if a friend has uploaded home movies to the site, they'll have a Video tab on their page; if they've scheduled or subscribed to an event, they'll have an Events tab. There might also be tabs for specific applications, such as LivingSocial or Goodreads. So everyone's Profile page will be different.

Facebook can display up to six visible tabs on a Profile page. If a person has more than six tabs, the additional tabs can be viewed by clicking the double right arrow (>>) tab at the far right of the tab list. This displays a drop-down menu of the other available tabs, as shown in Figure 5.21; click an item to open that tab.

Figure 5.21. *Accessing other tabs.*

All Comments Are Public

I'll say this several times throughout the book, but it's important to remember that Facebook is a *public* website. That means that just about everything you do on Facebook is visible to everybody else.

This is especially true in the comments you leave on your friends' status updates. It's easy to trick yourself into thinking that leaving a comment is a bit like replying to a private email, but a Facebook comment isn't private at all. Any comment you make is visible to all of your friend's friends, and possibly to everybody else on the Facebook site. (This last possibility depends on how your friend has configured his or her privacy settings.)

If you think you're leaving a private reply, you're more apt to write something that you really shouldn't. I'll give you an example. I was reading the comments on a friend's page a while back, and saw a comment to one of the updates there. A friend of my friend made a comment, my friend commented back, something along the lines of "how have things been going?," and the resulting comment was a long litany of how this person's wife was having an affair, and how awful his life was, and on and on in that fashion. Obviously, this comment was not private, since I was reading it, but the poster—the friend of my friend—either didn't know or care that his comment was a very public one.

The take-away here is that you shouldn't make any comment to any post that you don't want all your other friends to read. Facebook comments are not the place to post private messages; they're the Facebook equivalent of public announcements, and should be treated as such.

Chapter 6

Keeping Tabs on Your Kids

Facebook is a great place to reconnect with old friends. It's also a great place to connect with family members—especially your children.

Now, this assumes that your kids are on Facebook, which they probably are. (Almost all young people under 25 or so are.) It also assumes that your kids will want to be your Facebook friends—although there are things you can do if you're left unfriended.

The point is to not so much use Facebook as a way to communicate with your kids (although you can do that), but rather use Facebook to keep a watchful eye on what your kids are doing. Most young people use Facebook as a bit of a personal diary, posting all sorts of juicy details as to their private thoughts and activities; you can find out a lot about what your kids are up to just by reading their Facebook status updates.

Making Your Children Your Friends

The first step in using Facebook to watch your children is to add your kids to your friends list. This should be a fairly straightforward process—in fact, Facebook might suggest your children as friends when you first sign up, especially if you have your kids' addresses in your email contacts list.

Otherwise, you need to do a simple search for your kids on the Facebook site, as we discussed in Chapter 4, "How to Find Old Friends—and Make New Ones." You can search either by name or by email address, if in fact your kids have an email address and you know what it is. In any case, it shouldn't be too hard to find your children on Facebook and then send out the necessary friend requests.

What to Do If Your Kids Hide from You on Facebook

What do you do if one of your kids refuses your friend request? First, pat yourself on the back; you have a smart, technically savvy, and understandably wary offspring. He knows that you're probably going on Facebook to keep an eye on his activities, and he thinks he can block you out by not making you his friend.

Fair enough, as far as it goes. But you still have a few options.

Viewing Updates Without Being a Friend

First, you may not even have to make your child a Facebook friend to view his Profile page and status updates. Many people configure Facebook's privacy settings so that all users can view their status updates. If your child is this negligent, you don't have to be a friend to read everything he posts. Just find and go to his Profile page, and read to your heart's content. It's worth a shot.

Viewing Updates as a Friend of a Friend

Let's assume, though, that if your child was smart enough not to accept your friend request that he's also smart enough not to set his status update viewing setting to "everyone." Your next hope is that, instead, he set the viewing status to "friends of friends." This could be your foot in the door.

What you want to do now is find someone who you know is on your child's friends list. This might be a classmate, a cousin, the kid down the block, a guy on the football team, whatever. Just make sure that your child is on this person's friends list—look at the Friends box on that person's Profile page and see if your child's name is listed.

Now, invite this friend of your child to be on your Facebook friends list. Chances are you'll be accepted, but if not you can try inviting another of your kid's friends. Just keep trying until you get on someone's friends list.

After you are a friend of one of your child's friends, go your kid's Facebook Profile page. If he set the privacy levels to "friends of friends," you'll now be able to read all of his status updates, just as if you were a friend yourself.

Creating a Surreptitious Identity

Some youngsters are savvy enough (and care enough about their privacy) to configure Facebook's privacy settings to display their status updates only to friends. Some are even savvier, and know how to block specific people—like you—from viewing their updates. What to do, then, if you find yourself locked out from your child's innermost Facebook postings?

> **Note**
>
> The only downside to tracking your child when you're not an official friend is that his status updates won't appear in your News Feed. You have to manually access his Profile page to read his status updates.

Your only recourse at this point is to reinvent yourself—as someone else. That is, you need to create a second Facebook account under a different name and identity. Instead of being a forty-something mother, you need to be a teenaged girl or a college-aged dude. In other words, you need to become someone that your child won't automatically think to block on Facebook.

But wait—why would your child accept a friend request from a complete stranger, albeit one closer to their own age? Because, unfortunately, most teenagers and young adults have hundreds of Facebook friends, many of which they've never met in real life. They're friends of friends, acquaintances, people they bumped into once in the hall between classes, folks who just happen to live nearby or go to the same school or work at the same company. For better or worse, younger users are accustomed to accepting friend requests without question, as long as there are no obvious "red flags" concerning the person making the request. So as long as you don't stand out as an old weirdo, chances are you can fake your way onto your child's friends list.

Establishing a new identity does require some creativity, of course. First, you need to get the age right; within a year either side of your child's age is generally good.

Next, the gender. Is your son more likely to accept a request from a pretty girl or a guy he's never met? (I'd bet on the girl.) Is your daughter more likely to accept a request from a cool girl or a good looking guy? (Not to be sexist, but this one is a tougher question; many girls are less questioning about Facebook girlfriends than they are guys they've never met.)

You need to pick a new name, of course, something age appropriate. (That means something like "Colby" or "Dylan" instead of "Margaret" or "Bob.") Make sure the person you're inventing lives nearby; kids are less likely to make friends with people who live across the country.

As to school, this is also a little tricky. If your child goes to a smaller school where everyone is likely to know everyone else, you probably don't want to say you go to that school, too; instead, pick a neighboring school where he doesn't know everyone. If your child goes to a larger school, however, particularly a large university, you can fake the school allegiance and no one will be the wiser.

Then you need to fill in some personal information. The new person you're becoming should have a lot of the same likes and dislikes as your child—television shows, movies, music, and such. If you don't know what your kid likes…well, shame on you.

Finally, you need to have a second email address, one your child doesn't know about. It shouldn't be easily traceable to you—that is, it shouldn't include your real name in the email address. I recommend creating a new account at one of the big Web email services, such as Gmail or Hotmail, just for this purpose.

After you've created this new account for your fictitious self, you should first seek out some of your offspring's friends and invite them onto your friends list. Don't start by making your

 Tip

You don't have to—and probably shouldn't—add a photo to your fake Facebook account. Not every Facebooker has a Profile picture, so the absence of such shouldn't be suspicious. On the other hand, choosing the wrong photo could set off warning alarms. Plus, where are you going to get the picture, anyway? You could get into more trouble ripping off someone else's photo than you could being found out by your child.

child your first and only friend; you need to establish your identity before you ingratiate yourself with your child. It helps if you have a handful of friends already established, then it looks kind of normal when you ask your child to join your friends list.

After you're on the list, you don't have to—and probably shouldn't—interact with your child. Most Facebook friends are silent friends, so it won't look odd if you don't comment on your child's updates or make updates of your own. Just keep to the background and observe as best you can.

Yes, it's spying, but you're a parent—you're entitled.

Using Facebook to See What Your Kids Are Up To

The whole point of using Facebook to keep tabs on your kids is to look and listen without doing a lot of talking. You kind of want your child to forget that you're there, so she'll let her guard down. If your child thinks that you're watching, she'll be careful about what she posts. If she forgets a parent is watching, she'll be a lot more free with what she says on the site.

The main thing you want to do is read your child's status updates. Most young people on Facebook, for whatever reason, are surprisingly open about what they post; you'll get to see who your child is hanging out with, hear about her latest fight with her boyfriend, read about how much she hates her classes this semester or likes her new job or is creeped out by the guy who works at the Orange Julius stand at the mall. Your child's inner-most thoughts, both profound and mundane, will be there on her Wall for you to read.

It's kind of like eavesdropping on a private conversation—except that it's a public conversation that anyone can listen to. It's not like spying, not really; it's more like stalking. After all, your child's status updates are there on Facebook for everyone to read. You just happen to be actively interested in reading everything your child posts.

To be a successful parental Facebook stalker, however, you need to keep your presence someone muted. That is, you don't want to remind your child that you're reading what she writes. That means *not* commenting on your child's posts. This may be the hardest part of the whole process; most parents have to really restrain themselves from offering advice or support or consoling their kids when they make a post. You can't do that. You just can't. You have to stay invisible on your child's Profile page, so she doesn't know that you're there.

Note

Just because you shouldn't comment on your child's status updates doesn't mean that you can't make new status updates on your own Profile page. Chances are your child won't equate your occasional post showing up in her News Feed with the fact that you're eyeballing everything she posts online.

If you can't resist the urge and do post a comment to one of your child's status updates, let me tell you what is likely to happen. First, your child will become much less open on Facebook; the number of posts she makes will drop dramatically. Then she'll get smart and figure out how to configure Facebook so that you—and you alone—can't read her status updates. Then she'll go back to posting frequently, but you'll never know because you won't be able to see a thing she posts. In other words, you'll have blown your cover.

So heed my advice and, once you get inside, stay silent. Yes, you'll be listed as one of her Facebook friends, but you'll be one of those silent friends she soon forgets about. Out of sight, out of mind, if you want to stay in the loop.

Using Facebook to Contact Your Grown Kids

All this talk about snooping on your kids online really applies to younger kids—middle schoolers, high schoolers, college-aged kids. After your kids get a bit older and a lot more mature, your online relationship with them changes. Or should change, anyway.

As your children move away from home and establish families of their own, finding the time to talk is a major challenge. Days, weeks, even months might go by where neither of you can find the time to phone. Here is where Facebook can be of real value.

When you add a grown child to your Facebook friends list, that child now is privy to all the status updates you make—and vice versa. This is a great way to keep each other informed of all the little things happening in your lives.

For more detailed information, take advantage of Facebook's private messaging system. This is like email for Facebookers, where you use Facebook to send longer messages back and forth. It's not quite the same as exchanging written letters, but it's better than not writing at all.

And if you both happen to find yourself online at the same time (check the Friends Online section of your Home page), you can use Facebook's chat feature to instant message in real time with your child. It's almost like talking in person!

Note

Learn more about sending and receiving private messages in Chapter 9, "Exchanging Private Messages."

Note

Learn more about instant messaging in Chapter 10, "Chatting with Your Kids—Live."

Tracking Personal Info

The obvious thing to look at when you're snooping on (excuse me, observing) your child of Facebook is his status updates. These tell you what he's doing and thinking about at the moment.

But you also want to pay attention to the personal information he supplies to the Facebook site, in particular what's on the Info tab on his Profile page. There are a number of things to look for here.

First, it's always fun to observe your child's relationship status. Trust me, this might be the first place you learn that he's gotten a new girlfriend, or broken up with his old one.

I also like to look at what the kid is watching and listening to these days. An odd change in listening habits, for example, might signal other changes in behavior. It's not a perfect indicator, by any means, but you can get a sense of how a child is leaning by the music he listens to and the movies he watches.

Finally, take a look at the contact information at the bottom of the Info tab. If there's any information there at all, it's time to break your cover and have a talk with your child. Your child should not, under any circumstances, publicly list his or her phone number, mailing address, or email address. There should be no way for bad guys to contact your kids online, which means keeping all this contact information private. It's worth a few temporary bad feelings to keep your kids from putting too much of themselves online—and potentially putting themselves in harm's way.

Chapter 7

Organizing Your Friends List

After you've been on Facebook for any length of time, you'll find that you've added quite a few people to your friends list. Between old friends from your youth, current friends and co-workers, and assorted family members, you might end up with anywhere from a few dozen to a few hundred Facebook friends. Good for you!

The problem with having so many friends on Facebook, however, is managing them. That's a lot of people to track in your News Feed, for example. It's also difficult to find that one individual friend you want to email or send a photo to; when you have an ever expanding friends list, locating one single friend is a little like finding a needle in a haystack.

How, then, do you better manage the people on your friends list? There are ways, as I'll tell you next.

Creating Friends Lists

When it comes to managing large lists of friends, the key is to create *custom* lists within your main list. A Facebook list is simply a subset of your total friends list, organized however you wish.

For example, you might want to create a list that contains only family members. Or you could create a list of people you currently work with. Or one that contains other members of a club or outside organization. You get the drift.

When you have a custom list (or two or three), it's easy enough to find individuals on that list, or to send messages to all the members of the list. It's a lot easier to manage small lists of friends than it is to deal with all your friends at once.

Here's how to create a custom list:

1. Click the Account button on the Facebook toolbar and select Edit Friends from the pull-down menu.

2. When the Friends page appears, click Friends in the Lists section of the sidebar.

3. Facebook now displays the master list of all your friends, shown in Figure 7.1; you create your new list from this master list. Do so by clicking the Create New List button.

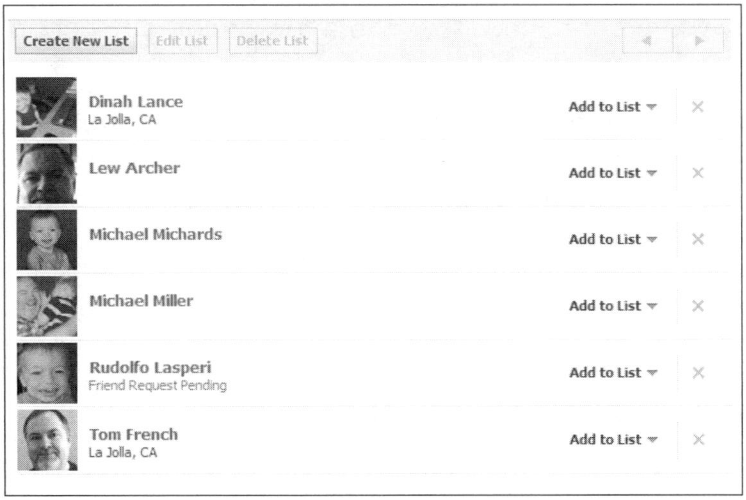

Figure 7.1. *Your master Friends list.*

4. When the Create New List window appears, as shown in Figure 7.2, enter a name for the list into the Enter a Name box.

5. Click those friends you want included in this list. You can select multiple people at the same time.

6. Click the Create List button.

That's it; your new list is now created.

Figure 7.2. *Creating a new custom friends list.*

Editing Your Lists

Your new list now appears in the Lists section of the sidebar on the Friends page. Figure 7.3 displays the lists that I've personally created, one for Family and one for Work.

Lists
- 👥 Friends
- 📄 Work
- 📄 Family
- 📄 Pages
- 📄 SMS Subscriptions

Figure 7.3. *All your Facebook friends lists—including your master list (Friends) and the custom lists you've created.*

To add or delete members from a given list, follow these steps:

1. Click the Account button on the Facebook toolbar and select Edit Friends from the pull-down menu.

2. When the Friends page appears, go to the Lists section of the sidebar and click the particular list.

3. Facebook now displays all members of the list, as shown in Figure 7.4. Click the Edit List button.

Figure 7.4.   *Viewing a custom friends list.*

4. When the Edit List dialog box appears, as shown in Figure 7.5, make sure the All button is selected.

Figure 7.5.   *Editing the members of a custom friends list.*

5. Current members of the list are shown with their names selected. To remove someone from this list, click his or her name to deselect them.

6. To add a new person to this list, click their name.

7. Click the Save List button.

You can also add people to any existing list from your master Friends list. Just display the Friends list and click the Add to List button to the right of that person's name, as shown in Figure 7.6. This displays all existing lists; check the list to which you want to add this person.

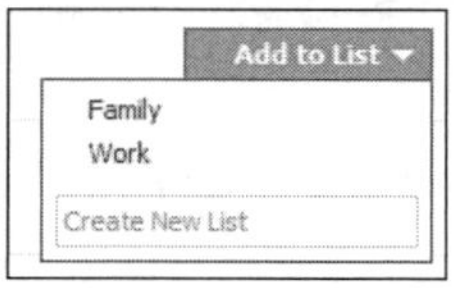

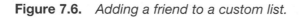

Figure 7.6. *Adding a friend to a custom list.*

Likewise, you can remove a person from any list from the master Friends list. Just click the *X* List(s) button next to that person's name and uncheck the list from which you want to remove that person. You can also add that person to another list at the same time.

Displaying Status Updates from List Members

One of the uses of a custom friends list is to view status updates only from the members of that list. This way you can see what all your family members are up to, for example.

To view the status updates of a custom friends list, follow these steps:

1. Go to the Facebook Home page and click Friends in the sidebar.

2. When the next page appears, the Friends section of the sidebar also expands to show all the custom lists you've created, as shown in Figure 7.7. Click the name of the list you want to view.

Figure 7.7. *Displaying status updates from the members of a custom friends list.*

Facebook now displays a News Feed of status updates from the members of this list.

Deleting Custom Lists

If you create a custom list that you later feel is unnecessary, you can easily delete it. Follow these steps:

1. Click the Account button on the Facebook toolbar and select Edit Friends from the pull-down menu.

2. When the Friends page appears, go to the Lists section of the sidebar and click the particular list.

3. Click the Delete List button near the top of the page, as shown in Figure 7.8.

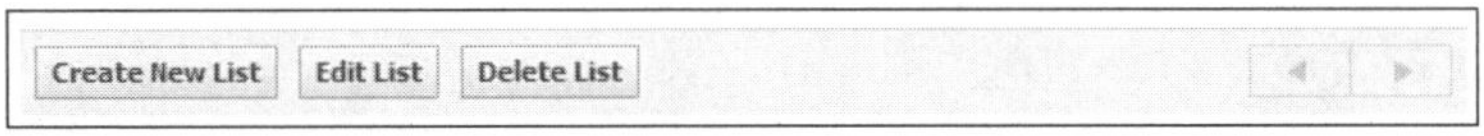

| Create New List | Edit List | Delete List | | ◄ | ► |

Figure 7.8. *Deleting a custom friends list.*

4. When prompted by the Delete List? dialog box, click the Delete List button.

Getting Rid of Unwanted Friends

While we're on the topic of managing your Facebook friends, what do you do about those friends who you really don't want to be friends with anymore? Maybe it's someone who's fallen off your radar, a co-worker who changed jobs, an acquaintance who's proven more annoying than friendly, or a black sheep family member you'd prefer to disown. Do you need to keep these people on your friends list forever?

The answer, of course, is that you don't. You can, at any time, remove any individual from your Facebook friends list. This is called *unfriending* the person, and it happens all the time. In fact, the person you unfriend doesn't even know he's been ditched; you just get rid of them and that's that.

Here's how to do it:

1. Click the Account button on the Facebook toolbar and select Edit Friends from the pull-down menu.

2. When the Friends page appears, go to the Lists section of the sidebar and click Friends.

3. Go to the person you want to unfriend and click the X to the far right of his or her name, as shown in Figure 7.9.

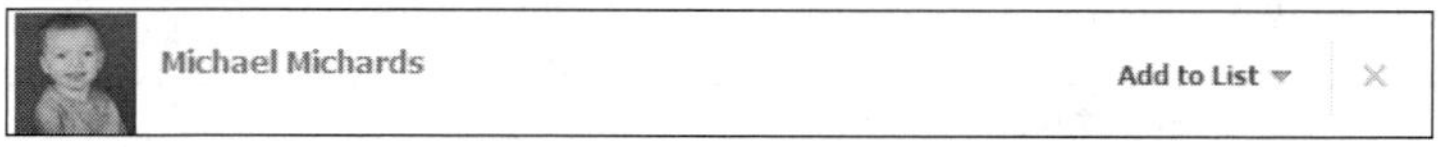

| Michael Michards | Add to List ▾ | × |

Figure 7.9. *Click the X to remove an individual from your friends list.*

4. When prompted if you want to remove the connection, click the Remove button.

That's it. The person is no longer your official Facebook friend.

Blocking Unwanted Users

Just because you remove someone as your friend doesn't mean that you become invisible to that person on Facebook. That person can still email you and, unless you alter your privacy settings, view certain content on your Profile page.

If you think that someone is acting like a stalker, it might be best to completely block all contact from that person. You do this by adding this individual to what Facebook calls your *block list*. Individuals on this list cannot view your Profile page, send you private messages, or even find you in search of the Facebook site. It's a great way to shield yourself from online stalkers—or just people you never want to hear from again.

To block someone in this fashion, follow these steps:

1. Click Account on the Facebook toolbar and then click Privacy Settings.

2. When the Choose Your Privacy Settings page appears, go to the Block Lists section at the bottom of the page and click Edit Your Lists.

Note

You can, at any time, re-add an unfriended person as a friend. You just have to go through the whole invite-a-friend process again, no big deal.

Note

Learn more about determining who can and can't view your personal information in Chapter 21, "Keeping Some Things Private."

3. When the Block Lists page appears, as shown in Figure 7.10, enter that person's Facebook name into the Name box, or enter his or her email address into the Email box.

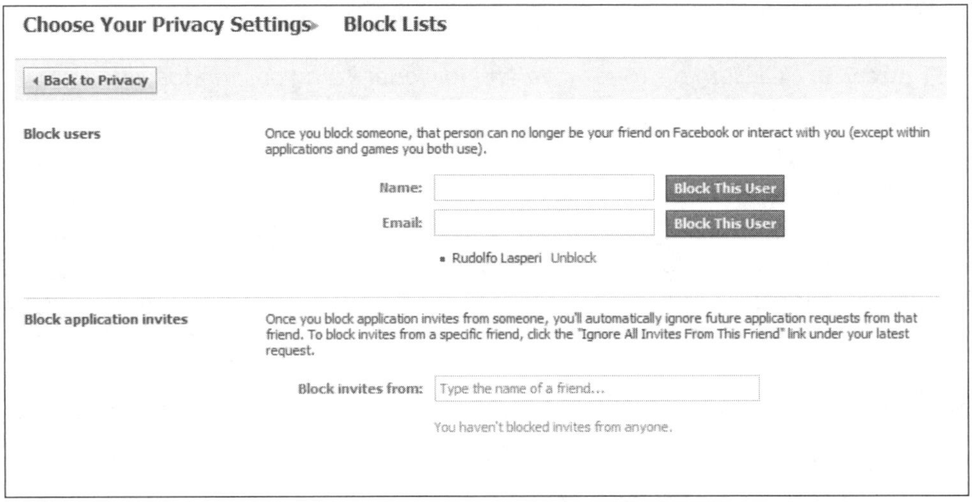

Figure 7.10. *Adding someone to your block list.*

4. Click the appropriate Block This User button.

People you've blocked are now listed on the Block List page. To unblock a given individual, click the Unblock link next to his or her name.

How Many Friends Is Too Many?

Younger Facebook users tend to have more friends than do older users. I'm not quite sure why this is the case; after all, we've met a lot more people in our years than younger users have in their limited time walking this planet.

Still, younger folks are more likely to use Facebook as the hub of their social interactions, and thus have lots of people on their friends list who they barely know, if they know them at all. Those of our generation, being older and wiser and more discriminate, tend to avoid friending mere acquaintances. Our friends lists are more likely to contain real friends.

That said, it's easy to build up a Facebook friends list that registers in the triple digits. I don't care how gregarious you are, it's unlikely that you have that many true friends. Really, take a look at your list—how many people on there really belong?

Because we tend to accumulate Facebook friends much the same way as our yards accumulate dandelions, from time to time you might want to cull the pretenders from your list of friends. Does that neighbor two streets over really need to be there? Or the checkout lady from the supermarket? Or, for that matter, weird cousin Ernie?

Sometimes who you let on your friends list is a matter of strategy. Take, for example, my stepdaughter, who is a nurse at a major metropolitan hospital. Her policy is to allow other nurses on her friends list, but not doctors or hospital administrators. To her thinking, her co-workers— people at her level—can be friends, but her bosses can't. Makes sense to me.

You might want to develop similar strategies for deciding who you do or don't let onto your friends list. Maybe it's as simple as saying anyone who gets a Christmas card (or you get a Christmas card from) gets on the list. Or only those people you talk or write to once a year get on the list. Or people who work in your department, but not those who work in remote offices. You get to make the rules.

The point is that even though Facebook is a social network, you don't have to network with everyone on the site. You can pick and choose those people you befriend—and sometimes a smaller circle of friends is better.

Keeping in Touch with Facebook

Chapter 8

Updating Your Friends on What You're Doing

We've talked a lot about Facebook being the perfect place to update your friends and family on what you're up to—things you're doing, thoughts you're thinking, accomplishments you're accomplishing, you name it. The easiest way to let people know what's what is to post what Facebook calls a *status update*.

Every status update you make is broadcast to everyone on your friends list, displayed in the News Feed on their Home pages. This way everyone who cares enough about you to make you a friend will know everything you post about. And that can be quite a lot—from simple text posts to photos and videos and even links to other Web pages.

What Is a Status Update?

Quite literally, a Facebook status update is an update of your status. Yeah, that's self-defining, but in essence it's a way to describe what you're doing or thinking about at the moment. It's a snapshot into your life, posted as a short text on the Facebook site.

A status update is, at its most basic, a brief text message. It can be as short as a word or two, or it can be several paragraphs long; that's up to you. (The official maximum limit is 420 characters, or three times the length of a similar Twitter message.)

Although a basic status update is all text, you can also attach various multimedia elements to your status updates, including digital photographs, videos, events, and links to other Web pages. You can also "tag" other Facebook users and groups in your updates, so that their names appear as clickable links (to their Profile pages, of course).

The nice thing about a status update is that it's a post-once, read-many process. That is, a single status update is broadcast to all the people on your friends list. If you have 100 friends, that's 100 people that read the single status update you posted.

Note

Various Facebook applications also let you attach application-specific items to your status updates. Learn more about these applications in Chapter 18, "Finding Fun Games and Applications."

Status updates appear in multiple places on the Facebook site. First, your status updates appear on your own Profile page, newest at the top, on your Wall tab, as shown in Figure 8.1. (Your most recent status update also appears at the very top of your Profile page, above the Publisher box, which is shown in Figure 8.3.) Your status updates also appear on your friends' Home pages, in their News Feeds, as shown in Figure 8.2. This way your friends are kept updated as to what you're doing and thinking.

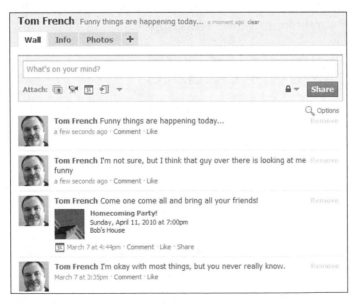

Figure 8.1. *Status updates on your Profile page.*

Figure 8.2. *Status updates on a friends' Home page.*

Where to Update Your Status

When you want to update your status, there are two different places you can do it.

First, you can go to your Home page, at the top of which resides the box you see in Figure 8.3. This box, which initially has the words "What's on your mind?" inside, is officially called the *Publisher box*; it's also sometimes referred to as the *Share box*. In any instance, this box is one place to enter your updates; click the Share button to post a new status update.

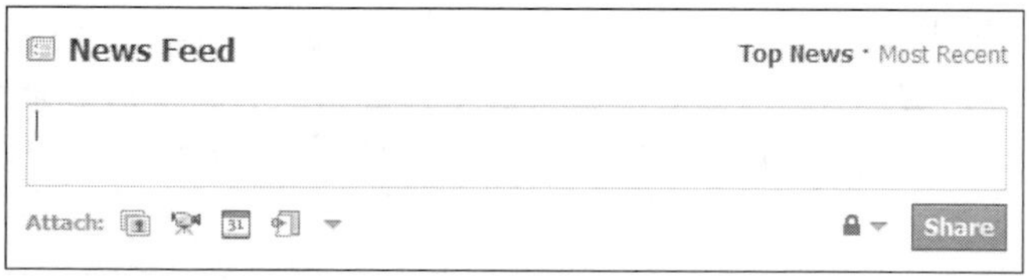

Figure 8.3. *The Publisher box at the top of your Profile page.*

You can also find a Publisher box at the top of your own Profile page. As you can see in Figure 8.4, it's the same box (save for a blue background around it) and works the same way.

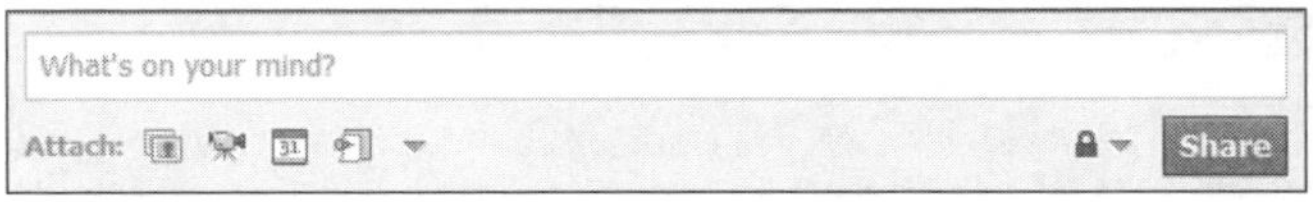

What's on your mind?

Attach: 📷 📹 📅 🔗 ▼   🔒 ▼   Share

Figure 8.4. *The Publisher box at the top of your Home page.*

By the way, you can also post status updates from your mobile phone, as a standard text message. Or, if you have a Facebook application for your iPhone or other smartphone, you can use that app to post your updates.

How to Update Your Status

Posting a status update is a relatively simple procedure. It can get a little more complicated, however, if you choose to attach a photo, video, event, or Web link to the basic text message.

Posting a Simple Text Update

Understandably, Facebook makes it extremely easy to post a status update. You have to be signed into Facebook, of course, but then you follow these simple steps:

1. Navigate to the Facebook Home page or your personal Profile page.

2. Type your message into the Publisher box at the top of the page.

3. Click the Share button.

! Caution

Do not confuse these Publisher boxes with the very similar box found at the top of your friends' Profile pages. The box on a friend's page is used to post a message to that friend on that friend's Profile page only. What you post on a friend's page is *not* a regular status update, and does not make it into anyone else's News Feed.

✎ Note

Learn more about posting to Facebook from your mobile phone in Chapter 19, "Using Facebook on the Go."

Attaching a Photo

So far, so good. But what if you'd like to attach a photo to a status update? You can, you know; it's a great way to share a special photo with your friends, without them having to navigate to and through your photo albums. In this instance, you follow these steps:

1. Begin by typing the desired text of your update into the Publish box at the top of the Home or Profile page.

2. Click the Photos button to display a new Photos panel beneath the Publisher box, as shown in Figure 8.5.

Note

Any additions you make to your Facebook photo albums are automatically added to the Wall on your Profile page. Any single picture you post with a status update is automatically added to the Wall Photos album. (Unless you posted it from your mobile phone, in which case it ends up in the Mobile Uploads album.)

Photos ☒
Upload a Photo from your drive   **Take a Photo** with a webcam   **Create an Album** with many photos
🔒▾ Share

Figure 8.5.   *Getting ready to attach a photo to a status update.*

3. To use a photo stored on your hard drive, click Upload a Photo. When the panel changes, click the Browse or Choose Button; when the Open dialog box appears, navigate to and select the photo you want. Then click the Open button.

4. To use a new photo taken with your computer's webcam, click the Take a Photo link. When the panel changes to display your live webcam, as shown in Figure 8.6, click the Photo button.

5. Click the Share button to post your update.

Note

Learn more about uploading photos to Facebook in Chapter 11, "Sharing Family Pictures."

Figure 8.6. *Using your webcam to create a photo for a status post.*

Attaching a Video

You can also attach videos to your status updates. This is a great way to share your latest home movies, assuming you've saved them in or converted them to a digital file.

Follow these steps:

Note

You can upload video files up to 20 minutes in length and 1024 MB (approximately 1 GB) in size.

1. Begin by typing the text for your update into the Publisher box at the top of your Home or Profile page.

2. Click the Video button to display a new Video panel beneath the Publisher box, as shown in Figure 8.7.

3. To attach a video already recorded and stored on your computer, click the Upload a Video link. When the panel changes, click the Choose File or Browse button; when the Open dialog box appears, navigate to and select the video file. Then click the Open button.

4. To attach a video recorded from your webcam, click the Record a Video link. When the panel changes to display a live picture from your webcam, as shown in Figure 8.8, click the Record button. Click the button again to end your recording.

Figure 8.7. *Getting ready to attach a video to a status update.*

Figure 8.8. *Recording a webcam video to attach to a status update.*

5. Click the Share button to post your update.

Attaching an Event

If you're hosting a party, planning a community get-together, or just planning a dinner date, you can share notice of that event with your Facebook friends by attaching it to a status update. Here's how it works:

> **Note**
>
> Learn more about uploading videos to Facebook in Chapter 12, "Sharing Home Movies."

1. Begin by typing any accompanying text for the update into the Publisher box at the top of your Home or Profile page.

2. Click the Event button to display a new Event panel beneath the Publish box, shown in Figure 8.9.

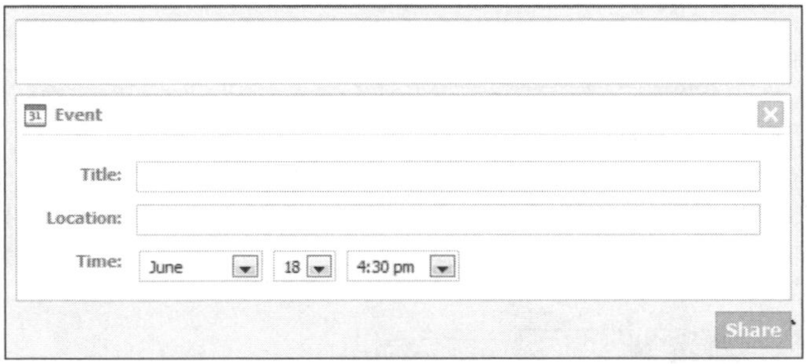

🗓 Event	✖
Title:	
Location:	
Time:	June ▾ 18 ▾ 4:30 pm ▾
	Share

Figure 8.9. *Creating an event attached to a status update.*

3. Type the name of the event into the Title box.

4. Type where the event is hosted into the Location box.

5. Pull down the time lists to select the start date and time of the event.

6. Click the Share button.

✎Note

Learn more about Facebook events in Chapter 13, "Sharing Birthdays and Events."

Attaching a Link to Another Web Page

Here's something else you can add to a status update—a link to a particular Web page or article you like. Not only does Facebook add a link to the specified page, it also lets you include a thumbnail image from that page with the status update.

Here's how it works:

1. Begin by typing any accompanying text into the Publisher box at the top of your Home or Profile page.

2. Click the Link button to display a new Link panel beneath the Publish box, as shown in Figure 8.10.

Figure 8.10. *Adding a Web link to a status update.*

3. In the Link box, enter the full Web address of the page you want to link to.

4. Click Attach.

5. When you are prompted to select a thumbnail image from this Web page to accompany your link, as shown in Figure 8.11, click the left- and right-arrow buttons to cycle through the available images, or check the No Thumbnail option to include the link without an accompanying image.

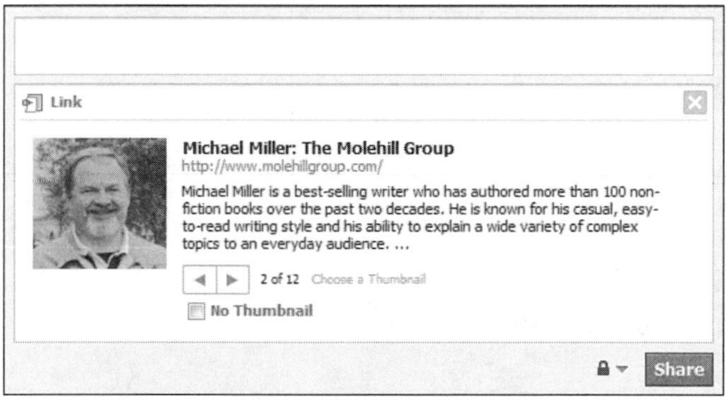

Figure 8.11. *Choosing a thumbnail image for a Web link.*

6. Click the Share button.

Tagging a Friend in a Post

Sometimes you might want to mention one of your friends in a status update. Or maybe you want to include a shout out to one of the Facebook groups to which you belong. Well, there's a way to "tag" friends and groups in your status updates, so that the update includes a link to the tagged person or group, as shown in Figure 8.12.

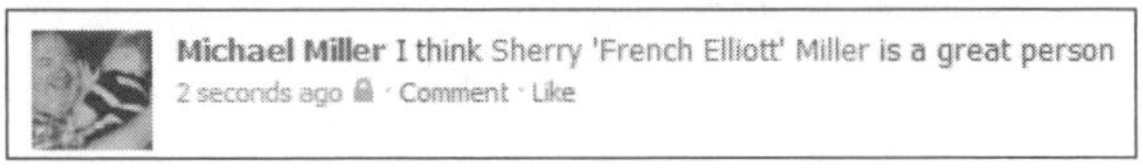

 Michael Miller I think Sherry 'French Elliott' Miller is a great person
2 seconds ago 🔒 · Comment · Like

Figure 8.12. *A status update "tagged" with a clickable link to a particular person on the Facebook site.*

To tag a person or group in a status update, simply type an @ sign before you start to type the name. Don't add a space after the @ sign, but then begin to type the name directly after. As you type, Facebook will display a drop-down list with matching entries, as shown in Figure 8.13; select the friend or group from the list, then continue typing the rest of your update, as normal.

Facebook lets you tag friends, groups, fan pages, events, and applications.

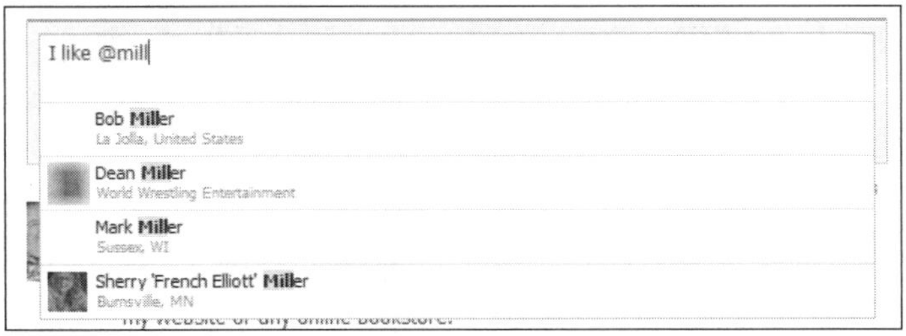

> I like @mill
>
> **Bob Miller**
> La Jolla, United States
>
> **Dean Miller**
> World Wrestling Entertainment
>
> **Mark Miller**
> Sussex, WI
>
> **Sherry 'French Elliott' Miller**
> Burnsville, MN

Figure 8.13. *Tagging a friend in a status update.*

Anyone reading this status update will see the tagged entity as a blue, underlined text link. Clicking the link will display the Facebook page for the person or item you tagged.

Determining Who Sees Your Status Updates

By default, when you post a status update, Facebook displays it to everyone on your friends list. That's fine for most things you might post, but what if you're posting something more inflammatory or intimate—something you *don't* want everyone to see?

We are now delving into the topic of Facebook privacy—who can see what. There are two ways to control who can see your status updates, and we'll discuss both here.

Setting Universal Status Privacy

The first thing you can do is determine the general privacy setting for all your updates. That is, you can determine who can see all the updates you post.

This is done via Facebook's privacy settings feature, which lets you control the privacy settings of dozens of different items. It's a little complicated, but we'll focus solely on the status updates settings.

Follow these steps:

1. From the Facebook toolbar, click Account and then click Privacy Settings.

2. When the Choose Your Privacy Settings page appears, as shown in Figure 8.14, go to the Sharing on Facebook section and click the Customize Settings link, under the big table.

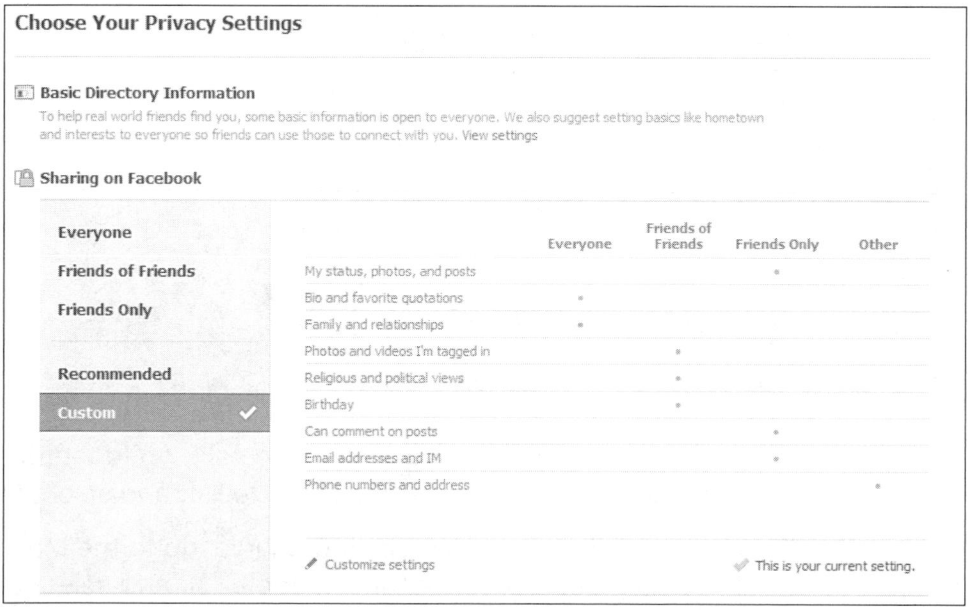

Choose Your Privacy Settings

Basic Directory Information
To help real world friends find you, some basic information is open to everyone. We also suggest setting basics like hometown and interests to everyone so friends can use those to connect with you. View settings

Sharing on Facebook

	Everyone	Friends of Friends	Friends Only	Other
Everyone				
Friends of Friends	My status, photos, and posts		•	
	Bio and favorite quotations	•		
Friends Only	Family and relationships	•		
	Photos and videos I'm tagged in		•	
Recommended	Religious and political views		•	
Custom ✓	Birthday		•	
	Can comment on posts		•	
	Email addresses and IM		•	
	Phone numbers and address			•

✎ Customize settings   ✓ This is your current setting.

Figure 8.14. *Getting ready to configure Facebook's privacy settings.*

3. When the Customize Settings page appears, as shown in Figure 8.15, go to the Posts by Me item (in the Things I Share section) and click the button to the far right.

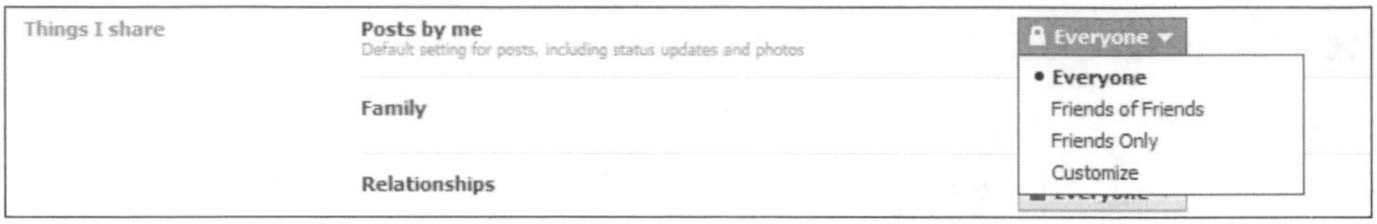

Figure 8.15. *Determining who can view your status updates.*

4. By default, this button says Everyone—which means that everyone on the Facebook site, not just your friends, can view all your status updates. You can instead opt to display your updates to Friends Only (only people on your friends list can see them) or to Friends of Friends (your friends plus their friends).

5. If you want to further limit who views your updates, click the button and select Customize. This displays the Custom Privacy dialog box, shown in Figure 8.16. You now have several options:

Figure 8.16. *Displaying or hiding your updates from selected people.*

- To hide your updates from everyone (but yourself), go to the Make This Visible To section, pull down the These People list, and select Only Me.

- To display your updates only to selected people, go to the Make This Visible To section, pull down the These People list, and select Specific People. You can then enter the names of the people with whom you want to share into the accompanying text box.

- To hide your posts from specific people (great for locking out your boss, your spouse, or people you don't like), go to the Hide This From section and enter the names of people you don't want to view your updates.

After you've made your selections, click Save Setting to close the Custom Privacy dialog box.

Setting Who Can View Individual Updates

The previous process let you configure how your status updates are displayed in general—whether everyone, your friends only, or your friends and their friends can view all your status updates. You can also restrict the viewing of your status updates on an update-to-update basis—that is, you can opt to display a

Note

If you belong to one or more networks, you can also opt to make your posts visible to members of those networks. You should see a Networks section in the Custom Privacy dialog box; pull down the list to select specific networks.

specific update only to select individuals, or to hide it from selected people. This is a perfect way to hide certain thoughts and actions from people who you don't want knowing about them.

To change the display settings for a specific status update, follow these steps:

1. Begin by typing your update into the Publisher box at the top of the Home or Profile page.

2. Click the Privacy button (looks like a padlock) next to the Share button.

3. When the pop-up menu appears, as shown in Figure 8.17, select who you want to see this message: Everyone, Friends of Friends, or Only Friends.

Figure 8.17. *Selecting who can view a specific status update.*

4. If you want to show this message to or hide it from specific people on your friends list, select Customize from the pop-up menu to display the Custom Privacy window. To display the message only to certain people, pull down

the Make This Visible to These People list, select Specific People, and then enter your friends' names into the accompanying text box. To hide the message from certain people, enter their names into the Hide This from These People box. Click the Save Setting button when done.

5. Click the Share button to post the status update to the people you selected.

Deleting an Accidental Status Update

By the way, if you change your mind about a status update you made, you can delete that post from Facebook. Here's how to do it:

1. From your Profile page, scroll to the post you want to delete and point to the post until the Remove button appears, as shown in Figure 8.18.

2. Click the Remove button.

3. When the Delete Post confirmation window appears, click the Delete button.

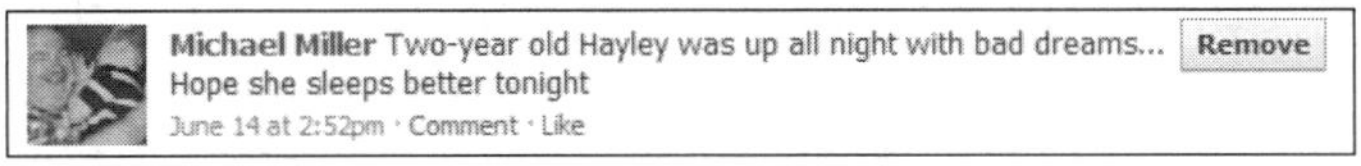

Michael Miller Two-year old Hayley was up all night with bad dreams... Remove
Hope she sleeps better tonight
June 14 at 2:52pm · Comment · Like

Figure 8.18. *Deleting a status update.*

Deciding What to Write About

When it comes to writing a status update, what qualifies as something worthwhile to post about? Unfortunately—and I really mean that—there are no rules or guidelines as to what's acceptable and what's not. So you run into a lot of useless drivel in your News Feed, along with useful updates and the occasional gem of an observation.

Let me demonstrate, by listing a random sampling of status updates culled from my own News Feed. These are actual updates from my actual friends, although some of the details have been changed to protect the innocent.

Our a/c has not turned off all day. It is raining, but it is still 90+F.

people have the swine flu and everyone wears a mask... millions have HIV and no one will wear a condom! Things that make you go Hmmmmm

Do the community giving thing ...it's easy and does something positive.

(John Smith) is nothing but salad for awhile. and protein bars.

Thanks to the Gods of Caffeine and Sugar, without whom I'd be unable to function.

Listening to a CD my daughter found-- Fruta Madura by Vienta De Agua, blends bomba and plena two major genres of Afro-Rican music. Great latin dance music with a big brass section & lots of percussion.

"Of course I'm ambitious. What's wrong with that? Otherwise you sleep all day." -- Ringo Starr

Please Lord, keep me mindful of my blessings, not on the things that have been taken from me

(Jane Smith) is frantically trying to finish my overdue library book!

Awake. Waiting for coffee.

Oh great. Heat and Humidity.

So...24 years of marriage has literally flown by! I have a wonderful husband and partner on this journey.

pathetic excuse for a day...

The cicadas have started.

In Vermont, It is illegal for women to wear false teeth without the written permission of their husbands.

Does everyone from Texas have Billy Bob somewhere in their name?

Two-year old Hayley was up all night with bad dreams... Hope she sleeps better tonight.

(John Smith) is going to see Craig Ferguson tonight! I'm excited, I was promised free chicken.

We saw James Taylor and Carole King at the Xcel Center last night.

Simply one of the best concerts we've ever seen. Enough great songs to fill a 3-hour concert with two encores.

(Jane Smith) doesn't trust cephalopods, and neither should you.

Last night I dreamt in 5/4.

First, note the variable grammar, spelling, and punctuation used; we'll discuss this in the following section. But beyond that, observe the variety of what people think is noteworthy. There are interesting observations, heartfelt tributes, funny quotations, petty complaints, and mundane statements of activity. In short, you can post pretty much anything you want and you won't get a lot of complaints.

That said, I can probably do without the more mundane observations. ("Awake. Waiting for coffee.") I don't need to know when you woke up, when you ate lunch, when you're going to sleep, and that sort of thing. Maybe some people care, but most don't.

It's better if you post on more interesting and unique topics. The fact that you went to a concert or read a book is interesting; it's even more interesting what you thought about it.

Also interesting are major life events, such as anniversaries and graduations and such. Some thoughts from some people are interesting; other thoughts from other people aren't. Some posts are funny; some are poignant; some are just silly. Some are simply factual, some speculate. Some are intimate, embarrassingly so. And a lot are self-centered; if you don't know the person, you might not care at all.

My point, then, is that there often is no point in what you post. You're updating your status, after all, and what's important to you might not be important to your friends. Try to keep a handle on that, and post about stuff your Facebook friends might be interested in. If you go too far outside, you might find your posts dropped from your friends' News Feeds, or even worse, get yourself unfriended. Not everyone cares about what you care about, after all; what you find interesting might not be interesting at all to anyone else.

Employing "Facebook Grammar"

A Facebook status update is a lot longer than a Twitter tweet, if you're aware of the whole Twitter thing. But at 420 characters max, you can't really write volumes in your updates; you still have to edit your thoughts to fit within the allotted space.

In addition, writing a Facebook status update is a bit like sending a text message on your cell phone. You do it quickly, without a lot of preparation beforehand or editing afterwards. It's an in-the-moment communication, and as such you can't be expected to take the time to create a grammatically perfect message.

As such, status updates do not have to—and seldom do—conform to proper grammar, spelling, and sentence structure. It's common to abbreviate longer words, use familiar acronyms, substitute single letters and numbers for whole words, and refrain from all punctuation.

For example, if you're posting about seeing your peeps (that's Facebook for "people") on Friday, instead of writing "I'll see you on Friday," you might post "C U Fri." You could even forgo capitalization and post "cu fri." Facebookers, especially more seasoned ones, will know what you're talking about.

It's also acceptable, at least to some users, to have the occasional misspelling. It's not something I personally like to do or see, but I'm a professional writer and pickier about these things; most people will let it slide if you get the spelling wrong once in a while.

To that end, you can use many of the same acronyms that have been used for decades in text messaging, instant messaging, and Internet chat rooms. Given that you're not a hip young communicator like your kids probably are, you might not be familiar with all these online shortcuts. For your edification, then, I've assembled a short list of the most popular of these acronyms, which you'll find in Table 8.1. Use them wisely.

Table 8.1 Common Facebook Acronyms

Acronym	Description
AFAIK	As far as I know
ASAP	As soon as possible
ASL	Age/sex/location
B/W	Between
B4	Before
BC	Because
BFN	Bye for now
BR	Best regards
BRB	Be right back
BTW	By the way
CU	See you
Cuz	Because
FB	Facebook
FTF	Face to face
FWIW	For what it's worth
FYI	For your information
GM	Good morning
GN	Good night
HTH	Hope that helps
IDK	I don't know
IM	Instant message
IMHO	In my humble opinion
IRL	In real life
JK	Just kidding
K	Okay
L8	Late
L8r	Later
LMAO	Laughing my ass off
LMK	Let me know

Acronym	Description
LOL	Laughing out loud
NSFW	Not safe for work
OH	Overheard
OMG	Oh my God
Pls or Plz	Please
Ppl or peeps	People
R	Are
Rly	Really
ROFL	Rolling on the floor laughing
SD	Sweet dreams
Tht	That
Thx or Tnx	Thanks
TY	Thank you
TTYL	Talk to you later
U	You
Ur	Your
WTF	What the f**k
WTH	What the hell
YMMV	Your mileage may vary
YW	You're welcome
Zzz	Sleeping

Armed with these helpful shortcuts, U should be able to FB with all the young ppl. Of course, YMMV. BFN.

How Often Is Enough?

How often should you update your Facebook status? That's an interesting question, without a defined answer.

Some of my Facebook friends post frequently—several times a day. Some only post occasionally, once a month or so. Most, however, post once a day or once every few days. So if there's an average, that's it.

Some of the more frequent posters are justified, in that they post a lot of useful business information. Others I find more annoying, in that their posts are more personal and less useful; every little tic and burp is immortalized in its own update. That's probably posting too much.

On the other hand, my friends who only post once a month or so probably aren't trying hard enough. I'd like to hear from them more often; certainly they're doing something interesting that's worth posting about. After a while, I tend to forget that they're still around.

So you need to post often enough that your friends don't forget about you, but not so often that they wish you'd just shut up. I suppose your update frequency has something to do with what it is you're doing, and how interesting that is. But it's okay to post just to let people know you're still there— as long as you don't do so hourly.

Chapter 9

Exchanging Private Messages

The whole goal of Facebook and social networking is to... well, to network *socially*. And, in this context, socially means publicly, which is where we get Facebook's very public status updates and Wall postings and the like.

But what if you see an old friend online and want to drop a more private note? What if you have something to say that you don't want the whole world to see? Do all your Facebook communications have to be public ones?

The answer, of course, is no; Facebook doesn't force you into all-public communication. There's a way to send private messages on Facebook, which is how you establish more personal relationships with your friends.

Understanding Facebook's Private Messages

It's not that Facebook doesn't like private messages between its users. It's that the Facebook community grows and benefits when communication is more public. A public status update or Wall posting goes into the Facebook system, where it's searchable and viewable by others, which leads to more connections and more communication. (It also helps Facebook target its ads to you, but that's another story—or is it?)

Despite its preference for public communication, Facebook does provide a couple of different methods for private communication. As you learn in the next chapter, Facebook offers an instant messaging service for real-time communication between users. It also offers a more traditional email system, which is what we're discussing in this chapter.

Facebook's email system is a private one. That is, you can email other Facebook users and your emails are delivered via the Facebook website. It's all member-to-member communication, facilitated by Facebook.

These Facebook emails aren't called emails, of course; that would be too easy. Instead, Facebook calls them *messages*. (Not to be confused with *instant* messages—which Facebook calls "chat.") In essence, you can use Facebook's email system to send private messages to anyone on your friends list.

These messages are just like those messages you send with any other email program or service. And, like traditional email (and unlike Facebook status updates), your Facebook messages are totally private, viewable only by you and the person you're corresponding with.

As such, Facebook messages are the preferred way to talk about more private stuff with your friends. If you want to dish on the details of a mutual friend's divorce, do it via private message, not via public status updates. Same thing if you want to talk trash about your job or your spouse or someone you both know. If it's something that not everyone should know, then take it private.

It's Just Like Email—Except It Isn't

Okay, I know I just said that Facebook's messages are just like traditional email. Except that's not exactly true; there are some important differences you need to be aware of.

The first big difference concerns attaching photos. Unlike traditional emails, where you can attach any number of photos to a message, Facebook only lets you attach one photo per message. So if you want to share a bunch of photos, you'd have to send multiple messages. A real pain, if you can imagine.

Then you have videos. Although you can attach any video file to a traditional email message, you can't do that with a Facebook message. You can shoot a new webcam video to attach to a message, but you can't attach an existing video file to a message. That's a strange limitation.

Speaking of limitations, just try attaching any other type of file to a Facebook message. You can't. That's right, Facebook doesn't allow you to attach Word files, Excel files, MP3 files, you name it. You can attach one photo file or your newly recorded webcam video file, and that's it, nothing else.

All of which adds up to the fact that you really can't use Facebook to send files to your friends and family. If that's what you want to do, stick with traditional email.

Reading and Replying to Messages

Even with these limitations, using Facebook's email system is similar to using any other email program or service. You receive messages from others in your inbox; you can then read, reply to, or delete these messages.

You access the contents of your inbox by clicking Messages on the Facebook toolbar. A list of your most recent messages displays, with the first line or so of each message visible, as shown in Figure 9.1. Click any message to read it in full; click the See All Messages link to view all the messages in your inbox.

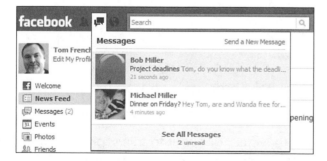

Figure 9.1. *Viewing recent messages from the Facebook toolbar.*

By the way, if you have a new, unread message in your inbox, Facebook displays a red number beside the Messages button on the toolbar, as shown in Figure 9.2. The number indicates how many unread messages you have. So, for example, if you have a single unread message in your inbox, you see the number "1;" if you have three unread messages, you see the number "3."

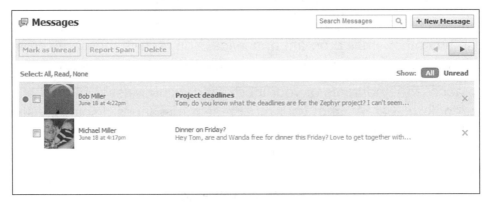

Figure 9.2. *The red number by the Messages button indicates how many unread messages you have waiting.*

To read or reply to a message, follow these steps:

1. Click the Messages icon on the toolbar to see the messages in your inbox. New messages are shaded.

2. To read a message in full, click that message.

3. To view all the messages in your inbox, click See All Messages. Your entire inbox displays, as shown in Figure 9.3. Click any message to read it.

Figure 9.3. *Viewing all the messages in your inbox.*

4. The message you clicked is now displays in its own page in your Web browser, as shown in Figure 9.4. Scroll down to read the entire message.

5. To respond to the message, enter your response into the Reply box.

6. If you want to attach a photo, video, or event to this reply, click the appropriate button under the Reply box. (More on this in a moment.)

7. Click the Reply button.

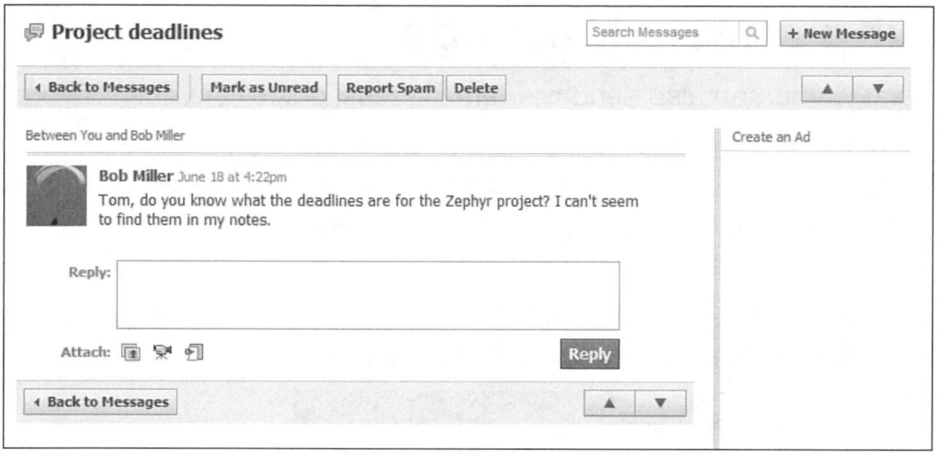

Project deadlines

Search Messages 🔍 **+ New Message**

| ◀ Back to Messages | Mark as Unread | Report Spam | Delete | ▲ ▼ |

Between You and Bob Miller

Create an Ad

Bob Miller June 18 at 4:22pm

Tom, do you know what the deadlines are for the Zephyr project? I can't seem to find them in my notes.

Reply:

Attach: 🖼 📹 ☐

Reply

◀ Back to Messages ▲ ▼

Figure 9.4. *Reading and responding to an email message.*

Deleting Messages

You can, at any time, delete old or unwanted messages from your inbox. Here's how to do it:

1. Go to your Facebook Home page and click Messages in the sidebar. Your message inbox displays.

2. To delete an individual message, click the X to the right of the message.

3. To delete multiple messages, check the messages you want to delete, as shown in Figure 9.5 and then click the Delete button above the message list.

Figure 9.5. *Deleting multiple messages from your inbox.*

Sending a New Message

Naturally, you can also send new email messages to anyone on your friends list. Here's how to do it:

1. Click Messages on the Facebook toolbar and then click Send a New Message. (Alternatively, you can go to your message inbox and click the New Message button.)

2. When the New Message window appears, as shown in Figure 9.6, start to enter the name of the recipient into the To box.

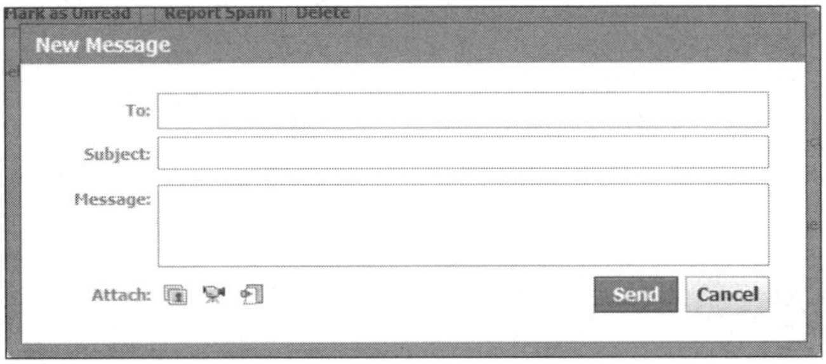

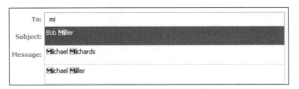

Figure 9.6. *Sending a new message.*

3. Facebook automatically displays the names of friends who match what you're typing, as shown in Figure 9.7. Select the desired recipient from this list.

Figure 9.7. *Facebook tries to determine who you're emailing to; select a name from the list.*

4. You can send a message to multiple recipients. Repeat Step 3 to add other recipients to your list.

5. Type a subject for this message into the Subject box.

> **✓ Tip**
>
> You can send Facebook messages to any Facebook member, whether they're on your friends list or not. You can also send messages to people *not* on Facebook, simply by entering that person's email address into the To box.

6. Type your message into the Message box.

7. Click the Send button.

Adding Attachments to a Message

As with traditional email, you can attach a photo, video, or Web link to any message you send. We look at each type of attachment in turn.

Attaching a Picture

To attach a digital photograph to a message, follow these steps:

1. Start a new message, as previously discussed.

2. Click the Photo button in the Attach section of the New Message window. The window expands, as shown in Figure 9.8.

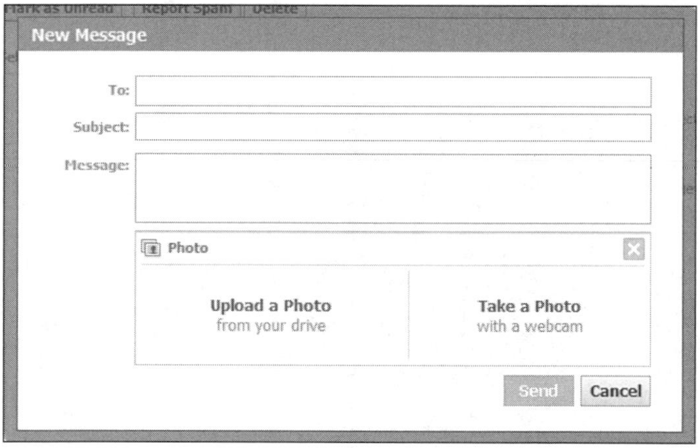

Figure 9.8. Attaching a photo to a private message.

3. To attach a photo stored on your computer, click the Upload a Photo link.

4. This changes the window yet again; click the Choose File button.

5. When the Open window appears, navigate to and select the photo you want to attach and then click the Open button.

6. Back in the New Message window, finish entering your message and then click the Send button.

Attaching a Video

Facebook enables you to record a new video, using your computer's webcam, and attach that video to a private message. You cannot, however, attach a previously recorded video file to a message.

To record and attach a webcam video, follow these steps.

1. Start a new message, as previously discussed.

2. Click the Video button in the Attach section of the New Message window.

3. The window expands to display a live picture from your webcam, as shown in Figure 9.9. Click the red record button to begin recording.

Figure 9.9. *Recording a webcam video to attach to a private message.*

4. Click the stop button to stop recording.

5. To view the video you just recorded, click the Play button.

6. If you don't like the video you recorded, click the Reset button and then redo Steps 3 and 4 to make a new recording.

7. When you're done recording, finish entering your message and then click the Send button.

Attaching a Web Link

Facebook also lets you link to other websites from a private message. Actually, you can only include one such link within a given message; that's a bit limiting, if you're used to including links in traditional emails. Still, it's better than not being able to link at all.

Here's how you do it.

1. Start a new message, as previously discussed.

2. Click the Link button to expand the window, as shown in Figure 9.10.

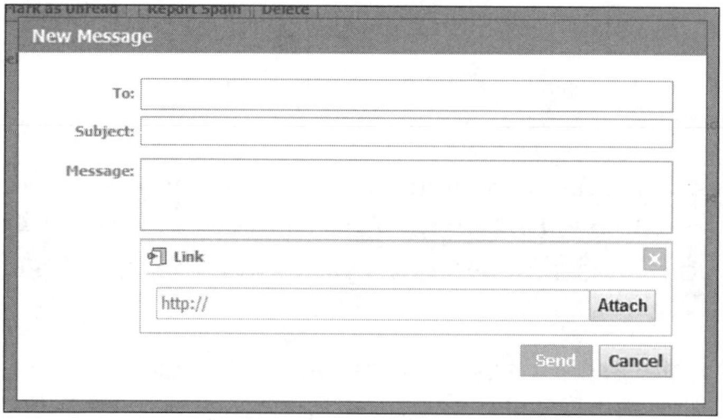

> **Note**
>
> You can also type URLs in the body of your message, but unless you include the full "http://" thing at the beginning, the link won't be clickable.

Figure 9.10.   *Attaching a Web page link to a private message.*

3. Enter the URL (Web address) of the page you want to link to into the box and then click the Attach button.

4. Facebook now displays a bit of text about the linked-to page, as shown in Figure 9.11. If the page includes graphics, you can then choose which thumbnail image from the page you want displayed in your message. If you'd prefer not to display a thumbnail image, check the No Thumbnail option.

Figure 9.11. *Choosing a thumbnail image to display with the link.*

5. Finish writing your message and then click the Send button.

Writing Wall-to-Wall

Facebook's email messages are what you want to use when you need totally private communication with a friend. Don't confuse these private messages with the public messages you can write on a friend's Wall on his Profile page.

And it's easy to get confused, especially when you start carrying on what Facebook calls a Wall-to-Wall conversation. This simply a string of messages and replies on a friend's Wall. You start by posting a message on his Wall, as discussed in Chapter 5, "Visiting Friends and Family on Facebook." Your friend replies to your message, which then shows up your Wall. (And on his, too, of course.) You reply to that reply, he replies to that one, and you have a whole string of messages back and forth.

That's well and good, but don't be tricked into thinking these messages are only between the two of you. Any person who is a friend of both of you (and you're sure to have a few of these mutual friends) will be able to read all of these Wall-to-Wall posts. So it's not a private communication, it's still a very public one.

Knowing that, Facebook does provide a way for you to view an entire thread of Wall-to-Wall messages between you and a friend. Simply go to one of the messages from your friend on your own Profile page, and click the See Wall-to-Wall link. This displays a new page titled something like "My Wall-to-Wall with John Smith," or whomever your friend is. This page displays all the messages between the two of you in one place, and only those messages. It's a good way to keep track of a longish conversation—even it if is a public one.

Chapter 10

Chatting with Your Kids—Live

In the previous chapter we discussed one way to communicate privately with friends and family online, via Facebook's email message system. Communicating via email can be slow, however, especially if the person you're writing to doesn't check her messages all that often.

If you want a more immediate means of communication, check out Facebook's live chat feature. This lets you communicate in real time with your friends, using one-to-one text messages. Like email messages, these are totally private communications; no one but you and the person you're talking to can read them.

What's Chat—and Who Uses It?

Okay, so here's the deal. What Facebook calls "chat," everybody else in the world calls *instant messaging*. You might or might not be familiar with instant messaging (or what those in the know call IM), but I guarantee your kids know what it is.

Understanding Instant Messaging

Instant messaging is like text messaging with your computer instead of your phone, and it's widely used by the younger generation. In fact, I'd bet big numbers that your kids already use instant messaging of one flavor or another.

And there are several flavors of instant messaging—that is, several different IM services. The most popular of these are Yahoo! Messenger, AOL Instant Messenger (AIM), ICQ,

Google Talk, Windows Live Messenger, and Skype. In general, these IM services don't talk to each other; you can only talk to other people who use the same service you do.

In reality, most younger users subscribe to more than one IM service. (All of them are free to use.) Yahoo! Messenger (YM) and AIM are the two most popular IM services, especially with those in their teens and twenties. It's common to find both YM and AIM windows open on a kid's computer, with multiple conversations taking place between your kid and a dozen or so of his or her friends.

Note

Skype is best known for its Internet-based telephone service, but also offers instant messaging between users.

Welcome to Facebook Chat

Facebook's chat works just like these more traditional IM services, but is exclusive to Facebook users. It runs within your Web browser only when you're logged into the Facebook site; it's well integrated with the Facebook interface.

As such, Facebook chat lets you carry on real-time conversations with any of your Facebook friends who are also logged onto the site. Obviously, you can't talk with someone who isn't logged on. But as long as a friend is online in Facebook at the same time you are, you can chat to your heart's delight.

Note

If you happen to subscribe to the AOL Instant Messenger (AIM) service, you can talk to your Facebook friends directly from the AIM program window.

Chatting, by the way, consists of sending and receiving sequential text messages to and from your friend. It's not a video chat and there's no audio involved; it's a text only thing. It's pretty much like sending and receiving one text message after another on your cell phone, except that the entire thread of the conversation appears in a single chat window—which makes it easier to keep track of who's saying what.

Knowing this, you shouldn't get Facebook chat confused with web-based chat rooms. (And if you don't know what a chat room is, ask your kids). Despite the similar names, Facebook chat is purely a one-to-one conversation; you can't have a multiple-person chat, as you can in a chat room on another site. A Facebook chat is between you and a single friend only.

That said, you can conduct multiple chats at the same time. That is, you can have one chat window open to talk with your friend John, another to chat with your daughter, and a third to chat with your boss. But these are three separate chats; your friend, your daughter, and your boss can't interact with each other. (Unless they open up separate chat windows to each other, of course.) You're talking to each one individually, not collectively.

Who's Chatting with Whom?

So who uses this chat thing, anyway?

Not surprisingly, Facebook chat is heavily used by younger members, and less so by older ones. It's much the same as with text messages on your cell phone; kids do it more often than their parents.

This means, of course, that Facebook chat could be a great way to actually get some face time with your kids. You can't get them to talk at the dinner table (assuming they even come to dinner anymore), you can't get them to return email messages (they might not even use their email accounts), but you can probably get them to answer a chat request. They're online seemingly 24/7, always have Facebook open in their browsers, and are comfortable doing the chat thing. It's second nature to them, so you might as well take advantage of it.

Not that you want to overdo it, of course; you never want to push things too hard with your kids. But when you need to talk to your kids, you should see if they're online and, if so, ask them to chat with you. Now, an exchange of short text messages will never be confused with a heartfelt face-to-face conversation, but it's better than nothing. You'd be surprised how willing your children will be to "talk" with you in this fashion; it's because you're meeting them on their own ground.

Who's Online to Chat With?

To chat with someone, both of you have to be online and signed into the Facebook site. How do you know, then, which of your friends are available to chat?

The first place to look is on your Facebook Home page. At the bottom of the left sidebar, as shown in Figure 10.1, is a box that says Friends Online. As you might suspect this box lists those of your friends who are currently online and logged onto Facebook.

Figure 10.1. *The Friends Online box.*

Or at least some of them. Unfortunately, this isn't quite a complete list. I'm not even sure how Facebook puts this list together. Is it your most favorite friends? (And if so, how does Facebook know?) Is it the friends you communicate with most often? I don't know. But I do know this little box doesn't always show me everyone who's available to chat.

Instead, you want to display the more complete chat list that pops up from the bottom corner of every Facebook page. You can display this list by clicking the See All link in the Friends Online box, or just by clicking the big Chat button thingie at the bottom right of the browser window.

However you do it, you end up displaying the Chat panel shown in Figure 10.2. This displays a full list of online friends, organized by the custom friends lists you create. Your custom lists appear first, with everybody not in a list appearing in the Other Friends section. So, for example, if you've created a custom list of family members labeled Family, online family members would appear first in the Family section.

Within each separate list, your online friends are organized into two sections. At the top of each list are friends who have a full green circle by their names; these friends are online and active, which means they're already chatting with someone else. Beneath these names are those with a blue half-moon by their names. These friends are online but idle, which means they're available to chat but not chatting yet.

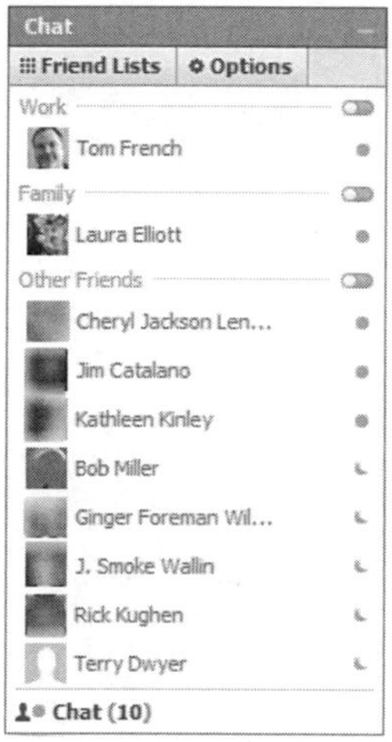

Figure 10.2. *The Chat panel, which displays all of your online friends; those who are actively chatting have a green circle next to their names.*

You can open a chat with anyone listed in the Chat pane, whether they're currently active or idle.

Doing the Chat Thing

When you want to start chatting with someone, it's a relatively simple process. Here's how it works:

1. Click the Chat button at the bottom right of any Facebook page, or click See All in the Friends Online box in the sidebar on the Home page. This opens the full Chat panel.

2. Click the name of the person you want to chat with. This opens a new chat panel for this person, as shown in Figure 10.3.

3. Type a text message in the bottom text box and press Enter on your computer keyboard.

Your messages, along with your friend's responses, appear in consecutive order within the chat panel. Continue typing new messages as you wish.

Note

When another user invites you to chat, you hear a short sound and see a new chat panel for that person open up on your Facebook page. Start typing to reply to your friend's initial message.

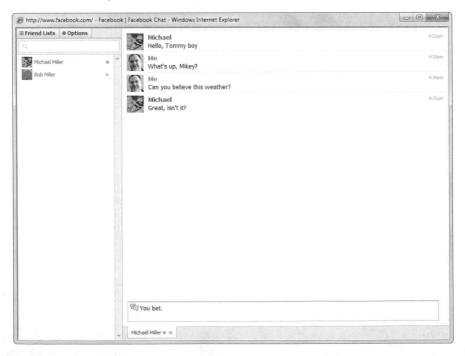

Figure 10.3. *Chatting in real time with a Facebook friend.*

It's pretty simple, really. You open a chat panel, you start typing, and that's that. When you're done chatting, you can close the chat window by clicking the X at the top of the panel.

By the way, you can display your chat in a larger window if you like. All you have to do is open the main Chat panel, click the Options button, and click Pop Out Chat. This opens a new Chat window, like the one shown in Figure 10.4.

Figure 10.4. *Chatting in a larger Chat window.*

There's nothing really special about this, other than it's a bigger chat space than you have on the normal Facebook page. To close this Chat window and return to the normal Chat panel, click the Options button and select Pop Out Chat.

Managing Your Chat Settings

There are a handful of settings you can configure for your Facebook chat sessions. You get to them by clicking the Options button in the Chat panel.

Here's what you find, as shown in Figure 10.5:

- Go Offline. Click this if you don't want to chat while you're browsing the Facebook site. You're still logged on, but your friends don't know you're there. To return to online status, just click the Chat button at the bottom of the browser window.

- Re-Order Lists. This lets you change the display order of your custom friends list in the Chat panel. Click this option and then drag and drop your lists into whatever position you like.

- Pop-Out Chat. As described previously, this opens your chat panel into a larger chat window.

- Play Sound for New Messages. This one is checked "on" by default. Uncheck it to not play a sound when you get a new chat request.

- Keep Online Friends Window Open. Check this option to keep the Chat panel displayed, even when you return to the underlying Facebook page.

- Show Only Names in Online Friends. By default, Facebook displays a small thumbnail picture of each person who's online. Check this option to display names only with no photos.

In addition, you can select which of your custom friends lists to display in the Chat panel. Click the Friend Lists button and check those lists you want to display; uncheck those you don't want to see.

Figure 10.5. *Configuring Facebook's chat options.*

Chatting Versus Private Messages

When it comes to talking privately with someone on Facebook, which should you use: The chat feature or private messages?

It kind of comes down to who you're talking to and why. If it's someone you don't talk to that often, or you have something long to say, use private messages. If it's someone you see all the time and just need to drop a short note—and they're online, of course—use chat.

The online thing is important. You can't chat with someone who isn't there. You can, however, send a message to someone who's not online at the time. They'll read your message the next time they log onto Facebook—which might not be today, and might not be tomorrow.

You can be sure, however, of getting your message across to someone who's online now and willing to chat. That makes chat ideal for talking to and collaborating with colleagues during work hours.

Chat is also good for talking to younger friends and family members, like your own children. They're likely to be on Facebook all hours of the day and night, which makes them uniquely available to chat. And, because it's more difficult to ignore a chat request than it is a message dumped in their inbox, you're more likely to actually connect with them. Which, knowing kids these days, is a big deal.

Sharing Your Life on Facebook

Chapter 11

Sharing Family Pictures

Here's something that I find somewhat amazing: Facebook is one of the largest photo-sharing sites on the Web. Nothing against Flickr or Shutterfly, but it's Facebook that more and more people are using to share their photos with friends and family.

Why is this? It's because Facebook is such a big community, period. It's also because Facebook makes it so easy to upload and share photos. Bottom line, if you're on Facebook and your friends and family are also, then Facebook is as good a way as any to give everyone a peek at your pictures.

What's Good—and What's Bad— About Sharing Photos on Facebook

Facebook is a social network, and one of the ways we connect socially is through pictures. We track our progress through life as a series of pictures, documenting events small and large, from picnics in the backyard to family vacations to births and graduations and weddings and everything else that transpires.

People of our age have collected a lot of pictures over the years, dating back from our childhoods through our children's childhoods and possibly to their children's childhoods. In my own household, we have literally tens of thousands of pictures, most in digital format now (either shot that way or scanned in), starting with my own baby pictures (and those of my wife, of course) and ending with pictures we shot yesterday of the grandkids. We're always taking new pictures, and love to share them with other family members.

Sharing pictures is also a great way for old friends to catch up on what we've been doing in the intervening years. It's fun to see pictures of friends' kids and grandkids; it's not quite the same as being there, but it certainly helps.

Facebook Photos: The Good

All of which brings us to using Facebook as a photo-sharing site. Facebook lets you upload any and all photos to your Profile page, on a special Photos tab. You can organize your photos into separate albums, just like you do (or used to do) with physical photo albums. Some users have hundreds and thousands of photos available for viewing on the Facebook site.

That's good. It's good because Facebook makes it so easy to do. Uploading photos takes little more than a few clicks of the mouse; it's easy enough that anyone can do it. Your photos are automatically visible to everyone on the Facebook site, so your friends and potential friends can view them. Again, very easy to do.

Facebook also lets you "tag" people in your photos. This lets you identify who is in each photo. So, for example, you have a photo of you and your cousin Ernie, you can tag both yourself and Ernie in the photo. This photo will appear on your own Profile page, of course, but also show up on Ernie's page, when someone clicks the View Photos of Ernie link underneath his Profile picture.

Facebook Photos: The Bad

That's all well and good, but Facebook is far from a perfect photo-sharing site. In fact, there are some very limiting and annoying things you'll run into once you start uploading pictures.

First, there's the fact that everyone by default can see your pictures. Maybe you don't want everyone to see your photos; maybe you don't want specific people to see specific photos.

Fortunately, there's a workaround for this, which involves setting the privacy levels for your photos albums. You can determine who can and can't view individual photo albums, so everyone doesn't have to see everything. But it does require a bit of work on your part, and the fact that the default setting is Everyone is not a good thing.

Next, we come to how the pictures look. It doesn't matter how high a resolution a photo is, when you upload it to Facebook it gets downsized to a 720 pixel width. So if you have shot a picture at 2592 × 1944 pixels (common for a 5 megapixel camera), Facebook downsizes it to 720 × 540 pixels. That's huge drop in image quality, and it's noticeable.

Now, why is this image resizing such a big deal? It probably isn't if all you're doing is viewing photos on your computer screen. But if you want to save a picture to your hard disk and then print out a hard copy, a low-resolution photo like the kind Facebook presents results in a singularly unsatisfactory print. It is not anywhere near the quality you get if you download a photo from a site like Flickr or Shutterfly.

Note

The 720 pixel width is actually a relatively recent development, added in summer 2010 to respond to newer widescreen digital picture formats. Prior to this, Facebook downsized photos to a measly 604 pixel width.

Of course, Facebook doesn't make it easy to download photos in the first place. There's no "download" button on a photo viewing page; in fact, you kind of get the impression that Facebook doesn't want you to download copies of users' photos. You can download photos, however, by using your browser's right-click "save as" process, as we discuss later in this chapter. But it's not easy, it certainly makes it slow to download more than one photo, and you end up downloading the crappy low resolution version of the photo, anyway.

Then there's the issue of printing photos. Not surprisingly, there's no "print" button on Facebook photo page. You have to use the right-click "print" method, or save the photo to your computer and open and print it from a photo-editing application. But because you're printing a low-resolution file, the results are likely to be disappointing.

So Is Facebook Good for Photo Sharing, or Not?

After reading the last few paragraphs, you might think I'm really down on using Facebook for photo sharing. That isn't necessarily the case.

What Facebook is good for is viewing photos, not necessarily saving them for posterity. So if you want to glance at photos of your friend's vacation or your nephew's graduation, great. You go to that person's Facebook Profile page, open the appropriate photo album, and start browsing through the photos onscreen. It's fast and easy and that's all you need.

But if you want to save a copy of a photo for your own collection, or make a print of an important picture, that's where Facebook falls down. The low resolution that Facebook uses for photo storage is a big enough negative to say that Facebook is horrible for photo *swapping*; okay for temporary sharing, but not for permanent keeping.

Here are two examples of where Facebook is good and where's it's not when it comes to photos. The good first. My nephews are in college now, and occasionally post photos of what they're doing on and off campus. I'm interested in what they're doing, and get a kick out of viewing their photos, but really don't need to keep permanent copies of them nor make prints. Viewing their photos on Facebook works just fine.

On the other hand, my stepdaughter likes to post pictures of her family, including my two adorable grandkids, on her Facebook page—and only on her Facebook page. I'd like to add those photos to my own burgeoning collection of digital photos that we view on our home computer and 60" plasma TV, as well as make prints of them from time to time. But it's a major league hassle to save pictures from a Facebook photo album, and when you do they look really crappy, thanks to the conversion to low-resolution files. If I want quality photos from my stepdaughter, I can't get them from Facebook.

Bottom line, then, Facebook is great for viewing other people's photos, and for letting them look at yours. But if you want others to download or print your photos, or if you want to download or print other people's photos, Facebook leaves a lot to be desired. For this type of archival sharing, a site such as Shutterfly or Snapfish would be a better choice.

> **Note**
>
> Facebook says you're only supposed to upload photos for which you have permission. That means uploading your own photos, not photos you've ripped off from someone or someplace else.

Creating a Photo Album

When it comes to sharing photos on Facebook, the first thing to do is to create a new photo album to hold the photos. You can then upload photos to this new photo album, or to any other photo album you've created.

Here's how it works:

1. Navigate to your Facebook Profile page and click the Photos tab. As you can see in Figure 11.1, this tab displays all the photos in which you are tagged, as well as your existing photo albums.

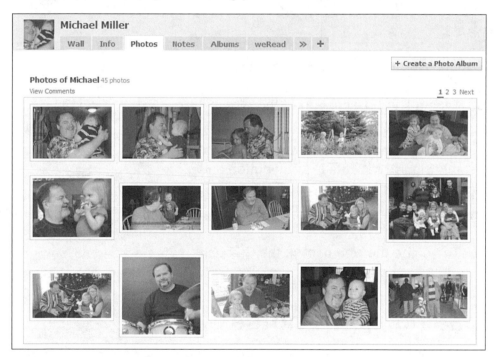

Figure 11.1.   *The Photos tab on a Facebook Profile page.*

2. Click the Create a Photo Album button.

3. When the Add New Photos page appears, make sure the Create Album tab is selected, as shown in Figure 11.2.

4. Type the name for this album into the Album Name box.

5. Type the location where these photos were taken into the Location box. (This step is optional; you can leave this box empty.)

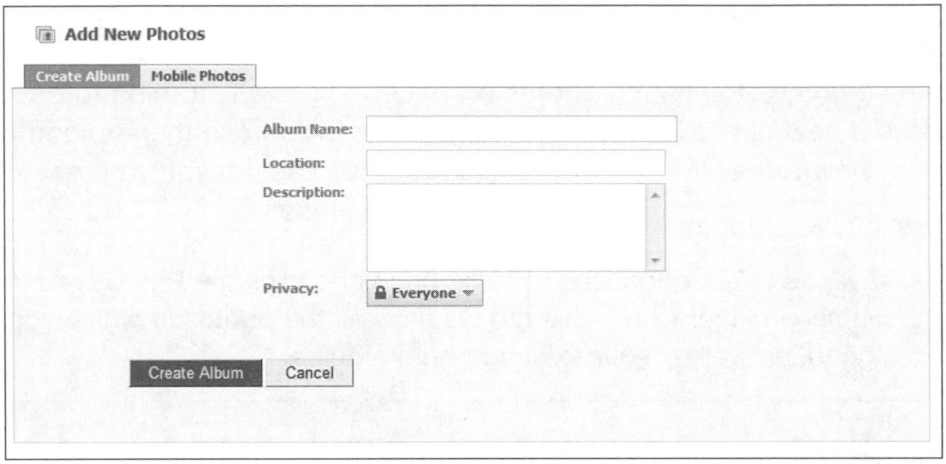

Add New Photos

| Create Album | Mobile Photos |

Album Name:

Location:

Description:

Privacy: 🔒 Everyone ▾

Create Album   Cancel

Figure 11.2. Creating a new photo album.

6. Type a short description of this album into the Description box.

7. To determine who can view the photos in this album, click the Privacy button and select one of the following: Everyone, Friends of Friends, Only Friends, or Customize.

8. To finalize the album, click the Create Album button.

Uploading New Photos

You can upload new photos while creating an album, as you just discovered. You can also add photos to an album at any time.

Facebook lets you upload photos in the JPG, GIF, BMP, and PNG file formats. The maximum file size you can upload is 15MB—although Facebook downsizes larger photos to its own low-resolution format. You're limited to 200 photos per album, but can have an

Note

When it comes to specifying a location for your photos, you can enter a ZIP code, city name, state name, or even just a country name.

Note

These instructions cover what Facebook calls the New Photo Uploader. If Facebook hasn't yet provided you with this new application, or if you're still using the old one (now called the Simple Uploader), you can access the new one by searching for New Photo Uploader, then clicking the button to install the plug-in.

unlimited number of albums, which means you can upload an unlimited number of photos.

Here's how to upload photos to a photo album:

1. Navigate to your Profile page and select the Photos tab.

2. Scroll to the bottom of the Photos page and click the album to which you want to upload new photos.

3. When the album page appears, click the Add More Photos link at the top of the page.

Note

The first time you upload photos to Facebook you are prompted to download and install the Facebook Plug-In. Follow the onscreen instructions to install this browser plug-in, which is necessary to upload photos to Facebook.

4. When the Select Photos window appears, as shown in Figure 11.3, use the tree lists to navigate to the directory where the photos are located.

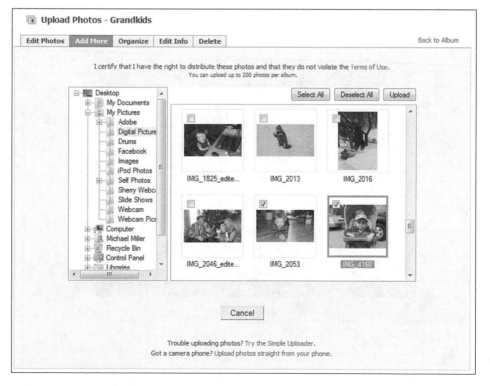

Figure 11.3. Selecting photos to upload.

5. Click each photo you want to upload. You can upload multiple photos at one time.

6. Click the Upload button.

Facebook now uploads the photos you selected and adds them to the current photo album.

Editing, Moving, and Deleting Photos

After a photo is uploaded, you can edit the description of that photo, move the photo to another album, or delete the photo. Follow these steps:

1. Navigate to your Profile page and select the Photos tab.

2. Click the album that contains the photo you want to edit.

3. When the album opens, click the photo you want to edit. This displays the photo page, like the one shown in Figure 11.4.

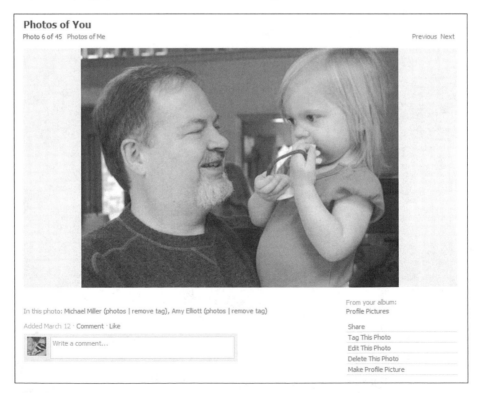

Figure 11.4. *A Facebook photo page.*

4. To edit the description of this photo, click the Edit This Photo link. When the Edit page appears, as shown in Figure 11.5, type a caption for this photo into the Caption box, then click the Save Changes button.

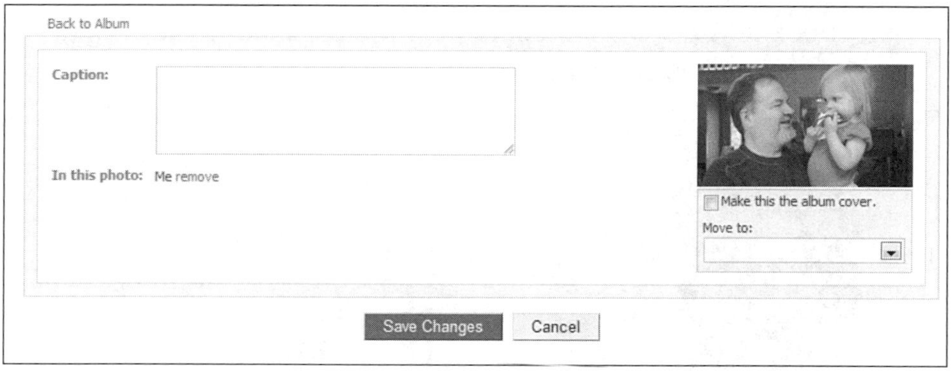

Figure 11.5.   *Editing a photo's description.*

5. To move this photo to a different album, click the Edit This Photo link. When the Edit page appears, pull down the Move To list, select the target album, and click the Save Changes button.

6. To delete a photo from Facebook, click the Delete This Photo link.

Pretty simple, when all is said and done.

Tagging People in Your Photos

One of the nice things about Facebook is that you can "tag" all the people who appear in your photos. Thus tagged, the photo appears on that person's photo page as well as your own. (And if you're tagged in someone else's photo, that photo appears on your photo page, too.)

You can tag any of your Facebook friends in photos. You can also tag a photo with the name of someone who's not yet a Facebook member, which is maybe a good way of identifying people in a photo.

Here's how to do the tagging thing:

1. Navigate to your Profile page and select the Photos tab.

2. Click the album that contains the photo you want to edit.

3. When the photo album opens, click the photo you want to edit.

4. To tag a person in the photo, click the Tag This Photo link under the photo.

5. In the photo, click on the face of the person you want to tag.

6. Facebook now displays a box around the selected person, along with a list of your friends, as shown in Figure 11.6.

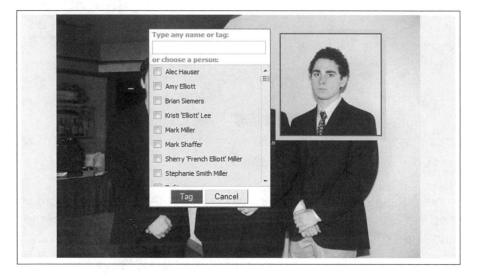

Figure 11.6. *Tagging a person in a photo.*

7. Click the correct friend's name in the list, or enter the person's name into the text box. (You can also tag yourself in the photo, of course.)

8. Click the Done Tagging button.

By the way, it's also easy to remove a tag from a photo. Just navigate to the photo page, and you see a list of people tagged in the In This Photo section under the picture. Click the Remove Tag link to remove any specific tag.

Note

If you enter the name of a person who isn't a Facebook member, Facebook prompts you to enter that person's email address. Facebook then emails that person a link to the photo and invites him or her to join Facebook and become your friend.

Sharing Photos with Others

Facebook makes it easy to share any photo you upload with others. You can share a photo publicly as a status update, or privately via an email message. Here's how it works:

1. Navigate to your Profile page and select the Photos tab.

2. Click the album that contains the photo you want to share.

3. When the album opens, click the photo you want to share.

4. When the photo page opens, click the Share link beneath the photo; this displays the Post to Profile window, shown in Figure 11.7.

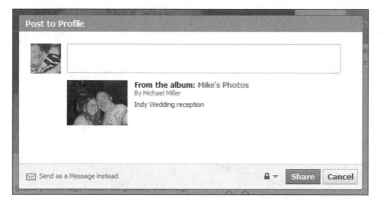

Figure 11.7. *Sharing a photo as a status update.*

5. To share this photo publicly via a status update, type a message to accompany the photo into the main text box. Then click the Share button.

6. To share this photo privately via Facebook email, click the Send as a Message Instead link. When the Send as a Message window appears, as shown in Figure 11.8, enter the recipient's name into the To box, enter an accompanying message into the Message box, and click the Send Message button.

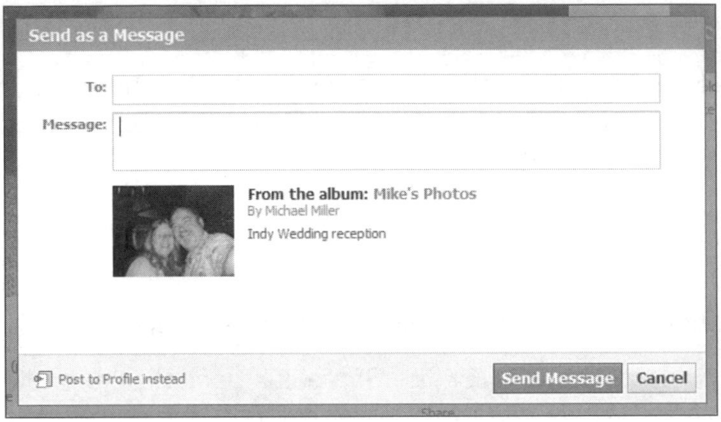

Figure 11.8. *Sharing a photo via private message.*

Managing Your Photos and Albums

After you upload a lot of photos to Facebook, you might want to spend a little time organizing your photos and albums. Here's what you can do, and how to do it:

1. Navigate to your Profile page and select the Photos tab.

2. Click the album you want to edit.

3. When the album opens, click the Organize Photos link at the top of the page. This opens the Edit Album page.

4. To change the order of photos in the album, select the Organize tab, shown in Figure 11.9. Click the photo you want to move and then drag it into a new position. Click the Save Changes button when done.

5. To reverse the order of photos in the album, select the Organize tab then click the Reverse Order button. Click the Save Changes button when done.

6. To edit the description of the album, select the Edit Info tab, shown in Figure 11.10. You can change the Album Name, Location, Description, or Privacy settings. Click the Save Changes button when done.

Figure 11.9. *Organizing the order of photos in an album.*

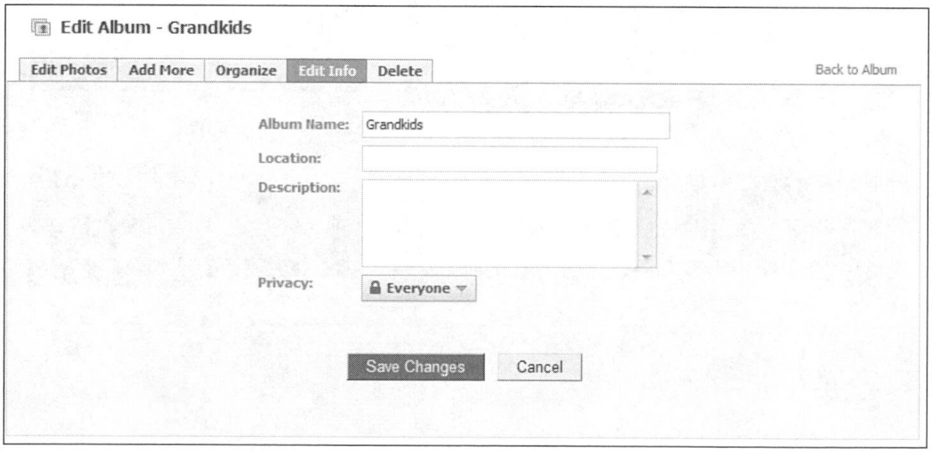

Figure 11.10. *Editing a photo album.*

7. To delete this photo album and all its contents, click the Delete tab. When prompted to confirm this action, click the Delete button.

Viewing Other People's Photos

Sharing your own photos is only part of the fun. You can also spend a lot of time viewing the photos that your friends have uploaded to Facebook.

Viewing Photos and Photo Albums

To view a friend's photos, go to her Profile page and click the Photos tab. As you can see in Figure 11.11, the top part of this page displays all the photos where your friend is tagged. The most recent 15 photos are displayed on this page; additional photos are displayed by clicking the Next link above the photos or by going directly to a specific numbered page of photos.

Figure 11.11. Viewing a friend's photos.

At the bottom of the photos tab are your friend's photo albums, as shown in Figure 11.12. The first four albums, plus the Profile Pictures album, are displayed here; click the Next link to view additional albums.

Figure 11.12. Viewing a friend's photo albums.

To view the pictures in an album, click that album's name or thumbnail. This displays a page full of pictures, as shown in Figure 11.13. To display additional pages, click the Next link; to return to your friend's Photos tab, click the Back to *Friend's* Photos link.

Note

The Profile Pictures album is automatically generated by Facebook, and contains all the photos you've used as Profile pictures.

Figure 11.13. Viewing photos in a photo album.

To view a given picture, click that photos' thumbnail. This displays the photo at its largest size, as shown in Figure 11.14. To view the next picture in the album, click the Next link or just click the picture; either method advances the display.

Figure 11.14. *Viewing a friend's photo.*

Adding Your Comments

You can comment on any picture you view. Just click the Comment link under the photo; this opens the Comment box, shown in Figure 11.15. Type your comment into the box and then click the Comment button.

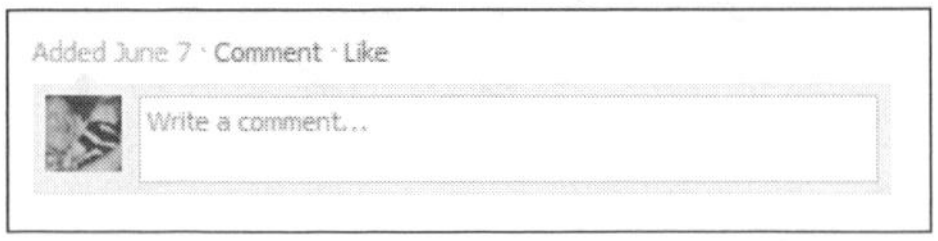

Figure 11.15. *Commenting on a friend's photo.*

You can also just "like" a photo. Click the Like link to voice your approval.

Tagging Yourself in a Photo

If you find yourself in a friend's photo, you can tag yourself therein. (You can also tag other people, not just yourself.) You do this the same way you add tags to your own photo. Click the Tag This Photo link, click your face in the photo, and then check your name in the accompanying list. Click the Tag button to make it stick.

Sharing a Photo

See a friend's photo that you'd like to share with others? You can share friends' photos just as you can share your own. Click the Share link under the photo, and then opt to share as a public status update to your Profile page or via private email message. Enter an accompanying message and then click the Share button.

Printing a Photo

Now we come to something a little more difficult. What do you do if you want to print a friend's photo? There's no "print" button on the page, after all.

What you have to do is take advantage of your web browser's ability to print photos on a Web page. If you're using Internet Explorer, for example, all you have to do is right-click the photo and select Print Picture from the pop-up menu. Other browsers have similar commands.

This prints the photo at its 720 × whatever resolution—which isn't great, but it's all you got.

Downloading a Photo

Similarly, there's no "download" or "save" button on a Facebook photo page, which makes it difficult to save a copy of a photo on your computer. Again, we turn to your Web browser to do the trick.

If you're using Internet Explorer, right-click on the photo you want to save and then select Save Picture As from the pop-up menu. When the Save

Picture dialog box appears, select a location for the stored photo, give it a name, and then click the Save button. Other browsers have similar features.

Downloading Multiple Photos

What if you want to save lots of photos? This manual method of saving files can be a bit cumbersome, after all.

To download large numbers of photos from Facebook, you have to turn to a third-party application, such as Photo Download or Photo Album Downloader. You can find these applications by entering their names into the Facebook search box; after you get to the appropriate Facebook page, click the Go to Application button and, when prompted, click the Allow button. You can then use the application to download photos in which you're tagged, photos in your own albums (great for archiving pictures you've uploaded), or photos in a friend's photo album.

For example, Figure 11.16 shows the Photo Album Downloader application at work. Select the album you want to download and the application downloads the album's photos to your computer's hard drive. It's not necessarily elegant, but it's a lot faster than downloading each photo manually.

Figure 11.16. *Downloading all the photos in an album with Photo Album Downloader.*

Other Ways to Share Photos on Facebook

This chapter talked about sharing photos via Facebook's photo albums. This is as good a way as any to share photos on Facebook, but it's not the only method available.

Previously in this book we talked about attaching a photo to a status update. (You do this by clicking the Photo button under the Publisher box.) This is a good way to share photos publicly; it's essentially the same as clicking the Share link under a photo in an album.

You can also share photos by attaching them to private messages. (Just click the Photo button under the message box.) This is probably the easiest way to privately share photos with friends, although you're limited by the one photo to a message rule.

By the way, if you want to view all the latest photos uploaded by your Facebook friends, go to your Home page and click Photos in the sidebar. This displays a page of thumbnails of the latest pictures uploaded. It's a great way to keep up on what your friends are up to, visually.

Chapter 12

Sharing Home Movies

Now you know how to share your digital photos with friends and family on Facebook. But did you know you can also use Facebook to share your home movies? All you have to do is have your movies in digital format (which you probably do, if you're shooting with a relatively new camcorder). You can then upload your digital video files for all your Facebook friends to see.

And that's not all. If you have videos already uploaded to YouTube, you can share those videos in your Facebook status updates. In fact, you can share just about *any* YouTube video—even those from other users—with your Facebook friends. It's pretty cool, once you get started.

The Ins and Outs of Sharing Videos on Facebook

Facebook lets you upload just about any type of video and share it as a status update—which means all your friends should see it as part of their News Feeds. Your uploaded videos also end up on a Video tab on your Profile page, much the same way that uploaded photos end up on your Photos tab.

Shooting Videos for Facebook

Where do you get videos to upload? It all starts with a digital video camera, or what some people call a camcorder. Today's camcorders save your movies in one of these common video file formats, which you can then transfer to your personal computer for editing.

Any video camera does the job, it doesn't have to be a fancy one. In fact, those inexpensive little "flip" cameras are just fine for Facebook use. But in practice, you can use any video camera you happen to own.

It helps, of course, if your camera is a digital one (all new ones are), as a digital camcorder by nature saves your movies as digital video files, which is what you end up uploading to Facebook. But even if you have an older camcorder that stores videos on old-school videotapes, there are ways to transfer your movies from tape to computer files.

What to Upload

What kinds of videos you can you upload to Facebook? Home movies are common, although you can upload other types of videos, as long as you're not uploading any copyrighted material. That means you can't upload commercial videos, or videos that contain commercial music in the background.

You can upload videos already stored as digital files, or create new videos in real-time from your computer's webcam. Videos must be no more than 20 minutes long, and no more than 1024MB in size. Facebook accepts videos in the following file formats:

- 3G2
- 3GP
- 3GPP
- ASF
- AVI
- DAT
- FLV
- M4V
- MKV
- MOD
- MOV
- MP4
- MPE
- MPEG
- MPEG4
- MPG
- NSV
- OGM
- OGV
- QT
- TOD
- VOB
- WMV

That's pretty much any video file format that's in use today.

As to resolution and aspect ratio and all that other technical stuff you probably don't know much about, not to worry; Facebook accepts videos at any resolution in either standard or widescreen aspect ratio. So if you have a video camera that shoots in high-definition widescreen, Facebook plays back your videos in all their HD glory. And if your camcorder is an older one without HD capabilities, that's okay, too.

Editing Your Videos

I do recommend editing your movies, as opposed to uploading raw video files. Editing lets you get rid of those scenes that don't work, for whatever reason (bad lighting, jittery camerawork, awkward action), and create a more concise movie. Today's video-editing programs let you cut and rearrange scenes, insert transitions between scenes, and add title cards, graphics, and other special effects. The end result can look quite professional, with little effort on your part.

Fortunately, some of the most versatile and easiest to use video-editing programs are free or relatively low cost. The free programs are those that come with your computer's operating system: Windows Movie Maker (for Windows users) and iMovie (if you have an Apple Mac). If you need more features than these programs offer, check out one of these programs:

- Adobe Premiere Elements (www.adobe.com/products/premiereel/, $99.99)

- Pinnacle Studio HD (www.pinnaclesys.com, $49.99)

- Sony Vegas Movie Studio HD (www.sonycreativesoftware/moviestudiohd/, $49.95)

Uploading Your Videos

To share a home movie on Facebook, you first have to upload the video to the Facebook site. This is a lot like uploading photos, except that you don't organize videos into albums as you do with your pictures. Videos are stored as a single group on the Video tab on your Facebook Profile page.

Displaying the Video Tab

Before you can upload photos to Facebook, you must first display the Video tab on your Profile page. (This tab is not displayed by default.) Here's how to do it:

1. Navigate to your Profile page.

2. Click the + tab at the end of the row of tabs, as shown in Figure 12.1.

3. Select Video from the list of available tabs.

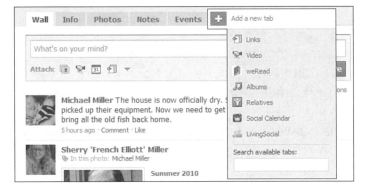

Figure 12.1. *Adding a Video tab to your Profile page.*

Voila! You now have a Video tab on your Profile page.

Uploading a Video File

After you've displayed the Video tab, you can now upload home movies—as video files—to Facebook. Follow these steps:

1. Navigate to your Profile page and select the Video tab, shown in Figure 12.2.

Figure 12.2. *Getting ready to upload a video from your Video tab.*

2. Click the Upload button.

3. When the Create a New Video page appears, as shown in Figure 12.3, make sure the File Upload tab is selected, then click the Choose File or Browse button.

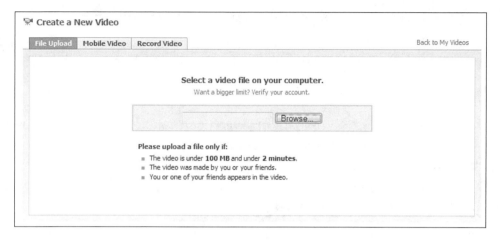

Figure 12.3.   *Uploading a video file.*

4.   When the Open or Choose File to Upload dialog box appears, navigate to and select the file to upload and then click the Open button.

5.   While the video is uploading, Facebook displays the Edit Video page, shown in Figure 12.4. Enter a title for this video in the Title box.

Figure 12.4.   *Entering information for an uploaded video.*

6. Enter a short description of this video in the Description box.

7. Click the Privacy button to determine who can watch this video: Everyone (default), Friends of Friends, Friends Only, or Customize.

8. Click the Save Info button.

When the file is finished uploading (which can take a bit of time, especially if you have a long video or are on a slow Internet connection), it appears on your Video tab.

Recording a Webcam Video

You can also upload videos recorded from your computer's webcam, in real time. This is a great way to do a quick–and-dirty video for your Facebook friends, no fancy hardware or software required. (Beyond the webcam, of course.)

Here's how to do it:

1. Navigate to your Profile page and select the Video tab.

2. Click the Record button.

3. When the Create a New Video page appears, make sure the Record Video tab is selected; you see a live shot from your computer's webcam, as shown in Figure 12.5.

4. Click the red Record button to begin recording.

5. When you're done recording, click the Stop button.

6. You can now watch the video you just recorded, as shown in Figure 12.6, by clicking the Play button.

Note

If you're prompted to okay the use of the Flash plug-in for recording, check Agree.

7. If you don't like what you see, click the Reset button to start over.

8. To save the video you just recorded, click the Save button.

Figure 12.5. *Getting ready to record a webcam video.*

Figure 12.6. *Saving your webcam video.*

9. Facebook now displays the Edit Video page, shown in Figure 12.7. Enter the names of you or any of your Facebook friends appearing in this video into the In This Video box.

10. Enter a title for this video into the Title box.

11. Enter a short description of this video into the Description box.

12. Click the Privacy button to determine who can watch this video.

Figure 12.7. *Editing a webcam video.*

13. If multiple thumbnails are available, go to the Choose a Thumbnail section and select which thumbnail image you want displayed for this video.

14. Click the Save button.

Editing Video Information

If you have been following my instructions, you've already entered information about your videos, as well as tagged any of your friends appearing in a video. If you didn't enter this info, however, you can enter it at any later time—or edit information you'd like to change.

Here's how to edit your video information:

1. Navigate to your Profile page and select the Video tab.

2. Click the video you want to edit. This displays the video page shown in Figure 12.8.

3. To edit video information, click the Edit This Video link beneath the video. When the Edit Video page appears, enter or change any of the following information: title, description, privacy level, or thumbnail image.

4. To add or remove a tag for someone appearing in the video, click the Tag This Video link. When the In This Video box expands (beneath the video itself), enter the names of any Facebook friends appearing in this video and then click the Done Tagging button.

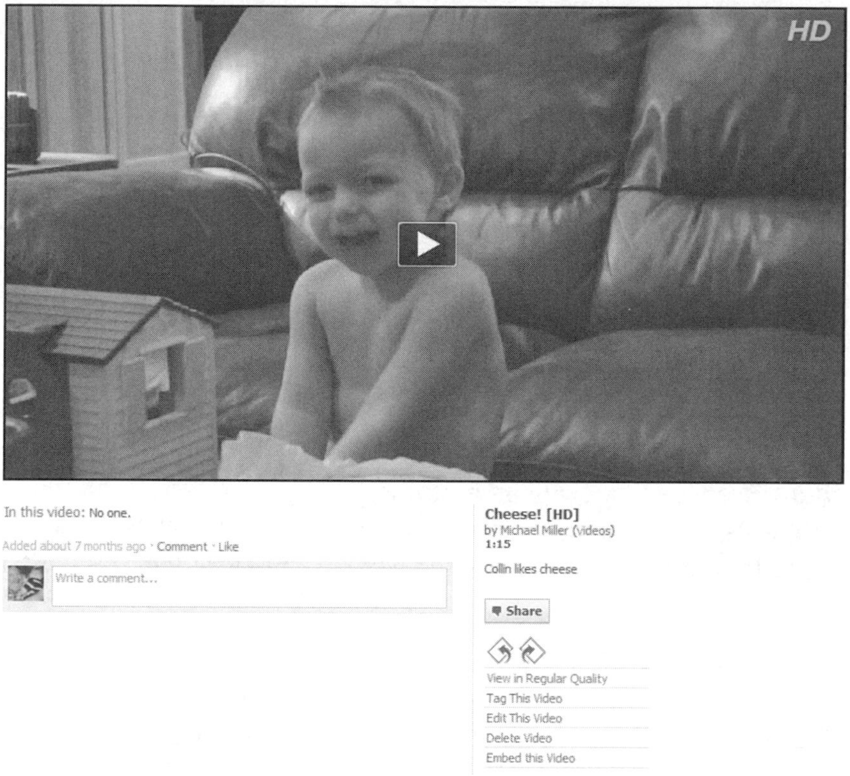

In this video: No one.

Added about 7 months ago · Comment · Like

Write a comment...

Cheese! [HD]
by Michael Miller (videos)
1:15

Collin likes cheese

Share

View in Regular Quality
Tag This Video
Edit This Video
Delete Video
Embed this Video

Figure 12.8. *Use this page to edit—or just watch—your video.*

5. To delete this video, click the Delete Video link.

Sharing Uploaded Videos

Just as with photos, any video you've uploaded to Facebook can be shared
publicly or privately with your friends and family—which is a great way for
the people you love to see your home movies. Here's how to do it:

1. Navigate to your Profile page and select the Video tab.

2. Click the video you want to share.

3. When the page for the selected video opens, click the Share button to dis-
    play the Post to Profile Page window, shown in Figure 12.9.

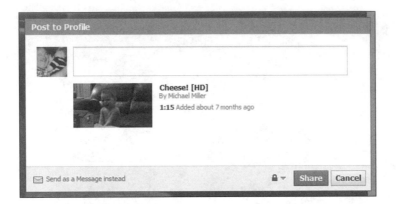

Figure 12.9.   *Posting a video as a status update.*

4. To share this video publicly as a status update, enter an accompanying message in the large text box and then click the Share button.

5. To share this video privately via Facebook email, click the Send as a Message Instead link to switch to the Send as a Message window, shown in Figure 12.10. Enter the recipient's name into the To box, enter an accompanying message into the Message box, and click the Send Message button.

> **Tip**
>
> You can also embed any Facebook video into your own Web page or blog. To get the embed code, go to the video's page and click the Embed This Video link. When the Embed Your Video dialog box appears, copy the embed code and paste it into your Web page's underlying HTML code.

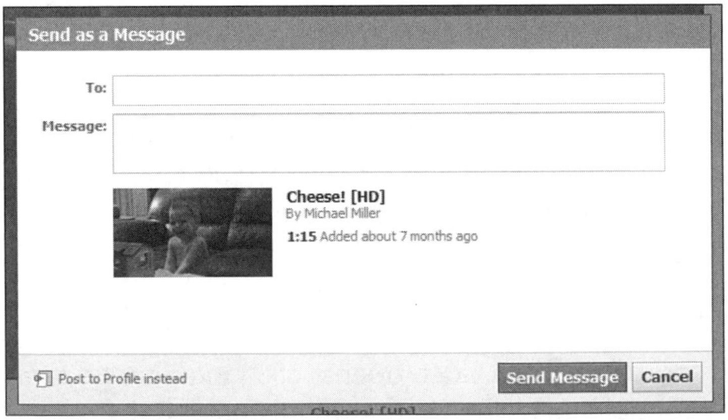

Figure 12.10.   *Sharing a video via a private message.*

Posting YouTube Videos

Here's another way to share videos on Facebook. If you're familiar with the YouTube video sharing site, you can post any YouTube video as a Facebook status update.

That's right, you can share *any* YouTube video on Facebook. This includes videos you've uploaded to the YouTube site, as well as any other public YouTube video uploaded by any other user, including all those videos of cute kittens and laughing babies. It's a great way to share not only your own videos but also any videos you find funny or useful or whatever.

There are two keys to posting a YouTube video file to Facebook. First, you have to have a YouTube account. (Don't worry; it's free.) Second, you need to link your YouTube and Facebook accounts, which is pretty much a one-click operation.

From there, it's all a matter of finding a YouTube video you want to share, and then clicking the appropriate buttons. Here's how it works:

1. Go to YouTube (www.youtube.com) and log into your YouTube account.

2. Navigate to the video you want to post to Facebook.

3. Underneath the video player, click the Share button to expand the Share panel, as shown in Figure 12.11.

4. Click the Facebook button.

5. The first time you share a YouTube video, you see the Facebook Login window. Enter your email address and Facebook password, then click the Login button. (You won't see this window again.)

6. When the Post to Profile window appears, as shown in Figure 12.12, enter an accompanying message into the large text box.

Note

YouTube is the world's largest online video community, with hundreds of millions of videos available for viewing. Learn more about YouTube in my companion book, *Sams Teach Yourself YouTube in 10 Minutes* (Michael Miller, Sams Publishing, 2009).

Tip

Because YouTube video files can be twice as large (2GB) as those allowed for direct uploading to Facebook, embedding a YouTube video might be a better way to share larger video files, such as those recorded in high definition.

Figure 12.11. Getting ready to share a YouTube video.

Figure 12.12. Sharing a YouTube video.

7. Select a thumbnail to display (if more than one thumbnail image is available), or check the No Thumbnail option to post the video without a corresponding thumbnail image.

8. Click the Share button.

This video is now posted as a status update to Facebook, like the one shown in Figure 12.13. To play a YouTube video embedded as a status update, simply click the video name or thumbnail in the post. A larger video player displays within the Facebook News Feed, complete with playback controls, as shown in Figure 12.14. Alternatively, click the title of the video in the News Feed and you open that video's playback page on the YouTube site.

Figure 12.13.   *A YouTube video shared via Facebook status update.*

Figure 12.14.   *Watching a YouTube video on Facebook.*

Watching Your Friends' Videos

With all this talk about sharing your own videos, how do you watch videos that your friends have posted to Facebook? There are two ways to go about it.

Watching a Video in the News Feed

When a friend first uploads a video, it should show up in your News Feed, looking something like the one in Figure 12.15. Click the video and it now gets larger on the page and starts to play, as shown in Figure 12.16. To control the video, simply hover your cursor over it; the various playback controls display, from left to right:

- Pause/Play

- Time slider (slide to move to another point in the video)

- Elapsed time/Total time

- Mute/Volume

- Full screen

Figure 12.15.   *A video posted as a Facebook status update.*

To pause playback, click the Pause button, which then changes to a Play button. To resume playback click the Play button.

To move to another point in the video, click and drag the Time slider left (earlier) or right (later). To mute the sound, click the Mute button; click this button again to unmute the sound. To adjust the video's volume, click and drag across the Volume control. And to view the video full-screen, click the Full-Screen button; press Esc to exit full-screen mode.

Figure 12.16. *Watching a Facebook video, complete with playback controls.*

Watching a Video on Its Own Page

You can also view any Facebook video on its own video page, like the one shown in Figure 12.17. This page displays the video a bit larger than on the News Feed page, which is a good thing. On this page, click the video to begin playback, then hover over the video to display the playback controls.

Figure 12.17. *A Facebook video playback page.*

The dedicated video page also displays more information about the video, including those people tagged in the video and any comments left by other viewers. To leave your comments, click the Comments link under the video and type into the text box that appears; click the Comment button when done.

Of course, you can also use this page to share this video with your other friends. Click the Share button to display the Post to Profile dialog box, shown in Figure 12.18. Enter your comments into the text box then click the Share button to post this update as a status update of your own. If you prefer to share the video privately, click Send as a Message Instead to display the Send as a Message dialog box; enter the recipient's name into the To box, enter your message into the Message box, then click the Send Message button.

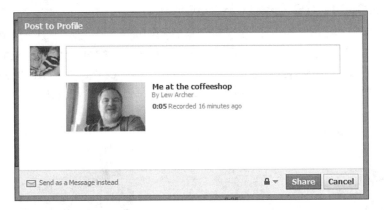

Figure 12.18. *Sharing a Facebook video.*

Viewing Your Friends' Most Recent Videos

And if you want to view the latest videos uploaded by your friends, go to the Facebook Home page and click Photos (that's right, Photos) in the sidebar. When the Photos page appears, click Video in the sidebar. This displays a grid of video thumbnails, as shown in Figure 12.19; these are chronologically the newest videos that your friends have uploaded. Click any thumbnail to play back the video on its own video page.

Figure 12.19. *Browsing your friends' most recent videos.*

Video Resolution

In general, higher resolution is always better. In terms of video play-back, a higher resolution video looks sharper than one recorded at a lower resolution; there's just more detail in the picture. The best picture quality comes from so-called high-definition videos, which have the highest possible resolution.

Facebook lets you upload videos at any resolution, low to high, and to watch videos recorded at any resolution, too. Great, you might think; I want to watch all my videos in the highest possible resolution.

The problem with this is that higher resolution means larger file sizes (more information in the video file), which then translates into longer download times. If you have a particularly slow Internet connection, this could result in stuttering playback, or unwanted pauses while the down-load catches up to your viewing.

The solution, if you have a slow Internet connection, is to watch your videos at a lower resolution. You can do this when watching videos on their own playback pages on Facebook.

Facebook labels videos recorded at a higher-than-normal resolution as HQ videos. Videos recorded in high definition are labeled as HD videos. By default, Facebook's video playback page plays videos at their highest resolution. To play back a video at a lower resolution, click the View in Regular Quality link beneath the video. That should speed things up for you.

Chapter 13

Sharing Birthdays and Events

Being as Facebook is a social network, what could be more social than sharing important events with your friends? You can use Facebook to let your friends know of upcoming birthdays in your tribe, community gatherings, business meetings, parties, you name it. It's all done via Facebook's Events feature, which lets you both respond to other people's events and create events of your own.

Why You Might Like Events

To be honest, events are probably one of the least used features on Facebook. I'm not sure why; they're quite useful for scheduling get-togethers with friends, family members, and co-workers.

I guess it helps to understand exactly what an "event" is. On Facebook, an event is like an item on your personal schedule. Events can be small and private, like a doctor's appointment or dinner with a friend. Events can also be large and public, like a museum opening or family reunion.

As such, you can use events to invite friends to cocktail parties, soccer games, or community meetings. You can also use Facebook events to remember friends' birthdays.

The events you work with don't have to be real-world, physical events, either. You can schedule virtual events, such as inviting all your friends to watch a specific TV show on a given evening. You can also schedule online events, such as seminars and conferences on sites that offer such options.

In other words, you don't have to meet someone in person to share an event with them.

There are tons of events scheduled on Facebook by other members of the site. The best way to find new events is by using the search box on the Facebook toolbar; you can also browse scheduled events being attended by your Facebook friends. When you find an event you want to attend, or when you've been invited to an event by a friend, you can then RSVP your intentions.

Of course, you can also create your own events. Maybe your child has a sporting event or concert coming up you want to invite family members to. Maybe you're hosting a big party for your real-world friends. Or maybe you just want to let everyone know about an important community gathering. Whatever the case, Facebook makes it relatively easy to create new events and invite some or all of your Facebook friends to these events.

Searching for and Attending Events

Let's start with the quest for new events to attend. You can search events by name, date, or type. Here's how it works:

1. Enter one or more keywords that describe the event into the search box in the Facebook toolbar and then click the Search (the magnifying glass) button or press the Enter key on your keyboard.

2. The search results page now displays, but these results include much more than just events. To display only events that match your query, click Events in the sidebar.

3. Now Facebook displays those events that match your query, as shown in Figure 13.1. To filter these events by date, pull down the Dates list at the top of the page and select All Dates (default), Today, Tomorrow, One Week, or One Month.

4. You can also filter events by type of event—Party, Causes, Education, Meetings, Music and Arts, Sports, Trips, and Other. (Plus All Event Types, of course.) To filter this list, pull down the Event Type list at the top of the page and make a selection.

> **Note**
>
> Most event types have their own subtypes; the Subtypes list appears after you select a main event type. For example, if you select Causes, you can then drill down further by selecting Fundraiser, Protest, or Rally as a subtype.

Figure 13.1. *Displaying events that match your search query.*

5. If you think you want to attend the event, click the RSVP link. The RSVP to This Event dialog box displays, as shown in Figure 13.2. Check your intention (Attending, Maybe Attending, or Not Attending), add an optional note to the event's organizer, then click the RSVP button.

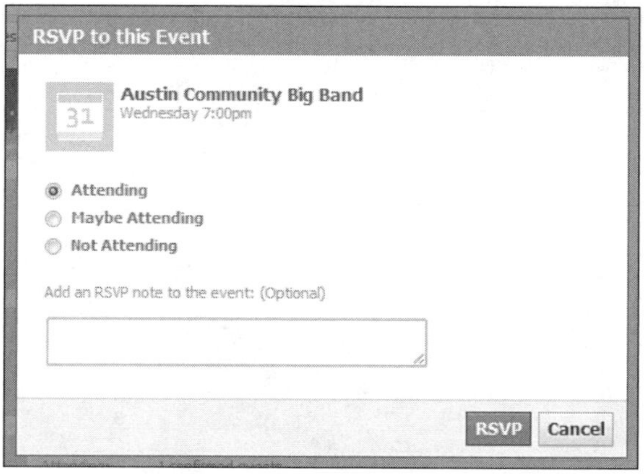

Figure 13.2. *RSVP'ing to an event.*

6. If you want to learn more about an event before RSVP'ing, click the event's title to view the Facebook page for that event.

RSVP'ing to Events

As you just saw, you can RSVP to an event directly from a search results page. You can also RSVP to an event from the Facebook page for that event, from a friend's status update post about an event, or from an email that a friend might send you about an event.

RSVP'ing from the Event Page

Let's start by going to the Facebook page for an event, seeing what's there, and then RSVP'ing or sharing notice of that event.

When you click on the title of an event anywhere on the Facebook site, you display the page for that event. As you can see in Figure 13.3, a typical event page contains more information about the event itself—the start and end times, location, description, even a list of guests attending.

Figure 13.3. *Viewing an event's Facebook page.*

You can use this page to RSVP to an event, download that event to any calendar application on your computer, or share notice of that event with your friends. Here's how it works:

1. To RSVP to an event, check the appropriate option in the Your RSVP box: Attending, Maybe Attending, or Not Attending.

2. To download this event to your computer's calendar program, such as Microsoft Outlook, click the Export button on the event page to display the Export Event dialog box, shown in Figure 13.4. Check the Download Calendar Appointment option and then click the Okay button.

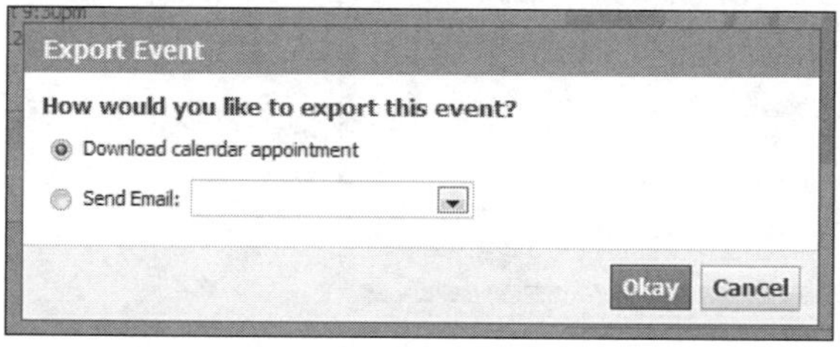

Figure 13.4. *Downloading event info to a calendar application.*

3. To email yourself a notice of this event, click the Export button on the event page to display the Export Event dialog box, check the Send Email option, verify your email address and then click the Okay button.

4. Likewise, you can also share notice of an event with your Facebook friends. To share an event as a public status update, click the Share button on the event page to display the Post to Profile dialog box, shown in Figure 13.5, enter some accompanying text and then click the Post button.

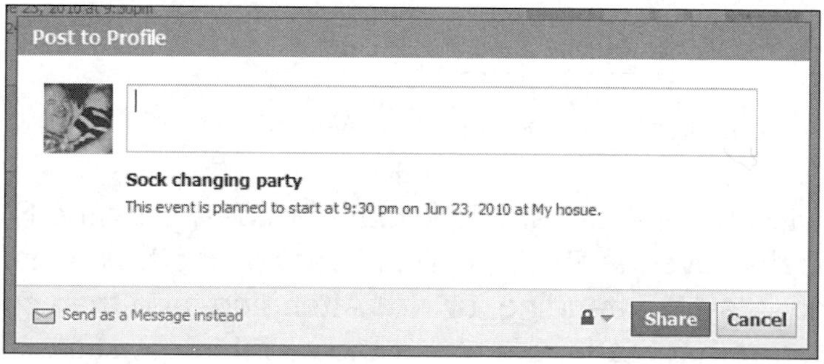

Figure 13.5. *Sharing an event as a status update.*

5. To email notice of an event to a friend via Facebook private message, click the Share button on the event page to display the Post to Profile dialog box then click the Send as a Message Instead link. When the Send as a Message dialog box appears, as shown in Figure 13.6, enter your friend's name into the To box, enter a short message into the Message box, then click the Send Message button.

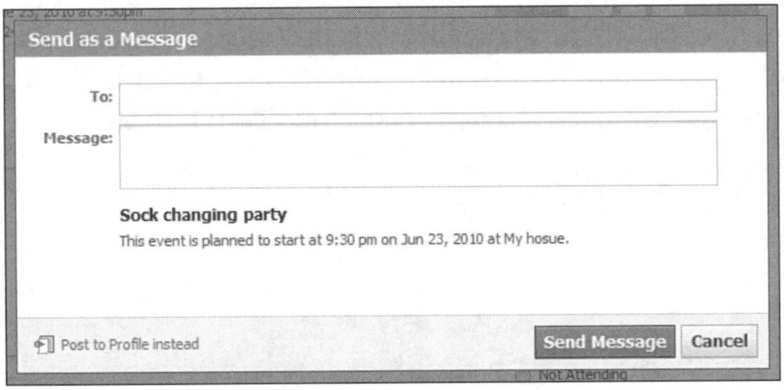

Send as a Message

To:

Message:

Sock changing party
This event is planned to start at 9:30 pm on Jun 23, 2010 at My hosue.

Post to Profile instead   Send Message Cancel

Figure 13.6. *Sharing an event via private message.*

RSVP'ing from a Status Update

Your friends will sometimes post notice of upcoming events that they've created, or are interested in. (Figure 13.7 shows how such an event looks in your News Feed.)

Dinah Lance Bring lots of stuff to eat!

Lance Family Reunion
31 Saturday, August 28, 2010 at 5:00pm
K of C Hall

31 18 seconds ago · Comment · Like · Share · RSVP to this event

Figure 13.7. *An event notification in the Facebook News Feed.*

To respond directly to one of these status update notices, click the RSVP to This Event link. This displays the RSVP to This Event dialog box, where you can check Attending, Maybe Attending, or Not Attending, and then click the RSVP button. If you'd rather read more about the event in question, simply click the event's titles in the News Feed.

RSVP'ing from an Email Invitation

Occasionally you receive event invitations from Facebook friends. These invitations show up in the Events section at the top right of your Home page, as shown in Figure 13.8. Click the link for an event to view its Facebook page; from there you can RSVP by selecting the appropriate action in the Your RSVP box.

Events	See All
What are you planning?	
31 **Lance Family Reunion** August 28 at 5:00pm RSVP: Yes · No · Maybe	

Figure 13.8. *Event notifications on the Facebook Home page.*

You can also receive invitations via regular email. (Not Facebook private message, but the regular old email address that you supplied to Facebook when you first signed up.) Figure 13.9 shows what an email invitation looks like; click the link in the email to open your web browser and display the event's Facebook page. You can RSVP from there.

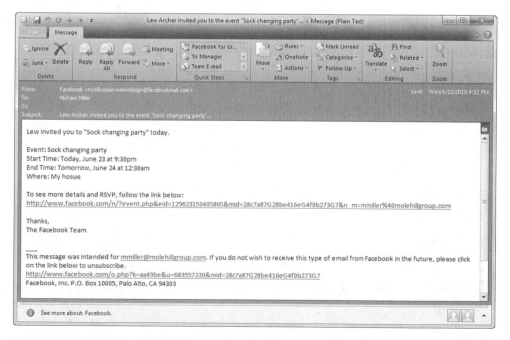

Figure 13.9. *An event invitation sent via email.*

Creating New Events

What if you're hosting an event, be that a block party or family reunion, and want to let friends know about it? It's time now to learn how to create Facebook events—and invite your friends.

Follow these steps:

1. Go to the Facebook Home page and select Events in the sidebar.

2. From the Events page, click the Create an Event button.

3. When the Create Event page appears, as shown in Figure 13.10, click the controls in the When section to set the start date and time for the event.

	Create an Event	
31	When?	Today 9:30 pm ▾ Add end time
	What are you planning?	
＋ Add Event Photo	Where?	
		Add street address
	More info?	
	Who's invited?	Select Guests
		☑ Anyone can view and RSVP (public event)
		☑ Show the guest list on the event page
		Create Event
	Facebook © 2010 · English (US)	About · Advertising · Developers · Privacy · Terms · Help

Figure 13.10. *Creating a new Facebook event.*

4. To set the end time for the event, click the Add End Time link to display the End Time section and then use the controls to set the end date and time.

5. Type the name of the event into the What Are You Planning? box.

6. Type the location of the event into the Where? box.

7. Add any additional information about the event into the More Info? box.

8. To invite friends to your event, click the Select Guests button. When the Select Guests dialog box appears, as shown in

> **Note**
>
> You can enter an exact address as the event's location, or just a city or state, or even just "My House" or "Room 223 in the Henry Building." It doesn't matter.

Figure 13.11, click those Facebook friends you want to invite or enter the email addresses of non-Facebook invitees, then click the Save and Close button.

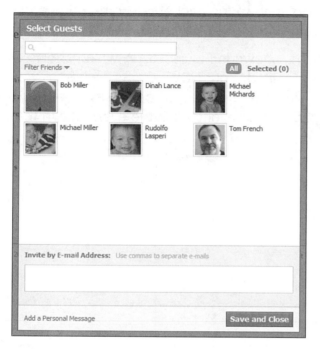

Figure 13.11.   *Inviting friends to an event.*

9. Back on the Create Event page, you have the option of making this a public or private event. To make this a public event that all Facebook members can view, check the Anyone Can View and RSVP (Public Event) option. To make this a private event, open to invitees only, uncheck this option.

10. By default, the guest list is displayed on the event page. Your guests might not always want their presence known; to hide this guest list, uncheck the Show Guest List on the Event Page option.

11. Click the Create Event button.

That's it. You've now created your event and invited some guests. To invite more guests or just monitor who's attending, navigate to the event's Facebook page and do what you need to do there.

Viewing Your Events

Where do you find the pages for those events you've created or have been invited to? All you have to do is go to the Facebook Home page and click the Events link in the sidebar.

This displays the Events page, shown in Figure 13.12, which shows all events to which you've been invited. Your RSVP status—whether you've accepted or declined the invitation—is displayed beside each event listed. To display the Facebook page for an event, click the event title in the list.

Figure 13.12. *The Facebook Events page.*

And here's something else you might find useful. Many users find that they're interested in events their friends are attending. To display your friends' events, go to the Events page and click the Friends' Events link in the sidebar. This displays your friend's upcoming events. Click an event title to view its Facebook page—and if you like what you see, RSVP from there.

Celebrating Birthdays

Facebook knows a lot about you and your friends, including when you were born. To that end, Facebook does a nice little social service by letting you know when someone's birthday is nigh.

First off, Facebook notifies you when it's one of your friends' birthday. The notice pops up in the Events section of your Home page, in the top right corner, as shown in Figure 13.13.

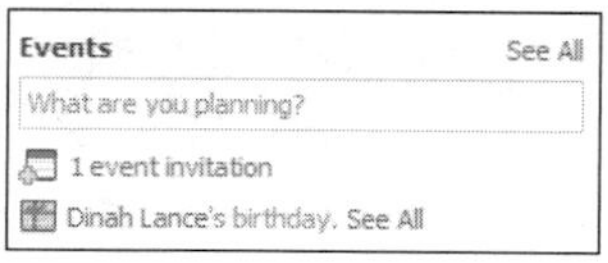

Events   See All

What are you planning?

1 event invitation

Dinah Lance's birthday. See All

Figure 13.13. *Today's birthdays on your Facebook Home page.*

To get a bit more notice of upcoming birthdays, click the Events link in the sidebar of the Home page to display the Events page and then click Birthdays in the sidebar. This lists all upcoming birthdays, soonest first, as shown in Figure 13.14.

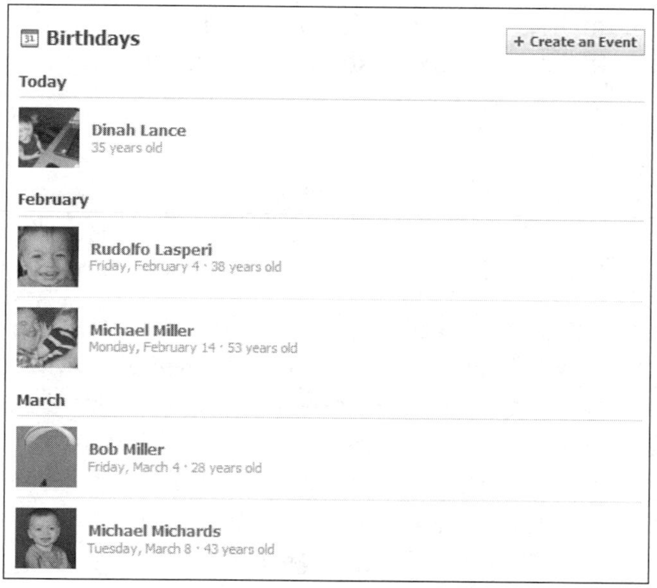

Birthdays   + Create an Event

Today

Dinah Lance
35 years old

February

Rudolfo Lasperi
Friday, February 4 · 38 years old

Michael Miller
Monday, February 14 · 53 years old

March

Bob Miller
Friday, March 4 · 28 years old

Michael Michards
Tuesday, March 8 · 43 years old

Figure 13.14. *A list of upcoming birthdays.*

And when it's someone's birthday, don't be shy about celebrating. Go to that friends' Profile page and leave them a happy birthday message. It's what people do on Facebook!

Selling Tickets

Facebook's Events feature is a good way to put events on your schedule, but it isn't perfect. While it's adequate for inviting friends to a private party, or letting people know about a big public gathering, it isn't that great when you're hosting an event that requires tickets to get in. That's right, Facebook doesn't let you sell (or give away) tickets to your event.

There's a way around this limitation, however, thanks to Facebook's integration with services like Eventbrite, EventPay, and Ticketing. These are services that make it easy to promote and sell tickets for events online. You can connect your Facebook event with the ticketing site, and then use that site to sell tickets to your event. Some of these sites even put "order tickets" links into your News Feed posts for new events. (Most also charge a fee, typically a small percentage of the ticket price.)

You activate these ticketing applications from within Facebook. Just enter the application's name into the search box and you see a link for that app; click the link to go to the application's Facebook page. When you're there, click the Go to Application button to get more instructions.

Let's look at Eventbrite as an example of how this all works. After you go to the Eventbrite page and click Go to Application, you see a long page that contains all the instructions you need to create a new ticketed event. Click the Create an Event button on this page to create an Eventbrite event, complete with ticket information. After you've created the event, Eventbrite invites selected friends to your event, and posts an update about the event to Facebook, where it appears in your friends' News Feeds. It's really quite simple.

Part **V**

Doing More with Facebook

Chapter 14

Personalizing Your Profile Page

Your Profile page is your personal page on Facebook. I'd say it's like a home page, except that Facebook's real Home page is something different. So while your Profile page might be your "home," it's actually a place where all your personal information is stored and displayed for your friends to see.

As such, wouldn't be nice if you could personalize your Profile page to better reflect your personality? Well, while you can't change the page's colors or backgrounds or how it looks in general, there are some things you *can* personalize. That's what we discuss in this chapter.

What Can You Personalize on Your Profile Page—and Why Would You Want To?

Before we look at what you can personalize on your Profile page, let's take another look at what's actually on the page. As you can see in Figure 14.1, your Profile picture is at the top left, with a sidebar full of informational boxes beneath it. The center of the page hosts a series of tabs, with the main Wall tab displaying your latest status updates, as well as posts made to you by your friends; other tabs on your Profile page hold your personal information, photos, videos, events, and so forth. Finally, there's a column on the right that displays a bunch of advertisements. (Along with birthday reminders, recommendations, and the like, of course.)

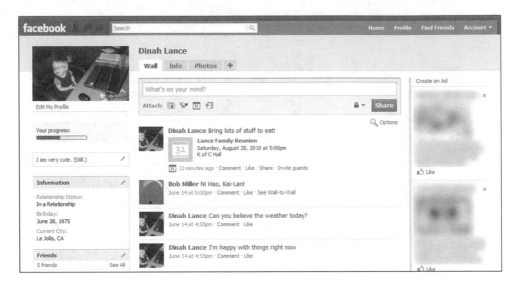

Figure 14.1. *A typical Profile page.*

Ignoring the column of ads, we can focus on the sidebar and the tabs, both of which are somewhat customizable. You can, for example, select which information boxes appear in the sidebar, and in which order. You can choose who can post to your Wall, as well as who can read your Wall postings. Finally, you can add a variety of new tabs, and arrange your tabs in any order. In short, you decide what people see—and what people post—on your Profile page.

Choosing What Posts to Display on Your Wall

Let's start with the posts on your Wall. By default, your wall displays your status updates, as well as public messages left by your friends. You can, however, opt to display only your status updates, or only messages from your friends. To do this, follow these steps:

1. On your Profile page, make sure the Wall tab is selected.

2. Click the Options link under the Publisher box; three options display, as shown in Figure 14.2. The default option is to display posts from *You +* Friends.

Figure 14.2. *Choosing what posts are displayed on your Wall.*

3. To display only your own posts, click Just *You*.

4. To display only messages left to you by others, click Just Friends.

Changing Other Wall Settings

While we're on the Wall, Facebook lets you configure quite a lot about what goes on your wall and who can put it there. You can change any and all of the following:

- **Stories Posted by You.** This setting lets you import posts (what Facebook calls "stories") from other sites, such as YouTube, Flickr, and Digg. When you post something to one of these sites, it also appears as a status update on Facebook.

- **Profile Story Comments.** By default, comments to your Wall posts are automatically expanded. If you prefer a cleaner look—with comments hidden (but displayed when a link is clicked)—you can turn off expanded comments.

- **Stories Posted by Friends.** You can choose to let friends post to your wall, or not. You can also choose who can see posts made by your friends.

You access these settings by following these steps:

1. On your Profile page, make sure the Wall tab is selected.

2. Click the Options link under the Publisher box.

3. Click the Settings button. This displays the settings panel shown in Figure 14.3.

4. To display posts from another website in your Facebook feed, go to the Imported Stories section and click a specific site. This expands this section to display a User name box for that site; enter your user name and click the Import button.

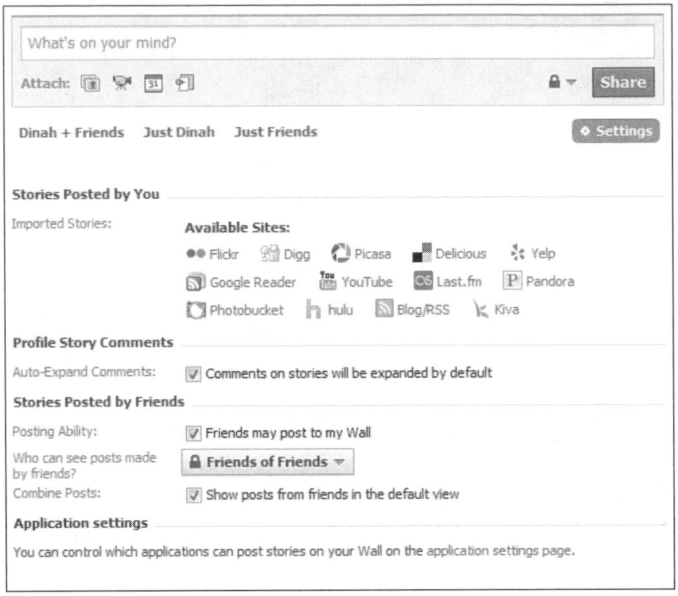

Figure 14.3. *Customizing Wall settings.*

5. All comments on your Wall are expanded by default. To not automatically expand comments, uncheck the Comments on Stories Will Be Expanded by Default option.

6. By default, your friends are allowed to post on your wall. If you don't want them posting, uncheck the Friends May Post to My Wall option.

7. To determine who can view Wall posts made by your friends, click the button in the Who Can See Posts Made by Friends? section, and select the appropriate option—Everyone, Friends of Friends, Friends Only, or, to select a custom list of friends, Customize.

8. By default, posts from your friends are displayed in line with your own status updates on your Wall. To not display friends' posts, uncheck the Show Posts from Friends in the Default View. (This is the same as selecting Just *You* when you first click Options.)

You don't have to click a "save" button or anything when you're done; your changes are applied as soon as you select them.

Changing Your Profile Picture

Here's something you'll probably end up changing quite a bit over time—the picture you display on your Profile page. Fortunately, Facebook makes it easy to change your Profile picture, at any point in time. Here's how to do it:

1. From your Profile page, point to your picture and click the Change Picture link that appears.

2. This displays a pop-up menu, as shown in Figure 14.4. Select how you want to obtain the picture: Upload a Picture (from your computer), Take a Picture (from your computer's webcam), or Choose from Album (to use a picture previously uploaded to Facebook).

Figure 14.4.   *Changing your Profile picture.*

3. If you selected Upload a Picture, Facebook displays the Upload Your Profile Picture window, shown in Figure 14.5. Click the Choose File or Open button to display the Choose File to Upload dialog box. Navigate to and select the picture you want to use and then click the Open button.

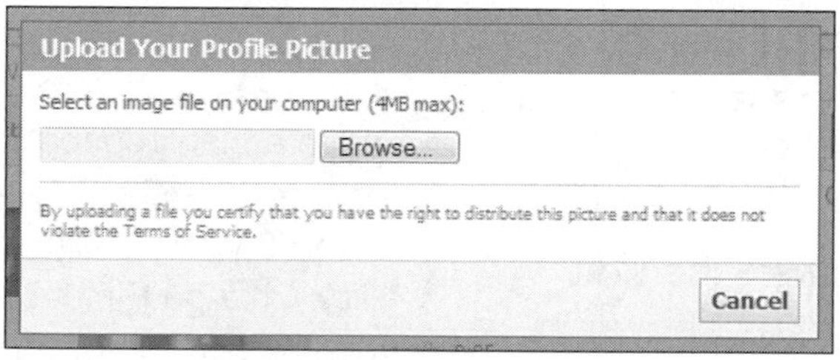

Upload Your Profile Picture

Select an image file on your computer (4MB max):

[Browse...]

By uploading a file you certify that you have the right to distribute this picture and that it does not violate the Terms of Service.

[Cancel]

Figure 14.5.   *Getting ready to upload a new Profile picture.*

4. If you selected Take a Picture, Facebook displays the Take a Profile Picture window, shown in Figure 14.6. Look into your webcam lens and smile and then click the camera button. You get a three-second countdown before the picture is snapped. If you like it, click the Save Picture button.

Take a Profile Picture

Save Picture | Cancel

Figure 14.6. *Taking a new Profile picture with a webcam.*

5. If you selected Choose from Album, Facebook displays your Profile Pictures album page, shown in Figure 14.7. Click the photo you want to use; this displays the selected photo on its own page. Click the Make Profile Picture link to make this picture your new Profile picture.

You can also edit the thumbnail version of your Profile picture that appears next to your status updates. To do this, point to your Profile picture, click Change Picture, and then select Edit Thumbnail. When the Edit Thumbnail dialog box appears, as shown in Figure 14.8, click and drag the thumbnail until it looks the way you want and then click the Save button.

> **✔ Tip**
>
> To remove the current Profile picture without replacing it with a new picture (resulting in a blank space where your picture should be), point to your Profile picture, click Change Picture, and then select Remove Your Picture.

Figure 14.7. *Choosing a new Profile picture from your Profile Pictures album.*

Figure 14.8. *Editing the thumbnail version of your Profile picture.*

Customizing the Tabs on Your Profile Page

Facebook uses tabs to display different types of information on your Profile page. By default, Facebook displays three tabs: Wall, Info, and Photos. You can add new tabs at any time, and then rearrange the order of the tabs. For example, you might want to add a tab to hold any home videos you upload, or to display your events, or to host information from an application you're using.

To add a new tab, follow these steps:

1. From your Profile page, click the + tab at the end of the row of tabs.

2. This displays a menu of available tabs, as shown in Figure 14.9. Click the tab you want to add.

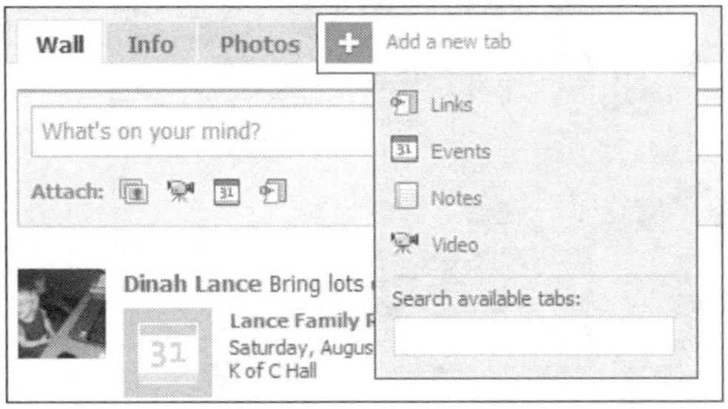

Figure 14.9. Adding a new tab to your Profile page.

Pretty simple, really. The new tab is added to the end of your previous tabs. To rearrange the order of your tabs, click a tab with your mouse and drag that tab to a new position.

Managing Sidebar Boxes

Now we come to your Profile page's sidebar, which displays various bits of personal information in individual boxes. There are two boxes that are always displayed on every person's Profile page: Information and Friends. These boxes cannot be moved or deleted.

> **Tip**
>
> Facebook displays up to a half-dozen tabs on your Profile page. If you have more than six tabs, you can view the others by clicking the right arrow tab and selecting the tabs from the list.

Adding New Boxes

You can, however, add other boxes to the sidebar. New boxes are typically added by the Facebook applications you use. For example, if you're using the FamilyLink app, you get a FamilyLink box in your sidebar.

To add a box for a given application, follow these steps:

1. From the Facebook toolbar, click Account and then select Application Settings.

2. When the Application Settings page appears, scroll down to the application you want to add and then click Edit Settings for that app.

3. When the Edit *Application* dialog box appears, make sure the Profile tab is selected, as shown in Figure 14.10.

Figure 14.10.   *Adding a sidebar box for an application.*

4. If the application lets you add a box to your Profile page, there will be a Box: Available section. Click the Add link to add a box for this app.

5. Click the Okay button.

Rearranging Boxes

You can also rearrange the boxes in your sidebar—save for the Information and Friends boxes, of course; they're fixed in place. To reposition a box, point to the title bar of that box until the cursor changes to a four-headed arrow; drag the box to a new position.

Deleting Boxes

You can delete any box from your sidebar. (Except for Information and Friends, natch.) To remove a box from your sidebar, click the Edit Box (pencil) icon for that box and select Remove Box from the pop-up menu. That's it.

Editing What You See in Sidebar Boxes

Some of the boxes in your sidebar contain information that can be edited. To edit the information in a given box, click the Edit Box (pencil) icon for that box. This typically displays a menu of items or options, such as the one in

Figure 14.11. All boxes have their own unique sets of options, but in general you check those items you want to display and uncheck those you don't. If additional editing can be done, look for and click the Edit Information link in the menu and then follow the onscreen instructions.

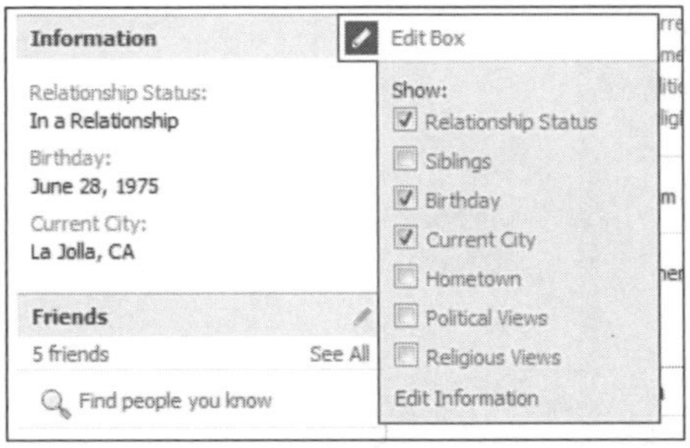

Figure 14.11. *Determining what information is displayed in the Information box.*

Editing Your Profile Information

Speaking of information, one of the default tabs on your Profile page is the Info tab. This tab displays information about you in the following section: About Me, Work and Education, Likes and Dislikes, and Contact Information.

You can easily edit the information displayed on this tab. Follow these steps:

1. From your Profile page, select the Info tab.

2. Click the Edit link for the About Me section.

3. When the next page appears, as shown in Figure 14.12, make any changes or additions to the information there, then click the Save changes button.

4. Back on the Info tab, click the Edit link for the Work and Education section.

5. When the next page appears, as shown in Figure 14.13, make any changes or additions to the information there and then click the Save Changes button.

6. Back on the Info tab, click the Edit link for the Likes and Dislikes section.

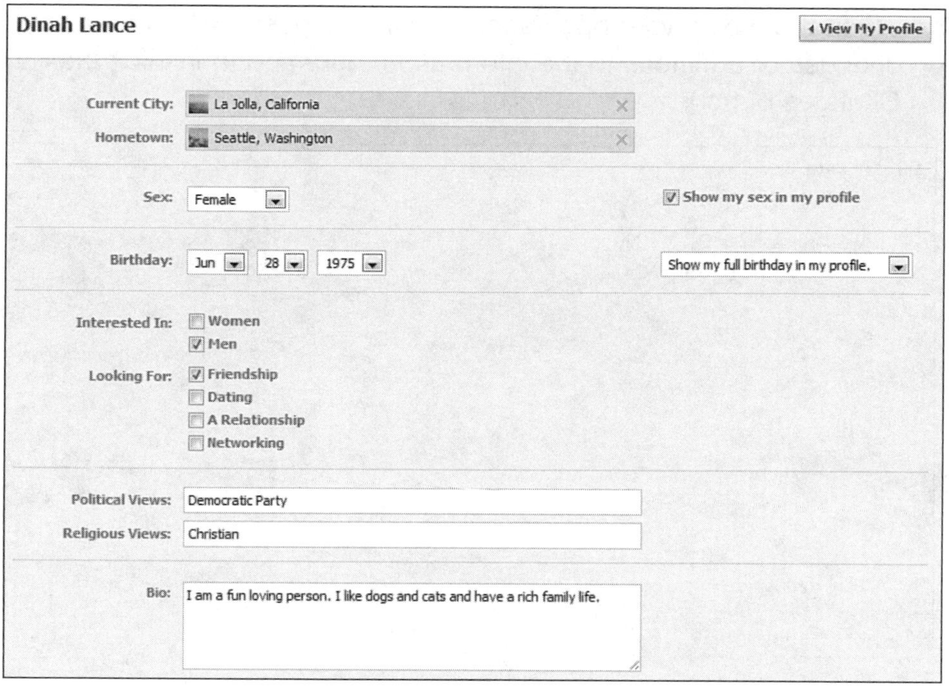

Figure 14.12.   Editing personal information.

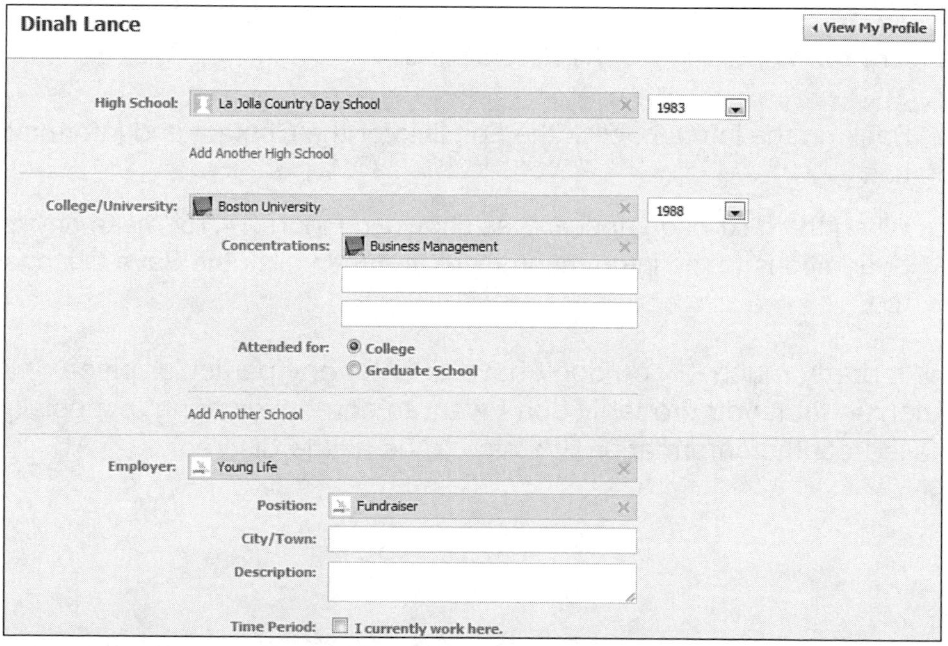

Figure 14.13.   Editing work and school information.

7. When the next page appears, as shown in Figure 14.14, make any changes or additions to the information there and then click the Save Changes button.

Figure 14.14. Editing your likes and dislikes.

8. Back on the Info tab, click the Edit link for the Contact and Information section.

9. When the next page appears, as shown in Figure 14.15, make any changes or additions to the information there and then click the Save Changes button.

That's pretty much it. You don't have to enter any particular piece of information; in fact, you probably don't want to enter everything, especially detailed contact information. It's nice to be a little discreet.

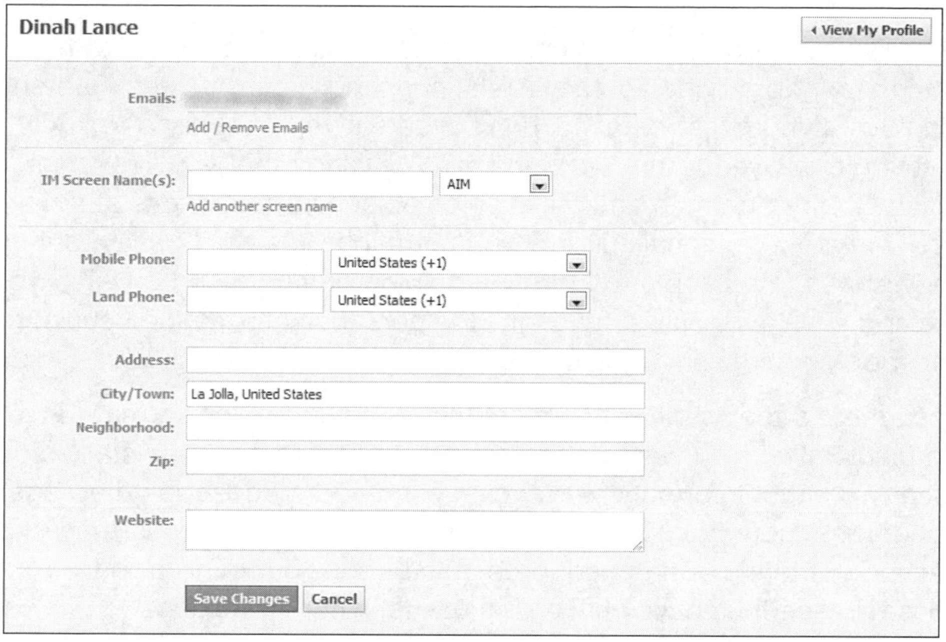

Figure 14.15. *Editing your contact information.*

Telling People About Yourself

How much personal information you display on Facebook is a source of great debate. Some people fill out each and every box in excruciating detail, choosing to tell everybody everything about themselves; others leave most of the boxes unfilled, choosing to keep their personal lives private.

Just how much personal information should you divulge to your Facebook friends? That depends.

I think it's okay to list your favorite movies and books and such; there's little harm in letting people know what you like to read and watch and listen to. Likewise, it's probably okay to list your past employers and where you went to school and such. This is all relatively public information anyway, plus it's a good way to help the people you used to work and study with find you on Facebook.

That said, you don't want to enter any information that could harm you in terms of job prospects, family relations, and the like. Does a potential employer (who might be a staunch conservative) really need to know that you're a dyed-in-the-wool liberal? Will listing that you like to listen to Bobby Sherman and the Archies poison your chances at a new job—or with a potential suitor, if you're dating? It's hard to say, but I do know that some people will form an opinion of you based on what you like and dislike. Rightly or wrongly, the personal information you list on Facebook could work against you.

Then there's the whole issue of contact information, which really is a lot simpler. Unless you want to encourage old flames and new stalkers, don't list any contact information. Let them send you a Facebook message, but don't encourage contact outside of Facebook. Your less-than-close Facebook friends don't need to be able to call you up or drop by your house. Leave the social networking online, where it belongs.

Chapter 15

Becoming a Fan

Do you like a given entertainer? I mean, do you really, really like him? Well, on Facebook you can "like" a celebrity in a way that lets you become a kind of friend of that person, receiving his status updates in your News Feed and letting you participate in discussions on his Facebook page.

The same thing with consumer-oriented companies, products, and brands. You can choose to "like" Starbucks coffee, Ludwig drums, Ford cars, you name it. This puts you on the list for all sorts of promotional status updates fed to your News Feed, which can be either informative or highly annoying, depending on what's sent your way and how interested in it you are.

In essence, then, Facebook lets you become a fan of the entertainers, celebrities, and companies you like. And that can be fun.

Understanding Fan Pages

Facebook offers something it calls *pages* for public figures and companies—musicians, actors, entertainers, writers, celebrities, and the like. A page—what I'll call a *fan page* to distinguish it from the generic use of the word—is the Facebook face of that person or company, kind of a super Profile page.

The Fan Page as Fan Club

I like to think of a Facebook fan page as an online fan club. They both function in much the same way, focusing on a particular person or group, disseminating information from and about the topic at hand, and encourage discussions among club/page members. There are no in-person meetings, of course, but a Facebook fan page is essentially your official contact to the person or organization at hand.

It makes sense, then, that most major musical acts have fan pages on the Facebook site. Subscribe to the Carole King page, for example, and you can find information about her tours and album projects, view recent photos of the artist, and participate in discussions with fellow fans. (Figure 15.1 shows Ms. King's page.) It's just like being in a fan club, except on Facebook.

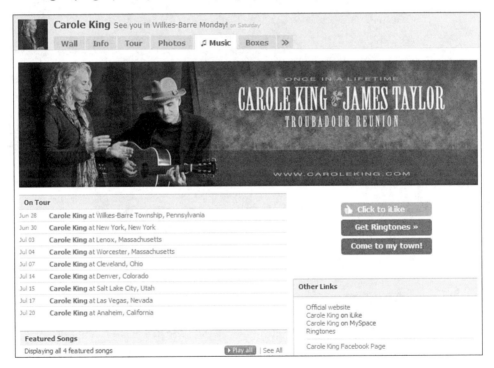

Figure 15.1. Carole King's Facebook fan page.

A fan page for a product or company is similar, although I'm not sure "fan" is the best word to use; maybe "loyal customer" would be better. The Starbucks page, for example, is pretty much all promotion, all the time. As you can see in Figure 15.2, there's information about Starbucks drinks and Starbucks stores and the Starbucks card, along with photos of said drinks and stores and cards. You get status updates, mainly promotional messages, from the folks at Starbucks. And there's a discussion forum where you can express your love for Frappaccinos and such to your fellow devotees.

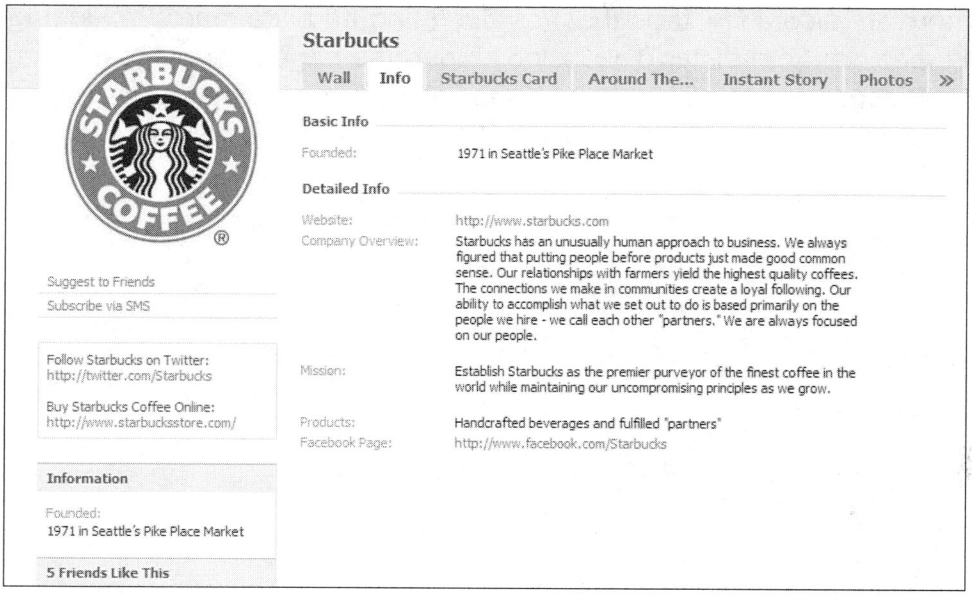

Figure 15.2. The Facebook fan page for Starbucks.

Liking a Page

Instead of "friending" a fan page, you instead opt to "like" it. You do this by clicking the Like button on the page; it's easy to do. When you like a page, you essentially subscribe to it, so that all of the status updates to that page appear in your News Feed on your Home page. Like I said, it's just like becoming a friend of that person or company, just without using the f-word.

Navigating a Fan Page

As you might suspect, a fan page is very similar to a standard Facebook personal Profile page. Fan pages have similar sections as do regular Profile pages, with a few extra features added. The typical fan page includes a side-bar along the left side, complete with photo, information box, list of group members, and other relevant information.

The center of the page has a familiar series of tabs. There's a Wall tab, with updates from the admins; an Info tab, with information about the target person or organization; and Photos tab, with any photos uploaded by the admins or people who subscribe to the page.

There are also a few tabs that you don't find on a standard Profile page but are necessary to foster discussion among the page's fans. Most common is the Discussions tab, like the one shown in Figure 15.3, which is kind of like a message forum or bulletin board. (Not all fan pages display a Discussions tab.)

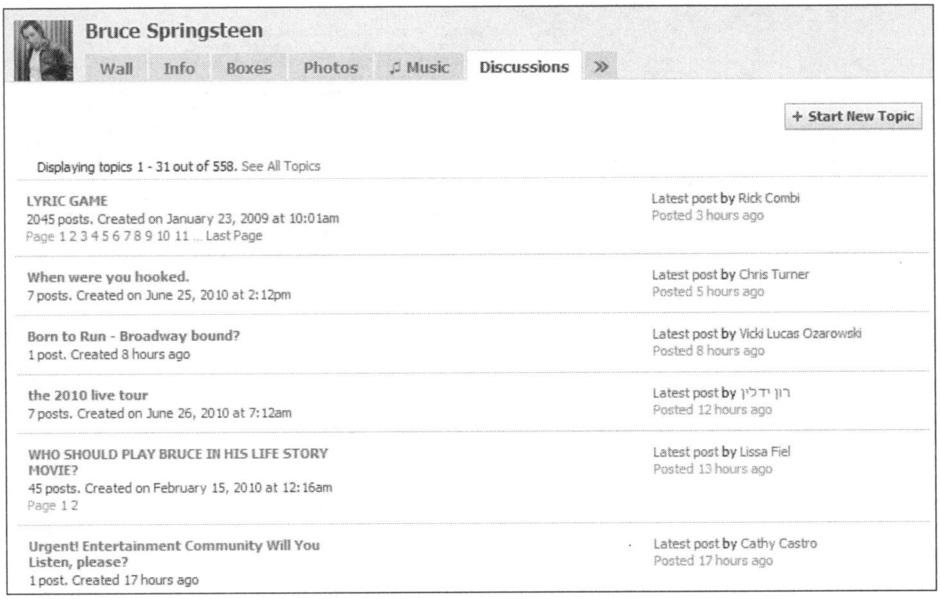

Figure 15.3. *A fan page's Discussions tab.*

Finding Fan Pages

So how do you find fan pages on Facebook? By searching for it, of course. Just follow these steps:

1. Enter one or more keywords that describe the entertainer or company in the search box in the Facebook toolbar and then click the Search button.

2. When the search results page appears, as shown in Figure 15.4, click the Pages link in the sidebar.

3. To view a specific fan page, click the Page's name.

4. To subscribe to the page, click the Like link.

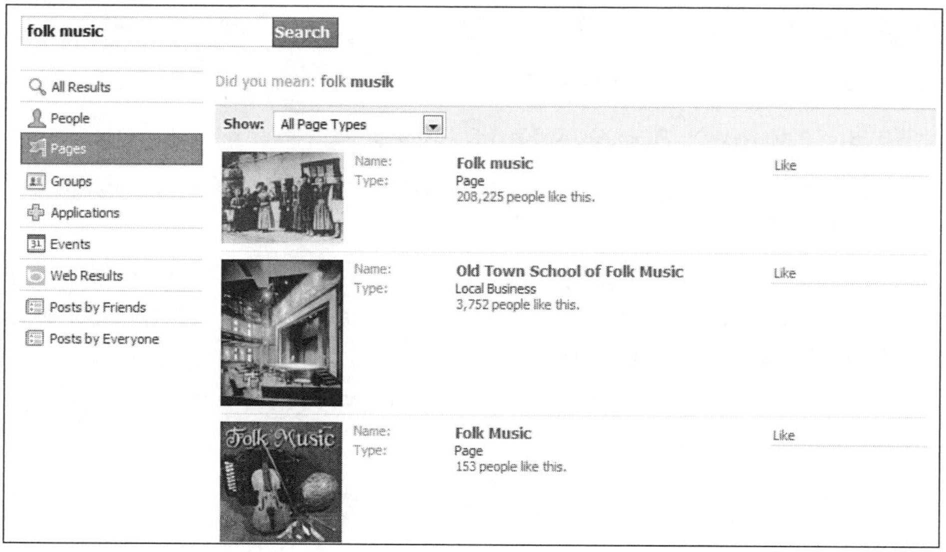

Figure 15.4. *Searching for fan pages.*

Creating Your Own Fan Page

Fan pages are designed for public figures and organizations to broadcast information to their fans. In fact, Facebook requires you to be an official representative of a given organization or person to create a fan page for that organization or person. So you can't just up and create a fan page for Mountain Dew, for example, or for the Doobie Brothers. That's something for the Dews or the Doobies to do for themselves.

That said, you *can* create a Facebook fan page for your own business or organization. Let's say, for example, that you help run a community youth soccer league. Assuming you have the approval of league officials, you can create a fan page for your league. Same thing if you run a local business; you can easily create a Facebook fan page for your company.

In fact, a Facebook fan page is a great way to keep in touch with your most loyal customers. You can use your fan page to announce new products and promotions, hold contests, and solicit customer opinions. Obviously, you can also link to your main website from your fan page, so customers can find out more information at the source.

Create a New Page

Here's how to create a fan page:

1. Navigate to www.facebook.com/pages/.

2. When the Browse All Pages page appears, click the Create Page button at the top of the page.

3. When the Create a Page page appears, as shown in Figure 15.5, select the category for your page: Local Business; Brand, Product, or Organization; or Artist, Band, or Public Figure.

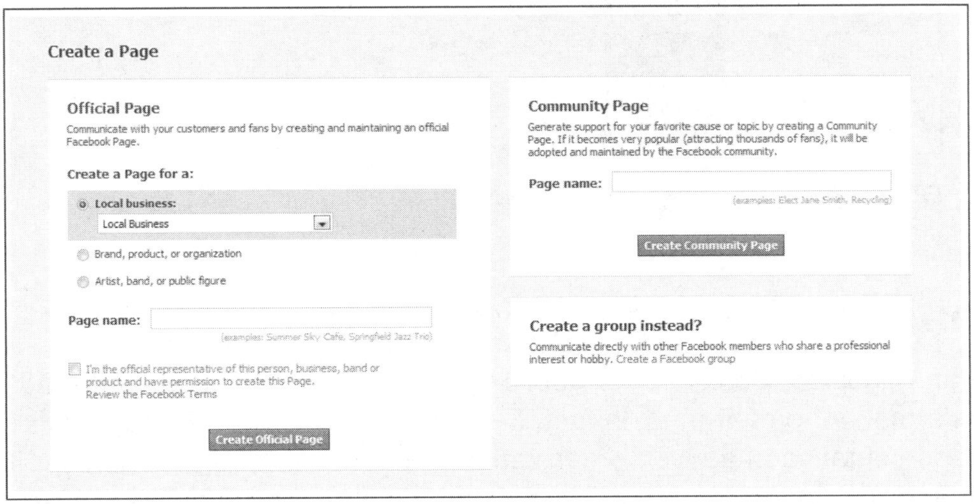

Figure 15.5. *Creating a new fan page.*

4. After you select the category, select the type of page you're creating from the list that appears. For example, if you're creating a page for a local business, you'd select the Local category and then make a further selection from the drop-down list: Automotive, Banking and Financial Service, Bar, Café, Club, and so on.

5. Enter the name of your page into the Page Name box.

6. Check the box stating you are the official representative of this person, business, band, or product and have permission to create this page.

7. Click the Create Official Page button.

That's it. You're now the proud owner of a brand new Facebook fan page.

Invite Others to Become Fans

Just having a fan page isn't enough, however. You also need to get yourself some fans.

Probably the best way to get fans is to invite them. Here's how to invite your current friends to become fans of your new page:

1. Navigate to your fan page and click the Suggest to Friends link in the sidebar.

2. When the Suggest to Friends window appears, as shown in Figure 15.6, click the names of friends you'd like to invite to be fans.

3. Click the Send Invitations button.

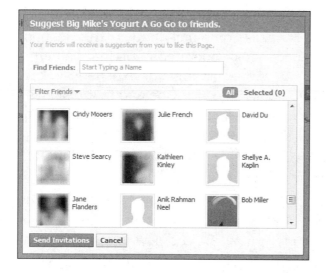

Figure 15.6. *Inviting your friends to become fans.*

Your friends will receive the invitations you send, and if they wish, can respond and choose to "like" your new page.

Community Pages

Facebook also offers a special type of fan page called a *community page*. These are pages for general topics or causes. For example, you can create a community page to support a candidate for elected office or to support a grassroots charitable movement. Unlike normal fan pages, you don't have to be an official representative to create a community page.

You create a community page the same way you create a standard fan page. Follow the previous steps until you get to the Create a Page page, where you see a Community Page section on the right side. Enter the desired name of the page into the Page Name box and then click the Create Community Page button. From there, it's pretty much like managing a regular fan page.

Don't confuse these types of community pages with those topic-oriented pages that Facebook also calls community pages. This second type of community page is a Facebook-generated page that gathers user-generated information about a specific topic or experience. For example, Facebook has a community page for Cooking that displays basic information about cooking, as well as posts from your friends that mention cooking. It's kind of like a Facebook-oriented Wikipedia; in fact, many of these community pages include information loaned from Wikipedia.

Facebook's intent with these topic-oriented community pages is to help you connect with others who share similar interests. I suppose that might work. But these community pages are too new to fully judge their effectiveness.

My initial opinion is that in creating topic-oriented pages, Facebook might have misjudged why people use their site. To me, Facebook is all about connecting with past and current friends; it's less about looking up general information that you can find elsewhere. I suppose you can use community pages to make new friends, but Facebook's other features—such as fan pages and groups, which we discuss in the next chapter—are much better for this task.

Chapter 16

Meeting Others in Groups

In the last chapter we talked about fan pages, those Facebook pages that are kind of like fan clubs for entertainers, celebrities, and companies. But fan clubs aren't the only kind of clubs out there; depending on your tastes and interests, you might be enticed to participate in a quilting club, or a photography club, or a chess club, or a club for Harley Davidson enthusiasts. It's all part of the social experience, after all, getting together—even if virtually—with others who share your interests.

As you might suspect, the millions of people who use Facebook share quite a few interests in common. If you're interested in coin collecting, for example, chances are there are more than a handful of other coin collectors on Facebook. The key is locating those people and then finding a forum for your communication and get-togethers.

Which is where Facebook groups come in. A Facebook group is an online club for users who share a common interest—and chances are you can find at least one group to participate in.

Understanding Facebook Groups

If you want to make some new friends on Facebook, one of the best ways to do it is to search out others who share your interests. If you're into gardening, look for gardeners. If you're into hang gliding, look for hang gliders. If you're a wine lover, look for other connoisseurs of the grape.

On Facebook, people who are interested in a given topic or hobby can congregate in virtual groups. These groups are nothing more than topic-oriented Facebook pages, a place for people interested in that topic to meet online.

Group Activities

What can you do in a Facebook group? Lots, actually. You can read the latest news, discover new information, view photos and movies, exchange messages with other group members, and engage in online discussions about the topic at hand. As you might suspect, each activity has its own tab on the group page.

Most groups are public, meaning they're open for all Facebook members to join. Some groups, however, are private, and require that the group administrator approve all requests for membership. You need to apply to join these private groups—and hope that your request is granted.

After you join a group, you have full access to the group's Facebook page. Most pages are like the one in Figure 16.1, with the standard sidebar along the left, familiar tabs in the middle, and annoying ads on the right. Which tabs you see depends on the group; some of these features are optional and aren't used by all groups.

Figure 16.1. *A typical Facebook group page.*

That said, the most common group tabs include the following:

- **Wall**: This is the same Wall you find on regular Profile pages, full of status updates from the group's leaders and posts from members.

- **Info**: This tab displays all the pertinent information about the group—category, description, contact info, and the like.

- **Discussions**: This is the place where the real talk takes place. Group members start topic-based discussions; other users reply to create message threads.

> **✔ Tip**
>
> Use the Discussions tab, not the Wall, to conduct your group discussions.

- **Photos**: This is where group leaders and members post their photos about the topic at hand.

- **Video**: Just like the Photos tab, except for videos uploaded by group members.

- **Events**: Open this tab to view upcoming group events—online chats, physical meet-ups, member reunions, and the like.

Running the Group

Remember, not all groups have all these tabs. What you see is up to the group leaders, called *admins*. That's short for *administrator*, of course, and the admin is the person who runs the group on a day-to-day basis.

In most instances, the admin is the person who first created the group, although other users can also be granted admin status. The admin is responsible for posting new content to the group, monitoring the Wall and discussion tabs, inviting new members to the group, approving new member applications (if the group uses that option), and just generally making sure that things run smoothly.

> **Note**
>
> In addition to admins, a group can also have group officers. An officer is merely an honorary title; he or she has no privileges beyond that of normal members.

Bottom line, Facebook groups are great places to commiserate with other people who are at least a little like you, and to learn more about your favorite hobby or interest. A group is also a great place to ask any questions you might have about the topic at hand; you're likely to find more than a few experts (real or self-appointed) among the group members.

Finding and Joining Groups

Before you can partake in all that a group offers, you first have to find a group that meets your interest. After you find a group, you can then officially join it—and then participate to whatever degree suits your fancy.

You find groups on Facebook by searching for them. Here's how it works:

1. Enter one or more keywords that describe what you're looking for into the search box in the Facebook toolbar and then click the Search button.

2. When the search results page appears, click the Groups link in the sidebar.

3. This narrows your search results to just Facebook groups, as shown in Figure 16.2. Scroll to a group that looks good and click that group's name to view the Facebook page for that group.

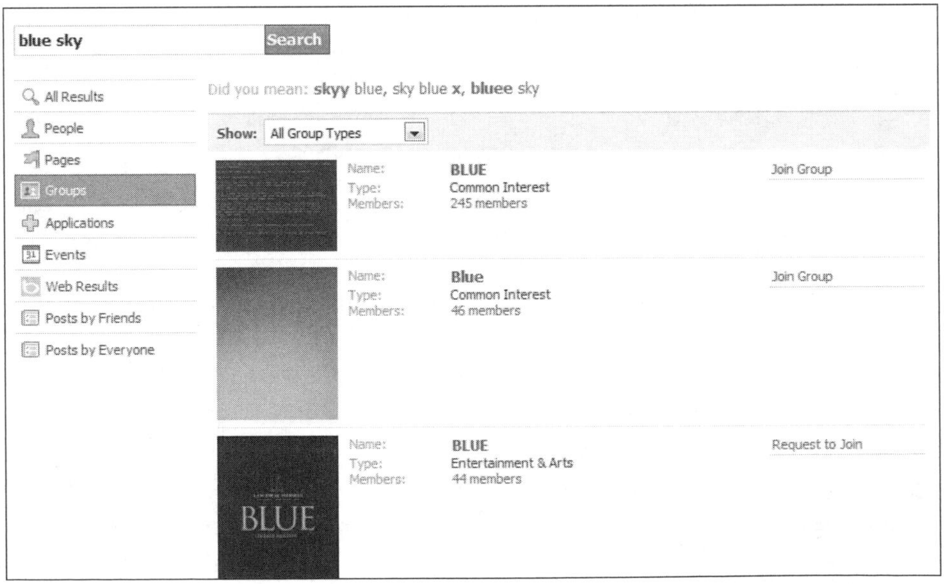

Figure 16.2.   *Searching for groups on Facebook.*

4. To join the group, click the Join Group or Request to Join links on the search results page.

Tip

You can also join a group directly from that group's Facebook page. Just click the Join or Request to Join button.

As noted previously, most groups are open to all Facebook members to join, which you do by clicking the Join Group link or Join button. Some groups, however, require that the group administrator approve requests for membership; these groups display a Request to Join link or button instead of the normal Join or Join Group link. Facebook notifies you when your membership request is approved.

Viewing Your Groups—and Your Friends' Groups

How do you get to the Facebook groups you belong to? It's simple, really. Just go to your Facebook Home page and click Groups in the sidebar. This displays your Groups page, shown in Figure 16.3, with all your groups listed. Click the name of a group to open that group's page.

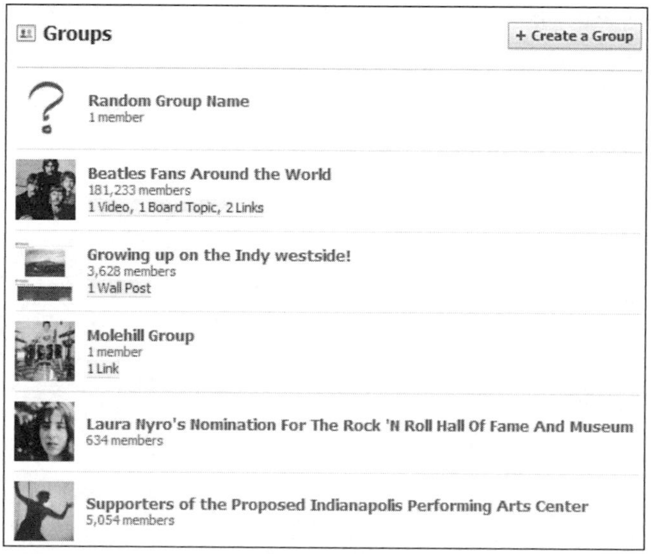

Groups   + Create a Group

? **Random Group Name**
1 member

Beatles Fans Around the World
181,233 members
1 Video, 1 Board Topic, 2 Links

Growing up on the Indy westside!
3,628 members
1 Wall Post

Molehill Group
1 member
1 Link

Laura Nyro's Nomination For The Rock 'N Roll Hall Of Fame And Museum
634 members

Supporters of the Proposed Indianapolis Performing Arts Center
5,054 members

Figure 16.3. *Viewing all your groups.*

By the way, sometimes it's fun to see the groups that your friends belong to. You can often find new groups to join by examining your friends' groups. To see your friends' groups, go to your Groups page and click the Friends' Groups link in the sidebar. You now see those groups that your friends subscribe to; click a group name to visit that group's page, or just click the Join or Request to Join button to join up.

Participating in a Group

After you join a group, then what? It all depends on whether you want to be a passive or an active participant.

Passive group participation means looking at what others post. This can range from viewing group photos and videos to reading ongoing discussions. All of this is easy enough to do; you don't need my help in that.

Active participation is another thing. The primary way to "talk" with other members of a Facebook group is on the Discussions tab, shown in Figure 16.4. A discussion is merely a series of messages and replies on a given topic; that forms a "thread" of messages that you can read through and reply to.

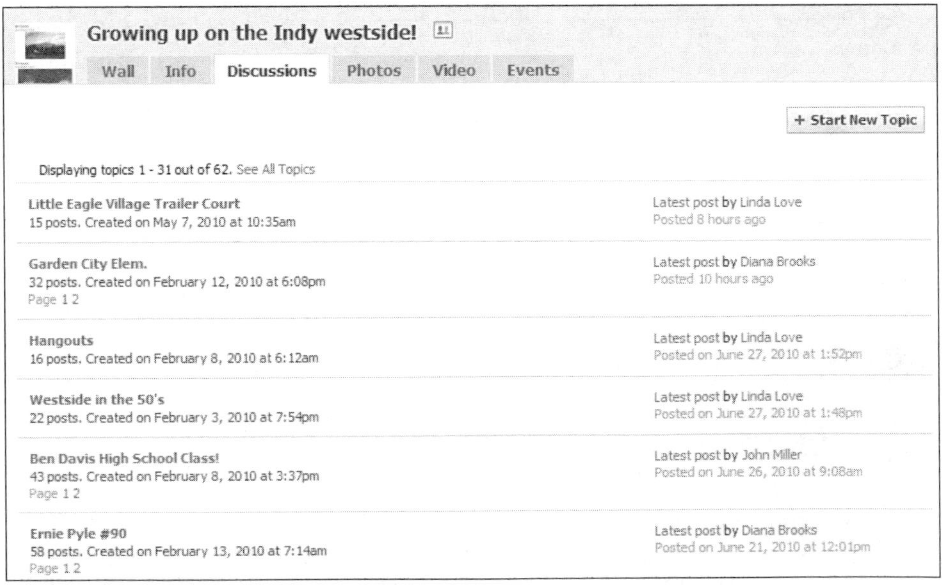

Growing up on the Indy westside!

| Wall | Info | **Discussions** | Photos | Video | Events |

+ Start New Topic

Displaying topics 1 - 31 out of 62. See All Topics

Little Eagle Village Trailer Court
15 posts. Created on May 7, 2010 at 10:35am

Latest post by Linda Love
Posted 8 hours ago

Garden City Elem.
32 posts. Created on February 12, 2010 at 6:08pm
Page 1 2

Latest post by Diana Brooks
Posted 10 hours ago

Hangouts
16 posts. Created on February 8, 2010 at 6:12am

Latest post by Linda Love
Posted on June 27, 2010 at 1:52pm

Westside in the 50's
22 posts. Created on February 3, 2010 at 7:54pm

Latest post by Linda Love
Posted on June 27, 2010 at 1:48pm

Ben Davis High School Class!
43 posts. Created on February 8, 2010 at 3:37pm
Page 1 2

Latest post by John Miller
Posted on June 26, 2010 at 9:08am

Ernie Pyle #90
58 posts. Created on February 13, 2010 at 7:14am
Page 1 2

Latest post by Diana Brooks
Posted on June 21, 2010 at 12:01pm

Figure 16.4. *Viewing group discussions.*

Most groups have dozens of different topics going at the same time. One post flows into another, members adding onto what other members have said, until you have a true discussion happening online. It's not in real time, of course, but it's still interesting.

Viewing a discussion thread is as simple as opening the Discussions tab and clicking the title for a given discussion. This displays all messages on the topic, as shown in Figure 16.5, oldest first; new replies are added at the bottom of the thread.

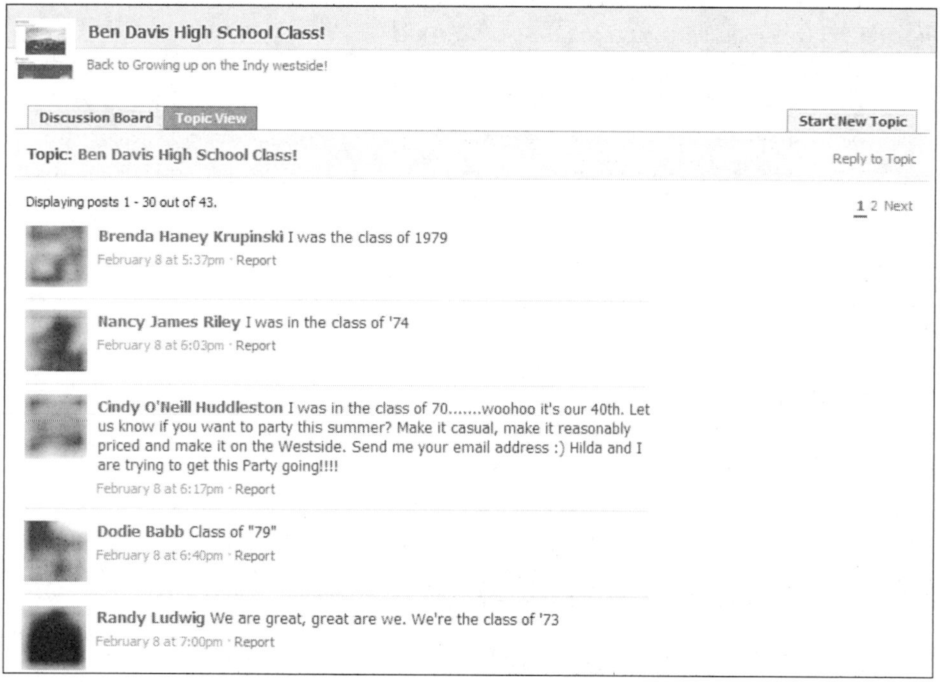

Figure 16.5.   Messages in a discussion thread.

To add your two cents worth, click the Reply to Topic link at the top of the list. This displays the Post Reply tab, shown in Figure 16.6. Enter your message into the Reply box and then click the Post Reply button.

To start a new message thread, go to the Discussions tab and click the Start New Topic button. When the Start New Topic tab appears, as shown in Figure 16.7, enter a title for the thread into the Topic box, and your initial message into the Post box. Click the Post New Topic button to post your message and get the discussion going.

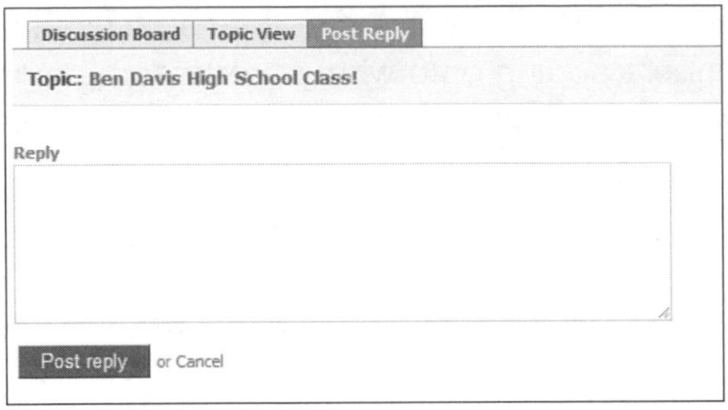

Discussion Board | Topic View | **Post Reply**

Topic: Ben Davis High School Class!

Reply

[ ]

Post reply or Cancel

Figure 16.6. *Replying to a discussion thread.*

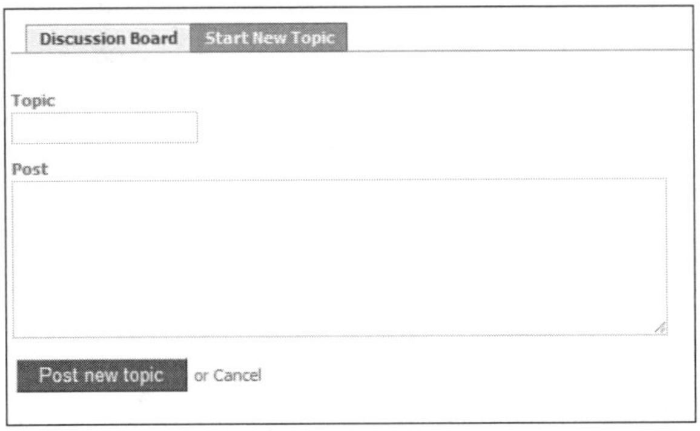

Discussion Board | **Start New Topic**

Topic

[ ]

Post

[ ]

Post new topic or Cancel

Figure 16.7. *Starting a new topic thread.*

Creating Your Own Group

There are tens of thousands of groups already on Facebook, so chances are you can find one for whatever interests you. But if there isn't a group for your particular interest, you can create one—which is pretty easy to do.

Here's the deal: Any Facebook member can create a new group. In fact, you can create more than one group, if you so wish.

Note

A Facebook member can create up to 200 groups.

Group Administration

As the creator of a group, you automatically become the group's admin. That means you're responsible for the day-to-day running of the group, such as it might be. Think about that responsibility before you launch a new group.

Access Levels

When you create a new group, you can choose from three different access levels that determine who can join the group, and how. These access levels are:

- **Open:** This type of group has open membership; any Facebook member can see and join the group without prior approval. This is the most common type of group.

- **Closed:** A closed group can be seen by all Facebook members, but the group administrator must approve all applications for membership.

- **Secret:** A secret group cannot be found in any Facebook searches; new members join by invitation (of the admin) only. Create this type of group when you want a totally private experience.

Group Features

As noted previously, Facebook groups can contain many of the same features found on a traditional Facebook Profile page, such as a Wall, photos, videos, events, and the like. In addition, groups can include a discussion tab, where members can engage in thread-oriented discussions, such as those found on web message forums.

Creating the Group

Those preliminaries out of the way, just how do you create a new group? Buckle yourself in, folks, because it's a somewhat lengthy process that goes something like this:

1. Navigate to the Facebook Home page and click the Groups link in the sidebar.

2. When the Groups page appears, click the Create a Group button.

3. When the Create a Group page appears, as shown in Figure 16.8, enter the name of your new group into the Group Name box.

Figure 16.8. *Creating a new group.*

4. Enter a short description of the group into the Description box.

5. Click For Group Type, click the Select Category arrow and select a category for your group: Business, Common Interest, Entertainment & Arts, Geography, Internet & Technology, Just for Fun, Music, Organizations, Sports & Recreation, or Student Groups.

6. Click the Select Type arrow and select the type of group you're creating. The options here differ depending on the category you selected in the previous step.

7. Enter any important announcements about this group into the Recent News box.

Note

If you're a member of a Facebook network, Facebook displays a Network list on the Create a Group page. To make your group available only to other members of a network, pull down the Network list and select a network. Select Global to make your group available to all Facebook members. (Learn more about networks in Chapter 17, "Networking for Business—and For Jobs.")

8. If the group has an official office, enter the office's name into the Office box.

9. If you want to display your email address, enter it into the Email box.

10. If you have a website, enter the site's URL into the Website box.

11. If you want to display your street address, enter it into the Street box.

12. If you want to display your city, enter it into the City/Town box.

13. Click the Create Group button.

Customizing Your Group

You're not done yet. After you've created the new group, you see the Customize page, shown in Figure 16.9, which includes numerous settings you can configure.

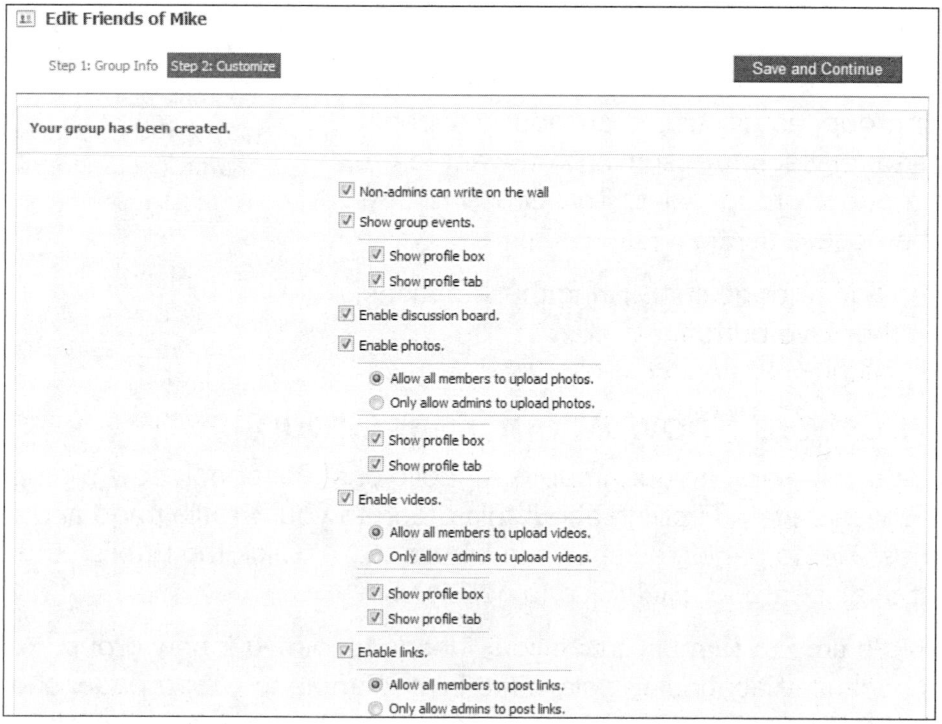

Figure 16.9.   Customizing your new group.

By default, the following options are enabled:

- Non-admins can write on the Wall

- Show group events

- Enable discussion board

- Enable photos

- Allow all members to upload photos

- Enable videos

- Allow all members to upload videos

- Enable links

- Allow all members to post links

To disable any of these features, uncheck their boxes.

You also need to select the access level for your group, as discussed previously: Open, Closed, or Secret. Assuming you want to create a public group, select This Group Is Open in the Access section.

When you're done configuring these options, click the Save button.

Note

You can also opt to display (or not) a profile box and profile tab for many of these items.

Letting Others Know About Your Group

There's still more. If your group is a public one, Facebook now prompts you to publish a status update about this group to your Profile page and to your friends' Home pages, as shown in Figure 16.10. Click the Publish button to post this update, or click Skip to not do so.

Now it's time to formally invite your friends to join your new group. You know this because Facebook displays the Invite People to *Group* page, shown in Figure 16.11. To invite Facebook friends to join your group, click each friend's name in the list. To invite non-Facebook members to join your group, enter their email addresses into the Invite People via Email box; use commas to separate multiple addresses.

Figure 16.10. *Publishing a notice about your group as a status update.*

Figure 16.11. *Inviting people to join your group.*

Enter a message to accompany this invitation into the Add a Personal Message box and then click the Send Invitations button. Everyone you selected receives an invitation to join your group.

> **Tip**
>
> You can also invite new members from the group's Facebook page.

Reconnecting

On the surface, it's easy to think of Facebook groups as like 21st-century versions of the homeroom clubs you had back in high school. You know, chess club, knitting club, model airplane club, and the like.

But while there certainly are a huge number of these club-like Facebook groups, there are also groups that are more about times and places than they are about hobbies and interests. As such, these groups attempt to reconnect people with shared experiences.

I belong to a number of groups that connect me back to the days of my youth. For example, I grew up on the west side of Indianapolis, and there's a Facebook group called Growing Up on Indy's Westside. It's a fun little group, with people posting faded pictures of old haunts, and lots of discussions about the way things used to be and what we used to do back then. I can't say I contribute too often, but it's always fun to read what others post.

I also belong to a "Where is and/or who do you remember?" group for my high school. This is a great place to find out what my old classmates have been up to in the decades since graduation. Lots of posts asking about individual students, teachers, and events. It's a nice stroll through memory lane.

The point is, Facebook groups—and their discussion boards—are great ways to reconnect with your past. You might even meet up with some of your old friends in these groups, or make some new friends you should have made way back then. It's kind of a virtual blast from the past, and we have the Facebook social network to thank for it.

Chapter 17

Networking for Business—and for Jobs

As you know, Facebook is a great place to connect with family members and old friends. It's also a good place to connect with current and former co-workers, as well as others in your industry or profession. For that matter, many people use Facebook to help them look for new jobs; with all those "friends" you have on the Facebook site, at least one of them must know somebody somewhere who can help you get an in for a new position.

How, then, do you use Facebook on a more business-oriented basis? It's a matter of taking advantage of the appropriate Facebook features, and of acting a bit more professional online.

Understanding Facebook Networks

You're familiar with Facebook groups and fan pages, which help you connect with others who share your personal interests. Well, Facebook has a similar feature that lets you connect with others on a more professional basis—in particular, people who work at the same company you do.

What Facebook offers is a special type of group, called a *network*, devoted to a specific company—large companies, in particular. To join a company's network, you have to be an employee of that company, and you have to provide an active email address from that company. That's how you join the network, by the way—by entering your work email address.

Note that networks exist only for established businesses; there's either a network for your business, or there isn't. And if there isn't, you're out of luck, as Facebook won't let individuals create new networks.

That said, it's worth your while to see if Facebook has a network for the company you work for—especially if it's a big company, with lots of offices in disparate locations. Let's face it, if you work in a five-person business, you don't really need a special Facebook group to connect with your co-workers. But if you work for an organization with thousands of employees across the nation or globe, connecting with your co-workers via Facebook could prove particularly useful.

What can you do in a work network? It's pretty much like any other Facebook group, with membership limited to your work colleagues. You can read status updates posted by company representatives, peruse company information, view photos of remote offices and work-related events, and join in lively discussions with colleagues near and far. It's a meeting place for the people you work with, plain and simple.

Note

Networks also exist for many schools and universities. Access to a school network is limited to current students, former students, and teachers who have valid school email addresses. Because you probably graduated long ago and no longer have a school email address (if, in fact, you ever did), joining your old school network is probably out of the question. So we limit our discussion of networks to business networks only.

Joining Your Work Network

To join a company for your current employer, you must have a valid email address; this keeps non-employees and former employees from joining in the festivities. Assuming you have a work email address, follow these steps to join your company's network:

1. From the Facebook toolbar, click Account and then select Account Settings.

2. From the My Account page, click the Networks tab, shown in Figure 17.1.

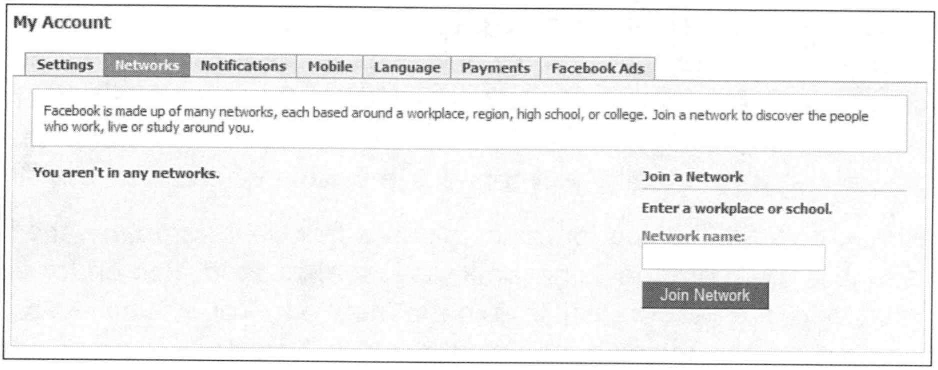

My Account

| Settings | Networks | Notifications | Mobile | Language | Payments | Facebook Ads |

Facebook is made up of many networks, each based around a workplace, region, high school, or college. Join a network to discover the people who work, live or study around you.

You aren't in any networks.

Join a Network

Enter a workplace or school.

Network name:

Join Network

Figure 17.1. *Joining a work network.*

3. Enter the name of your company into the Network Name box. As you type, matching networks appear in a drop-down menu.

4. Select your company from the list.

5. Enter your work email address into the Work Email box.

6. Click the Join Network button.

You should now receive a confirmation email at your work email address. Click the link in this email to finalize things. You now have access to your company's Facebook page, and everything that goes with it.

Networking Professionally

Although Facebook has its roots in personal social networking, it has also become a useful site for establishing professional connections. That's right, Facebook is more than just a site for friends and families; it's also a place to connect with co-workers, other professionals in your industry, and other business people in your city.

Finding Other Business Professionals on Facebook

There are many ways to find other business professionals (and potential employers) on the Facebook site. Let's look at a few.

One approach is to browse for friends of your business friends. Begin by identifying a colleague or business professional who is already in your friends list, then go to that person's Profile page and browse his or her friends list. If you find someone with whom you would like to connect, invite that person to become your friend. Peruse that person's friends list to identify further potential business connections—and so on and so on. It's like a six degrees of separation thing; eventually, you connect to people who can be of value.

Of course, if you're looking for connections within your company, the best bet is to join your company's network, as just discussed. Search for your company and, if a network exists, join that network. You will have access to all company employees who are Facebook members and who have joined that network.

You can also use Facebook's search function to search for relevant company names, industry buzzwords, and the like. Filter the search results by people, and you see a list of people who work for the company or in the industry in question. Invite these people to be your Facebook friends.

Managing Your Professional Contacts

After you've added a number of professional contacts to your Facebook friends list, it's good practice to create a list of just these professional friends. You can then easily send email messages to this list of professional contacts. Create a single message and then enter the list name into the message's To box. The message is sent to all members of this list.

You can also filter the status updates and other information you send to the members of this professional contacts list; Facebook lets you configure its privacy settings so that members of a list can see only select information. Doing so enables you to display personal information to your personal friends and hide that personal information from your professional friends.

Note

Learn more about creating custom friends lists in Chapter 7, "Organizing Your Friends List." Learn more about sending messages in Chapter 9, "Exchanging Private Messages."

Note

Learn more about determining who can view your status updates and personal information in Chapter 21, "Keeping Some Things Private."

Networking via Facebook Groups

Facebook hosts a large number of groups focused on professional topics. These are groups devoted to a particular company, industry, or profession, and tend to be where you find like-minded professionals on the Facebook site.

Note

Learn more about Facebook groups in Chapter 16, "Meeting Others in Groups."

Use Facebook's search function to search for keywords related to your company, profession, or industry. When the search results page appears, filter the results by group. You can then join those groups that are most closely related to what you're looking for professionally.

After you join a professional group, become an active participant. Participate in group discussions, respond to questions asked by other group members, and start your own conversations with others in the group. And when you post, be sure to provide useful and relevant information and advice to the group. Over time you become familiar with other group members, and you can invite them to join your friends list.

Caution

Avoid making group posts that sound like advertisements or overt solicitations, especially solicitations for employment. You should offer genuine contributions, not self-promotion disguised as posts.

You should also consider creating your own professional group, related to your profession or industry, and see which professionals it attracts. When you create such a group, make sure that it offers unique value not found in other similar groups. Invite your professional Facebook friends to this group; you should also invite non-Facebook members to join, via the email join feature. Encourage all group members to invite their professional friends to join the group, as well. The more successful your group, the more professional connections you will make.

Job Hunting on Facebook

In addition to simple professional networking, you can also use Facebook to connect with prospective employers and seek out new jobs. To that end,

Facebook is second only to LinkedIn for job hunters—and for employers seeking to fill new positions.

The key here is finding employers who use social networking sites such as Facebook to find prospective job applicants. Many companies look online to fill positions before paying for a job listing in a newspaper or on a job site such as Monster.com. Better to fill the position for free than pay for the listing, the thinking goes.

For that matter, you can often connect with potential employers before positions exist. You connect with someone on Facebook, make friends with them as it were, and they'll think of you when something crops up in the future.

Reworking Your Profile

When you're in the job market, you need to present a professional face to potential employers. The first place to start is your Facebook Profile page, which can be reworked to function much like an online resume.

First, eliminate all unnecessary and potentially damaging personal information from your profile. That means deleting information about your political and religious views, your favorite TV shows, likes and dislikes, and the like. Employers don't want or need to know that you're a fan of *I Dream of Jeanie*, follow Phish from concert to concert, and support the Libertarian party. That information seldom works in your favor, and often works against you. Better to keep it short and sweet with the personal details.

Next, load up your profile with all sorts of professional information, including employment history, professional accomplishments, and the like. There are sections in your profile for much of this information; what doesn't fit naturally can be added to the Bio section in your profile.

After you have your profile cleaned up, make sure that it's set for public viewing. No sense going to all that work and then hiding it from a future employer.

> **✓ Tip**
>
> You should also sort through your Facebook photos and delete those that present you in a non-professional matter. That includes some "recreational" photos; include too many golf photos and an employer might think you spend too much time on the links and not enough at the office.

Becoming a Fan of Potential Employers

Facebook fan pages are a great way to learn more about companies you want to work for. Not only can you find basic information about a company, you get first notice of company news and events.

To that end, you want to sign up as a fan for any potential company that has a Facebook page. That means "liking" the company, of course; after you do so, status updates from the company automatically appear in your News Feed.

Note

Learn more about fan pages in Chapter 15, "Becoming a Fan."

Asking for a Job

Finally, let's not dismiss the simple act of using Facebook to tell people that you're looking for a job. You can do this by posting a status update to that effect—"Hey, I'm job hunting, anybody know of open positions?"

Of course, this probably isn't an option if you currently have a job and want to jump somewhere else. You don't want to tip off your current employer that you're looking, after all.

That said, this is a very direct way for the unemployed to make their interests known. Telling your Facebook friends that you're available sometimes turns up interesting work. Who knows which of your friends has knowledge of a decent job opportunity—or is looking to hire someone himself?

Keeping Your Personal and Professional Lives Separate

When you're using Facebook for professional purposes, you have to be careful about mixing your personal and professional lives. For example, you probably don't want to broadcast gossip (or even pictures!) about your drunken behavior at a weekend party to your boss, or to potential employers. It makes sense to practice discretion about what you post in your status updates, and to utilize Facebook's numerous privacy settings to limit what you display to whom online.

This goes beyond the obvious to the quite subtle. If you do a lot of spouting off about politics or religion or other sensitive subjects in your Facebook status updates, some potential employers might think twice before giving you a hearing. For that matter, complaining about your current employer is sure to both get back to your boss (and nothing good will come of that) and cause potential employers to think you're either a whiner or a troublemaker, or possibly both. And nobody wants to deliberately hire someone like that.

To some degree, it comes down to the image conveyed by your Facebook presence. If you're less than discreet online, potential employers have to ask the question, what kind of judgment does this person possess? Poor judgment about what you say or post could carry over into what you do at work. In an employer's eyes, that would not be a good thing.

Speaking of images, know that your so-called friends on Facebook can work against you. Off-color remarks posted by a friend on your Wall are seen by others. If you're tagged in a questionable photo posted by a friend, that photo is going to show up in your stuff. And that includes photos from long ago and far away; a lot of people keep busy scanning old pictures and posting them on Facebook, tagging everyone included. You might not want these pictures made publicly available, but unless you can convince your friends to take them down, there you are.

And don't think that employers don't check you out on Facebook and other social networking sites. They most certainly do. You can't hide in plain sight, when you're an active job prospect they're going to search for you and see what they find. If there's something up there that presents you in poor light, they'll find it.

Although you can try to hide some personal information by reconfiguring Facebook's privacy settings, there are ways around this. A large company might have someone on staff who went to the same school you did, and thus be able to view your information via the school network ties. Sometimes they deal in subterfuge, getting an intern to pose as a friend of a friend or whatever to get onto your friends list. In other words, if a company wants to see your stuff, they'll find a way.

So don't assume that your "private" information on Facebook will remain private. Instead, assume that a potential employer will look for and find everything posted by you and about you on Facebook. Take the effort to clean things up as much as you can—and refrain from mixing your personal and professional lives online.

Chapter 18

Finding Fun Games and Applications

Mafia Wars. FarmVille. LivingSocial. FamilyLink.

You've seen them. Possibly you've played them or used them. Maybe you've even been annoyed by them—or rather, by posts about them from your friends. But what are they?

Mafia Wars, FarmVille, LivingSocial, et al are Facebook applications. That is, they're games and little utility programs that run on the Facebook site. And they're very, very popular.

Understanding Facebook Applications

A Facebook application is simply a program or game that runs on the Facebook site. These applications are accessed from their own Facebook pages, and you use them while you're signed into Facebook.

Now, these aren't big fancy applications like Microsoft Office or Quicken. No, they're small, typically single-purpose applications, web-based in nature, that add a bit of functionality to your Facebook experience.

Some applications build on the social networking nature of the Facebook site. Others are designed for more solitary use.

> **Note**
>
> Some applications, such as the default Photos and Videos applications, are developed by Facebook. Most applications, however, are created by third-party application developers. Most applications are available free of charge.

Some are strictly functional. Others are more fun. The reality is that there are a wide range of these available; you're bound to find some that look interesting to you.

For example, the aforementioned FamilyLink is designed to help you connect with other family members on Facebook. LivingSocial offers a variety of applications that track and publicize the books you're reading, music you're listening to, and so forth. And the Causes application, shown in Figure 18.1, helps you mobilize your Facebook friends to support various charities and organizations.

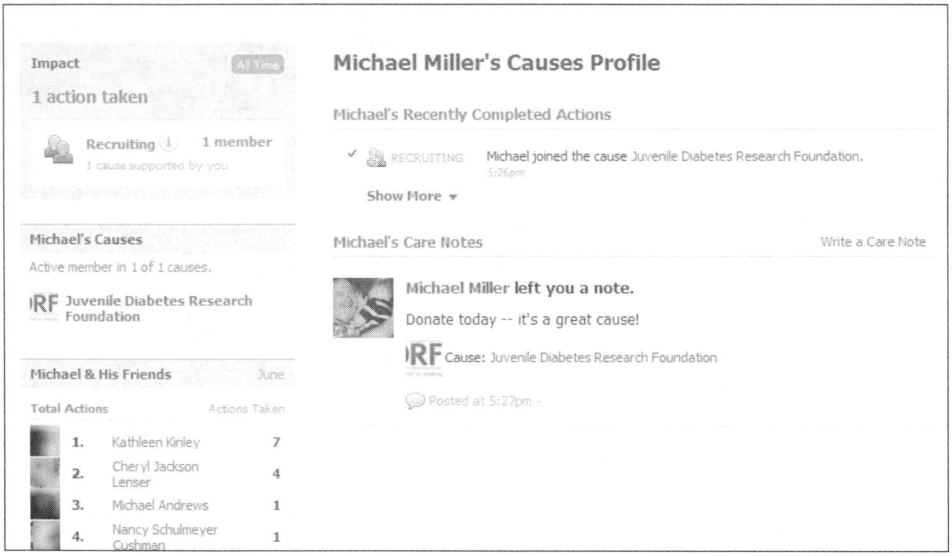

Figure 18.1.   *Facebook's Causes application.*

Then there are the apps that are a little less serious. Honesty Box is a quiz you can send to friends to find out what they really think about you. Which Star Trek Captain Are You?, shown in Figure 18.2, is another quiz that determines whether you're more like Kirk or Picard. The iHeart and @Hugs applications let you send your love to your Facebook friends. And Bumper Sticker lets you create and post fun sayings to your Facebook page.

Some Facebook applications are actually games—social games, to be exact. These are single-player or multi-player games that you play on the Facebook site, while you're logged on. Mafia Wars, FarmVille (shown in Figure 18.3), and PetVille are probably the most popular of these games, but there are a lot more than just these, some of which have millions of users. These games can be fairly addictive and become big time-wasters—which isn't necessarily a bad thing.

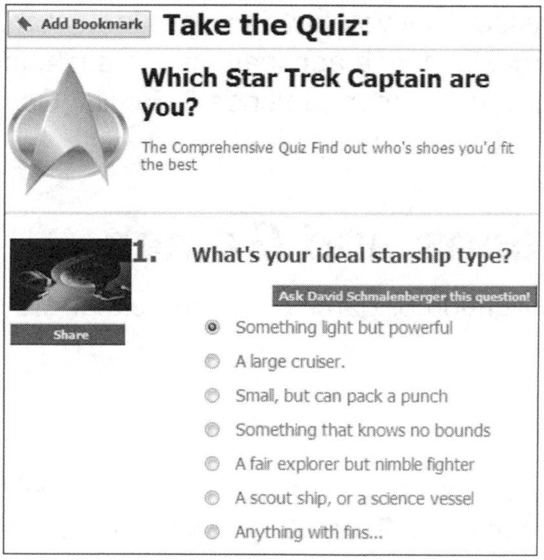
Add Bookmark
Take the Quiz:
Which Star Trek Captain are you?
The Comprehensive Quiz Find out who's shoes you'd fit the best
1. What's your ideal starship type?
Ask David Schmalenberger this question!
Share
Something light but powerful
A large cruiser.
Small, but can pack a punch
Something that knows no bounds
A fair explorer but nimble fighter
A scout ship, or a science vessel
Anything with fins...

Figure 18.2. *The Which Star Trek Captain Are You? application.*

Free Gifts
Play
My Neighbors
Invite Friends
Add Farm Coins & Cash
Love FarmVille?
323
Add Coins & Cash
5
3
01
Michael's Farm
Add Neighbor
Michael

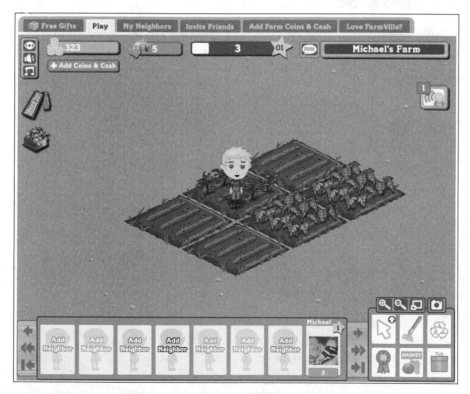

Figure 18.3. *The ever-popular FarmVille application.*

To give you a flavor of what's available, all you have to do is look at the categories that Facebook uses to organize these applications. As such, look for apps in the Business, Education, Entertainment, Friends & Family, Games, Just for Fun, Lifestyle, Sports, and Utilities categories.

Discovering Applications and Games

How do you find a Facebook application or game? You can either browse or search for apps; it's up to you.

Browsing for Apps

If you're not sure what specific app or game you're looking for, it might be useful to browse applications by category. This lets you see all related applications, and choose from there.

Just follow these steps:

1. Navigate your Web browser to the Facebook application directory, located at www.facebook.com/apps/. (Figure 18.4 shows this directory.)

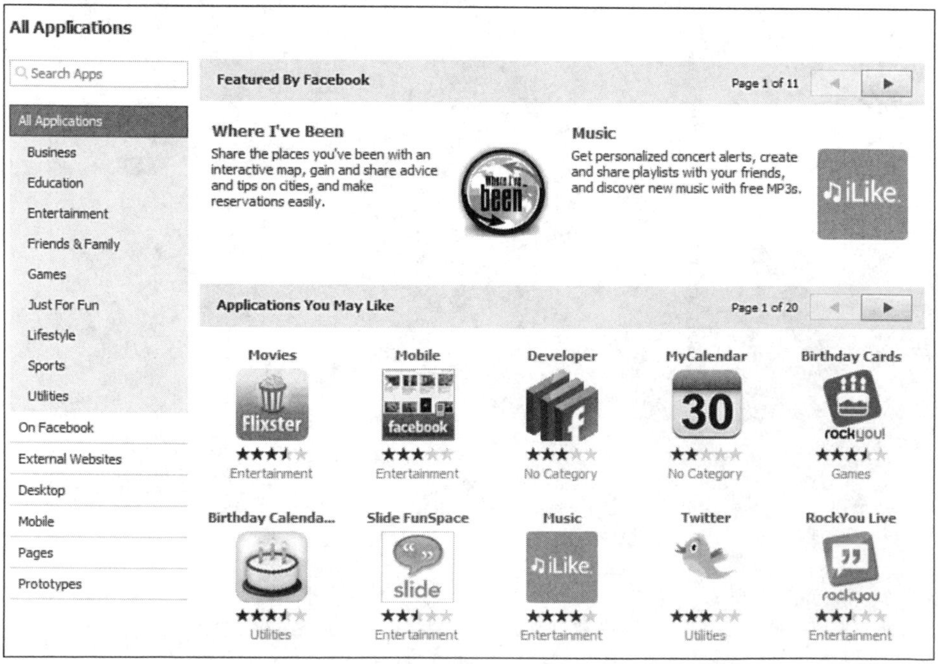

Figure 18.4.   *Browsing for apps in the Facebook application directory.*

2. From the sidebar, click the category of application you're looking for.

3. Click the link for an application to display the Facebook page for that app.

Searching for Apps

Browsing is fine, but if you have a specific app or game in mind, it's quicker to search for it. Follow these steps:

1. Enter the name of the app into the search box in the Facebook toolbar and then click the Search button.

2. When the search results page appears, click Applications in the sidebar to display only applications in the search results, as shown in Figure 18.5.

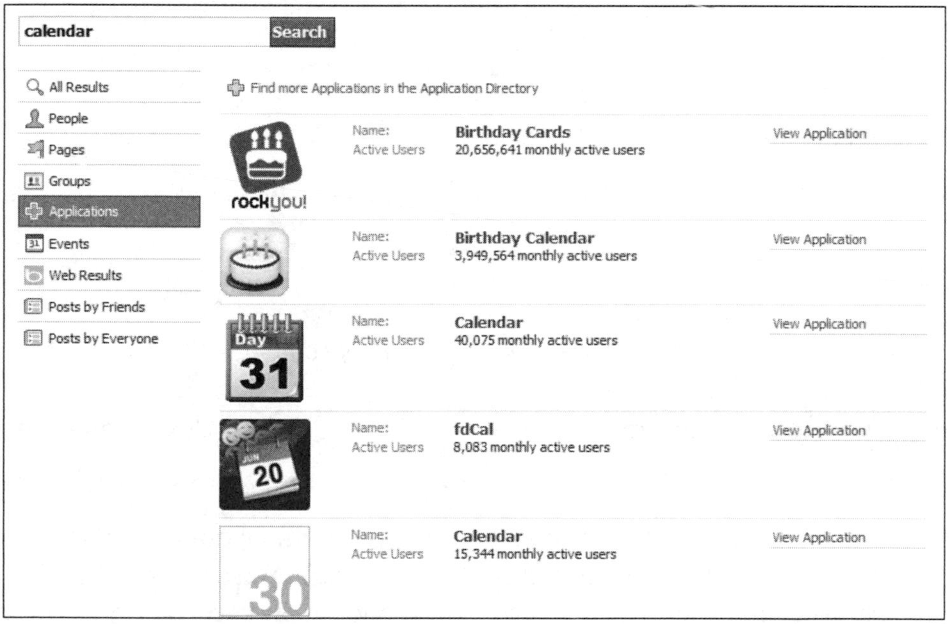

calendar	Search

- All Results
- People
- Pages
- Groups
- **Applications**
- Events
- Web Results
- Posts by Friends
- Posts by Everyone

Find more Applications in the Application Directory

| | Name: | **Birthday Cards** | View Application |
| rockyou! | Active Users | 20,656,641 monthly active users | |

| | Name: | **Birthday Calendar** | View Application |
| | Active Users | 3,949,564 monthly active users | |

| | Name: | **Calendar** | View Application |
| Day 31 | Active Users | 40,075 monthly active users | |

| | Name: | **fdCal** | View Application |
| JUN 20 | Active Users | 8,083 monthly active users | |

| | Name: | **Calendar** | View Application |
| 30 | Active Users | 15,344 monthly active users | |

Figure 18.5. *Searching for applications.*

3. Click the link for an application to display the Facebook page for that app.

Using an Application or Game

When you find an application you like, click the link for that application to go to that application's Facebook page. This page, like the one in Figure 18.6, contains important information about that application—including, in many instances, reviews from users of that app.

Figure 18.6. *The Facebook page for a typical application.*

If you want to use that application or play that game, follow these steps:

1. From the application's Facebook page, click the Go to Application button.

2. When the Request for Permission page appears, like the one shown in Figure 18.7, you see what actions the application wants to take. This might include accessing your personal information, sending you email, posting to your Wall, and accessing your friends' info. If you're okay with all this, click the Allow button. If you're not, click the Leave Application button.

What happens next depends on the application. You might be returned to the app's Facebook page, or you might see a new page with information on how to start using the app. For games, you'll probably be taken to the game's page, where you can start playing the game.

Figure 18.7. *Giving permission for an application to do all sorts of stuff.*

Viewing and Managing Your Applications— and Those Your Friends Are Using

Want to see which applications you're using? There are probably a lot more than you might remember.

Viewing Your Applications and Games

If all you want to do is see which apps you're using, go to your Facebook Home page and click Applications in the sidebar. This displays the Applications page, as shown in Figure 18.8, with your apps listed at the top. Click any link to view the page for that application.

As to games, even though they're technically Facebook applications, you view them separately. Go to the Facebook Home page and click Games in the sidebar. This displays the Games page, with your games listed at the top.

By the way, you can view those apps and games your friends are using from the Applications and Games pages. Your friends' apps and games are listed below yours on these pages.

> **Note**
> Facebook isn't always consistent as to what it labels an application or game. For example, weRead, which I would clearly call an application, is listed as a game. For this reason, you might need to look in both places to view everything you're using.

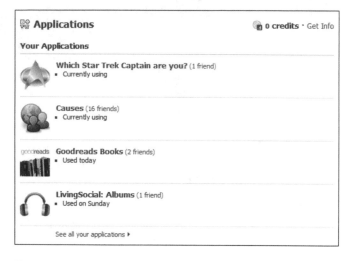

Figure 18.8. Viewing the applications you're using.

Managing Your Apps and Games

Viewing which apps you're using is nice, but what if you want to manage them—specifically, to delete those you're no longer using? Well, Facebook lets you do this too. Just follow these steps:

1. From the Facebook toolbar, click Account and then select Application Settings.

2. When the Application Settings page appears, as shown in Figure 18.9, you see those applications and games you've used in the past month. To delete an application or game, click the X on the far right of its listing.

3. To determine how an application is used and where it's displayed, click the Edit Settings link for that listing. This displays the Edit *Application* Settings dialog box, like the one in Figure 18.10. Each application has its own unique settings; make your changes and then click the Okay button.

What about these application settings? Well, the most common ones concern where an application is displayed and who can see it.

Figure 18.9. *Managing your applications.*

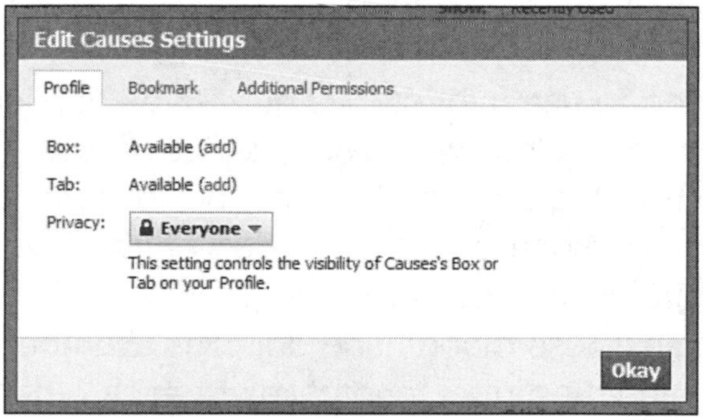

Figure 18.10. *Editing application settings.*

From the Edit *Application* Settings dialog box, click the Profile tab. There are likely several options here, possibly including the following:

- **Box**: If this option is enabled, a box for this application appears either on a Boxes tab on your Profile page or possibly in a box in the sidebar of your Profile page.

- **Tab**: If this option is enabled, a tab for this application appears on your Profile page.

- **Privacy**: Click this button to determine who can see information about this application on your Profile page: Everyone, Friends Only, or Friends of Friends. Select Customize to select visibility options for specific friends.

Note

Some apps have an Additional Permissions tab that lets you give permission for the app to publish content to your Wall, access your email address, and the like.

Not all apps or games have all these options. (It can never be that simple, of course.) You need to configure each application as necessary, using the options available.

Apps for Grown-Ups

Young people and older people use pretty much the same Facebook features, but they often use them in different ways. This is certainly the case with Facebook applications, where the apps used by the younger crowd tend to be much different than those used by those of us with a few more years under our belts.

Younger users, for example, tend to use a lot of the "quiz"-type applications, such as Honesty Box, IQ Test, Who Were You in a Past Life?, and Do You Really Know Me? They're also big on apps that purport to discover your true personality (My Personality, Personality Analysis), deliver horoscopes and predictions (Daily Horoscope, Numerology), link together their Facebook friends (Top Friends, My BFFs), express moods and opinions (Bumper Sticker, Pieces of Flair), and send little virtual *tchotchkes* to each other (Pass a Drink, Send a Rose). In other words, a lot of virtual time wasters.

Older users, however, tend to be a little less frivolous and bit more practical in their choice of apps. People our age like to use apps that help them connect to family members online, manage their schedules, track their favorite books and music, connect with business associates, and do good things. It's a different bag of apps than what your kids or grandkids use.

With that in mind, here are some of the apps I find most useful for or interesting to those of us of a certain age:

- **Birthday Calendar:** This app goes a few steps beyond Facebook's built-in birthday notifications, compiling all the birthdays of your friends and family members into a single calendar interface. It helps you plan ahead for upcoming birthdays, which is a good thing if you have a large family to deal with.

- **Business Cards:** This app lets you create a custom business card and attach it to your Facebook messages.

- **Causes:** This is a very popular application, designed to help publicize worthy causes and raise money for them.

- **Circle of Moms:** This is a social network within the Facebook network that lets moms connect with other moms to address the challenges of motherhood. This one has more than a million users.

- **Family Tree:** A great tool for finding your relatives—and staying in touch with them.

- **FamilyLink:** Another app for connecting with your relatives online.

- **GoodReads:** This app helps you manage your book library, review books, and share your favorite books with your Facebook friends.

- **iLike:** Okay, this one's popular with the kiddos, too, but it's also a great app for us music-loving oldsters. iLike lets you share your favorite songs and playlists, as well as discover new music.

- **Jobster Career Network:** A great app for those of us in the job market. Jobster lets you post your resume, receive job alerts, and search for openings from within Facebook.

- **LinkedIn Profile:** Great for job hunters, or just those who want to connect with professional colleagues. This app adds your LinkedIn profile information to your Facebook Profile page.

- **MeetingWave:** This tool helps you meet up with people offline. Good for making local business contacts, discovering sales prospects, and even hooking up with potential employers.

- **My Diet:** A nice app for helping you take off a few pounds. Includes food and activity diaries, weight ticker, weight chart, journal, support wall, and the ability to compare your activities to those of your friends.

- **MyCalendar:** An application that helps you keep track of friends' birthdays and Facebook events.

- **TripAdvisor—Cities I've Visited:** A neat little app that creates an interactive travel map of places you've traveled, which you can then share with your Facebook friends.

- **Twitter:** If you're into the Twitter thing, this app enables you to follow your Facebook friends who also tweet and post your own tweets to Facebook.

- **Visual Bookshelf:** Another good app for book lovers, a good way to share your literary likes with your Facebook friends.

Note

You can learn more about and start using any of these apps just by searching for them from the Facebook toolbar.

- **Weekly Schedule:** This app posts a graphical display of your weekly activities for all your Facebook friends to see.

- **Where I've Been:** Another travel app that tracks all the places you've visited, to share with your Facebook friends.

Then there's the games. While I'd like to say that older, more mature users are less likely to play Facebook's social games, I don't think that's the case. I see too many posts about FarmVille, Mafia Wars, Bejeweled Blitz, and Texas Hold'em Poker to think otherwise. No, I'm pretty sure that a lot of old geezers waste as much time playing these games as do their more spritely offspring. It also appears that older users play many of the same games as do their younger counterparts.

That said, I'm not going to go through a list of popular games here. You know what you like to play; you don't need me to tell you that. So feel free to search for what you like or just browse through Facebook's games category in the application directory. There are plenty of games to waste your time with there.

Blocking Annoying Games and Apps

Some people really like Facebook apps, especially playing games like Mafia Wars and FarmVille. I don't. I'm not a big game player, period, and I especially don't care to hear about the games that my friends are playing. That's their business, and I don't want to be bothered.

The thing is, I get bothered, because many games and apps insist on posting status updates to my friends' feeds. Some apps post updates when a friend reads a new book or listens to a new CD. Some games post updates when a friend reaches a certain level or posts a certain score. (Or, in the case of Mafia Wars, when they "off" someone important.) These unwanted updates clog my News Feed and annoy the hell out of me.

Fortunately, there's a way to block these app-generated updates from your News Feed. Block an app or game once, and you'll never see an update about that app again.

I talked about this trick back in Chapter 5, but it bears repeating here. To block an app or game from posting status updates to your News Feed, you first have to find one of these annoying posts. Point to the post to display the Hide button; this displays a box underneath the post with three more buttons: Hide *Friend*, Hide *Application*, and Cancel. (For example, if it's a Farmville post, the button reads Hide FarmVille.) Click the Hide *Application* button and it blocks all future posts from this application or game from any of your friends.

Needless to say, I use this technique a lot. And I don't get too bothered by unwanted application and game posts. Hurray!

Chapter 19

Using Facebook on the Go

Most people connect with Facebook from their personal computers. But that isn't the only way to connect; you can also use your mobile phone to post status updates and read posts in your News Feed. Connecting in this fashion helps you keep in touch while you're on the go—or just waiting in line at the supermarket.

You can connect to Facebook from any mobile phone, using simple text messages. But if you have a smartphone, like the Apple iPhone, you can use phone-specific Facebook applications to gain access to most of Facebook's features on the go. Even if all you have is basic Web access (no Facebook app), you can still connect to the Facebook site via your phone's Web browser.

Connecting from Your iPhone

Because Apple's iPhone is the most popular smartphone on the market today, let's start by examining how you can connect to Facebook from your iPhone.

It all starts with the Facebook for iPhone application. You can find this app in the iPhone App Store, just search the store for "Facebook" and then download the app—it's free.

> **Note**
>
> You can learn more about Facebook for iPhone by going to the app's Facebook page, at www.facebook.com/iphone/. The first time you launch the app, you need to enter your email address and password to log onto the Facebook site.

Figure 19.1 shows the Home screen of the Facebook for iPhone application. As you can see, you have icons for nine specific functions:

- **News Feed**: This displays the most recent posts from your friends.

- **Profile**: This displays your Profile page.

- **Friends**: This displays an alphabetical list of all your friends.

- **Inbox**: This displays any messages in your Facebook email box.

- **Chat**: This lets you instant message in real time with your friends.

- **Requests**: This displays any pending friend requests, and lets you respond to those requests.

Tip

The Photos features on Facebook for iPhone is actually a great way to carry your photo collection around with you, virtually. When you want to show someone your favorite pictures, just whip out your iPhone, launch the Facebook app, and press the Photos icon; you can then browse through and display photos from all your Facebook albums.

- **Events**: This displays any upcoming events you have scheduled.

- **Photos**: This displays the photos you've uploaded to Facebook.

- **Notes**: This displays any notes you've uploaded to Facebook.

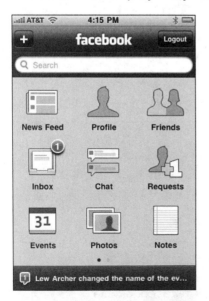

Figure 19.1. *The Facebook for iPhone Home screen.*

There's also a Notifications bar at the bottom of the screen. Any unread Facebook notifications are noted here; press the bar to view the notifications.

By the way, you can navigate back to this Home screen at any time by pressing the Home button at the top left of any subsequent screen, as shown in Figure 19.2.

Tip

You can add a shortcut button for any of your friends to a second page of the Home screen. Just click the + button at the top left of the Home screen; this displays your friends list. Tap the name of a friend and you create a button for that person's Profile page.

Home ——

Figure 19.2. *Tap the Home button to return to the Home screen.*

Viewing the News Feed

If you're like me, you use your iPhone to catch up on friends' posts while you're on the go, or just lounging on the couch. This is probably what I use Facebook for iPhone for the most.

To display the News Feed, tap the News Feed icon on the Home screen. This displays the News Feed screen, shown in Figure 19.3. This is your Top News feed, by the way; at present, there's no way to configure this to display your Most Recent feed.

Each post is similar to what you see on the web-based News Feed. You see the name the poster, the post itself, and any photos or other attachments.

Tip

To view a friend's Profile page from the News Feed, tap his or her name in a post.

To comment on or "like" a post, press the + icon. This displays a blue bar with Like and Comment buttons, as shown in Figure 19.4.

Press the Comment button to display the Comment screen, shown in Figure 19.5; type your comment and then click the Post button. To like a post, all you have to do is press the Like button.

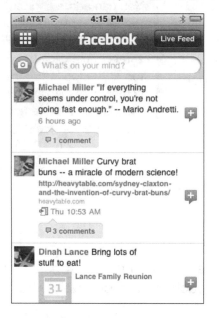

Figure 19.3. *The Facebook for iPhone News Feed.*

Figure 19.4. *Like or comment on a friend's status update.*

By the way, if a post has a picture attached, tap the picture to view it full screen. If there's a YouTube video attached, tap the video to begin playback. Unfortunately, at this point in time, the Facebook for iPhone app does not support playback of regular Facebook videos.

Tip

To view other comments to a post, tap the Comment box underneath the post.

Figure 19.5. *Entering a comment.*

Posting a Status Update

What I really like about using Facebook on my iPhone is being able to post status updates at any time, no matter where I am. Yeah, you have to hunt and peck with the iPhone's onscreen keyboard, but that's easier than trying to construct a text message from a traditional numeric keypad.

You can post status updates from either the News Feed or Profile screens. Just follow these steps:

1. From the Home screen, tap either News Feed or Profile.

2. When the next page appears, tap within the Publisher ("What's on your mind?") box.

3. This displays the Status Update screen, shown in Figure 19.6. Type your message into the text box.

4. Tap the Share button to post your update.

Figure 19.6. *Posting a new status update.*

Posting a Picture

You can also post pictures you take with your iPhone. You can post either new pictures at the time you take them or photos you already have stored on your iPhone.

Follow these steps to take a new photo:

1. From the Home screen, tap either News Feed or Profile.

2. When the next page appears, tap the Photo icon next to the Publisher box.

3. When the Photo panel appears, as shown in Figure 19.7, tap Take Photo.

4. This launches the iPhone's camera. Point your phone where you want to shoot and then tap the Photo button.

5. When the photo appears on the next screen, as shown in Figure 19.8, tap Retake if you don't like it, or Use if you do.

Figure 19.7. *Getting ready to post a picture.*

Figure 19.8. *Viewing the picture you're ready to post.*

6. When the next page appears, tap Write Caption to add some text to your update. When the Caption screen appears, enter your text then tap Done.

7. Tap Upload to upload the photo (and accompanying text) as a new status update.

To upload an existing photo as a status update, follow these steps:

1. From the Home screen, tap either News Feed or Profile.

2. When the next page appears, tap the Photo icon next to the Publisher box.

3. When the Photo panel appears, tap Choose from Library.

4. When the Photo Albums screen appears, as shown in Figure 19.9, navigate to and tap the photo you want to upload.

Figure 19.9. *Choosing a picture to upload.*

5. When the next page appears, tap Write Caption to add some text to your update. When the Caption screen appears, enter your text then tap Done.

6. Tap Upload to upload the photo (and accompanying text) as a new status update.

Viewing Friends' Profiles

Viewing a friend's profile on your iPhone is relatively easy. Just tap Friends from the Home screen to display a full list of your Facebook friends. Scroll to and tap the name of the friend you want to view.

Figure 19.10 shows a typical Profile page on the iPhone. There are three tabs at the bottom of the page: Wall, Info, and Photos. The Wall tab displays your friend's Wall, complete with recent status updates. The Info tab displays very basic (not complete) information about your friend. And the Photos tab displays your friend's photo albums.

Figure 19.10. *Viewing a Profile page with Facebook for iPhone.*

You can post a message to your friend's wall simply by tapping the Publisher box near the top of the page. When the Wall Post screen appears, enter your message and then tap Share.

Checking Messages

You can also use your iPhone to check your Facebook messages while you're on the go. Just tap the Inbox icon on the Home screen to display the Inbox screen, shown in Figure 19.11. Tap a message snippet to read the entire message.

Figure 19.11. *Viewing the Facebook for iPhone inbox.*

Chatting with Friends

Finally, you can indulge in on-the-go instant messaging via the Facebook for iPhone app. Click the Chat icon on the Home screen to display a screen of online friends. Tap a friend's name to begin the chat session.

Figure 19.12 shows what the Chat screen looks like on the iPhone. Use the onscreen keyboard to type a message, then tap the Send button. Your chat session is displayed at the top of the screen.

Figure 19.12.   *Chatting in real time with Facebook for iPhone.*

Connecting from Other Smartphones

The iPhone isn't the only smartphone supported by Facebook. There are Facebook apps for all the following phones:

- Android
- Blackberry
- INQ
- Nokia
- Palm
- Sidekick
- Sony Ericsson
- Windows Mobile

All these apps work similarly to the Facebook for iPhone app. For example, Figure 19.13 shows the News Feed on Facebook for Android; it looks a lot like the News Feed screen on the iPhone.

Figure 19.13. *The News Feed screen on Facebook for Android.*

If your web-enabled phone doesn't have a dedicated Facebook app, you can still use your phone's Web browser to connect to the Facebook Mobile website. Just navigate to m.facebook.com and you see a version of the Facebook site that's optimized for mobile browsers. As you can see in Figure 19.14, the Home page displays your News Feed, with the Publisher box at the top. Other tabs display your Profile page, your Friends list, and the messages in your Inbox.

Figure 19.14. *The Home page of the Facebook Mobile site.*

Connecting via Text Message

How can you connect to Facebook if you don't have a fancy smartphone? It's easy, really, as Facebook enables you to post via simple SMS text messages from any mobile phone. You can also receive text messages when your friends post to their Walls.

To use Facebook via text, you first have to activate your individual phone. Here's how to do it:

1. Click Account on the Facebook toolbar and then click Account Settings.

2. When the My Account page appears, click the Mobile tab.

3. When the Mobile tab appears, click the Register for Facebook Text Messages link.

4. When the Activate Facebook Texts dialog box appears, as shown in Figure 19.15, select your country and mobile phone carrier from the lists and then click Next.

Figure 19.15. *Activating Facebook texts.*

5. The next dialog box contains instructions on how to register your phone. You need to use your phone to text the short message displayed here to the number listed (32665 or FBOOK) and then click Next.

6. Facebook replies to your text with a unique mobile activation code. Enter this code into the next dialog box on your computer screen and click Confirm.

7. Facebook displays the confirmation page shown in Figure 19.16. This page lists all the different notifications that can be sent to your phone—messages, wall posts, comments, friend requests, and the like. Check those notifications you want to receive as text messages and uncheck those you don't.

Figure 19.16. *Configuring text messaging for your Facebook account.*

8. Scroll down to the Whose Status Updates Should Go to My Phone? section and enter the names of those friends whose status updates you want to receive as text messages.

9. To limit when you receive text messages (for example, to not receive messages while you're sleeping), scroll to the What Times Should Texts Be Sent to My Phone? section and specify a time range, or check the Anytime option.

10. If your phone's text plan is limited, scroll to the How Many Texts Should Be Sent? section and enter how many daily texts you want to receive, maximum.

11. If you want to receive a confirmation text every time you make a post, scroll to that section and check Yes.

12. When you're done configuring, click the Save Preferences button.

After you have your phone activated and configured, you can send status updates to Facebook via text messages from your phone. All you have to do is send your texts to 32665 (or FBOOK) and you're good to go.

Facebook Mobile? Really?

Okay, I almost hesitated to add this chapter to the book. That's because using Facebook on a mobile phone is something that the young folks do—a lot. It's a less popular option for us older, texting-challenged people.

As you're well aware, the young people today are born with mobile phones grafted onto their palms. They emerge from the womb texting about the experience: "dr hit me rdy 4 lnch."

To the younger generation, texting is as natural as breathing. It's no surprise that they often opt to do the Facebook thing via cell phone, too. They always have their phones with them; their computers, not so much. So they do the configuration thing and receive friend's updates and messages via text messages, and make their own posts via texts, as well. It works well for them.

Us older folks, however, are less comfortable with and often less skilled at the whole texting thing. My stepdaughter can do ten texts in the time it takes me to peck out a single one, and I've yet to figure out all the shortcuts and abbreviations she uses. It's kind of like a foreign language to me, one that requires the punching of teeny buttons with pudgy fingers. It's not a good fit.

So my sense is that grown-ups use Facebook on their phones far less often than do their offspring. That doesn't mean it doesn't have its place in your bag of tricks, or that you'll never do it. But I'm guessing you'll use your phone to make a few posts when you're away from home or the office, but probably not opt to receive text updates. Our generation is a more patient one; we can wait to check our News Feed when we're back at the computer, thank you very much.

Chapter 20

Buying and Selling in the Facebook Marketplace

Facebook is all about making social connections. But there's also a part of Facebook is more about commerce than connections. The Facebook Marketplace, as it's called, is kind of like classified ads for and by Facebook members. You can use the Marketplace to find items for sale by your friends and others on Facebook, or put stuff of your own up for sale.

Understanding the Facebook Marketplace

The Facebook Marketplace isn't a true marketplace, per se. It's really a database of classified advertisements. In this respect it's more like Craigslist than it is eBay.

Like Craigslist, the Facebook Marketplace is a listing service for online classified ads. You don't actually purchase an item from the Facebook Marketplace; you contact a seller and arrange the purchase directly from him. Facebook doesn't get involved with payment or shipping or anything like that.

The Facebook Marketplace is also like Craigslist in that there are no buyer or seller protections. If you send somebody money based on a Facebook ad and they don't ship the item, you're out of luck. Same thing if you sell something to someone and their check bounces. Don't even bother contacting Facebook about it.

It's all about personal transactions. You see an ad in the Facebook Marketplace, you contact the seller (via Facebook email), you agree on a purchase price, and you pay the seller directly. The seller then ships you the item or, if you live nearby, you go and pick it up. As I said, Facebook really isn't involved, saved for hosting the initial listing.

What can you buy or sell on the Facebook Marketplace? That's easy enough to see by examining the categories of goods and services listed on the Facebook site:

- **Stuff:** These are the "merchandise for sale" categories, including Adult; Baby & Kid Stuff; Clothes & Accessories; Collectibles; Computers; Crafts & Hobbies; Electronics; Free; Furniture; Garage & Yard Sales; Health & Beauty; Home & Garden; Movies, Music & Video Games; Musical Instruments; Office & Biz; Sporting Goods & Bicycles; Textbooks; and Everything Else.

- **Vehicles:** That's right, you can find all manner of vehicles listed for sale in the Facebook Marketplace, including Airplanes, Boats, Cars, Commercial Trucks, Heavy Equipment, Motorcycles, Parts & Accessories, Power Sports, RVs, and Everything Else. (You can also shop by make of vehicle, in case you're specifically looking for a Ford or a Honda or whatever.)

- **Rentals:** The Facebook Marketplace isn't just for buyers and sellers; it's also for renters. The categories here include Apartments, Commercial, Condos, Homes, Open Houses, Roommates, Short Term, Vacations, and Other.

- **Houses:** If you're looking to buy or sell property, look here for Commercial, Condos, Foreclosures, Homes, Land, Mobile Homes, Multi Family, Open Houses, Vacation Property, and Other.

- **Jobs:** Just like traditional classified ads, the Facebook Marketplace includes lots and lots of job listings that you can search by location.

- **Services:** It's not just about buying and selling things; the Facebook Marketplace is also a good place to buy and sell services, from music lessons to lawn care. Categories include Auto; Career; Child & Elderly Care; Cleaning; Coupons; Creative; Financial; Food & Restaurants; Health & Beauty; Home, Lawn & Garden; Legal; Lessons; Moving & Storage; Party & Entertain; Pet Services; Real Estate; Tech Help; Travel & Transportation; and Everything Else.

- **Tickets:** Want to buy tickets for a sold-out concert? Have some spare tickets to sell? Then check out these Tickets categories: Concerts, Group Events, Sports, Theater, and Other.

You can filter the items in these categories by location (X number of miles from your ZIP code), or just look at listings from your friends or friends of your friends. You can browse the categories or just search for something specific. And it's all done from within the main Facebook site.

> **Note**
>
> Even though it's very well integrated into the Facebook site, the Facebook Marketplace is actually a third-party application by Oodle, which is wholly endorsed by Facebook.

Shopping for Something to Buy

The thinking behind the Facebook Marketplace is that buyers will be more comfortable buying from people within or connected to their social circle. There's also the conceit, I suppose, that sellers who are Facebook members are somehow more reliable than sellers you find on other websites. I'm not sure I buy into that conceit, but do find that there's a lot of good stuff for sale on the Facebook Marketplace.

Browsing the Marketplace

When you're looking for something to buy, follow these steps:

1. Go to the Facebook Home page and click Marketplace in the sidebar.

2. This opens the Facebook Marketplace page, shown in Figure 20.1. By default, the page opens to listings in the city you specified in your profile information. To change the city listed, click the Change link after the city name; when the Location dialog box appears, enter a new city name or ZIP code and then pull down the Radius list and select how far away you want to search. Click the Submit button when done.

3. Click the tab for the category you want to browse: All, Stuff, Vehicles, Rentals, Houses, Jobs, Services, or Tickets.

4. When the category page appears, like the one in Figure 20.2, click the subcategory you want to browse. (The Jobs category is the only one that doesn't have subcategories.)

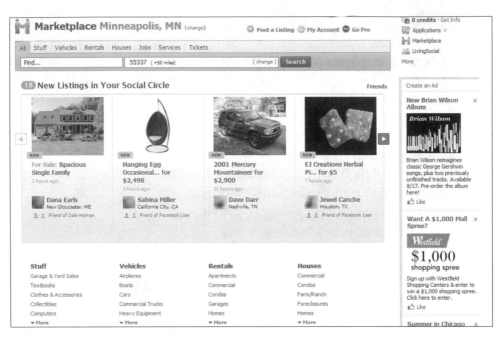

Figure 20.1.   *The main Facebook Marketplace page.*

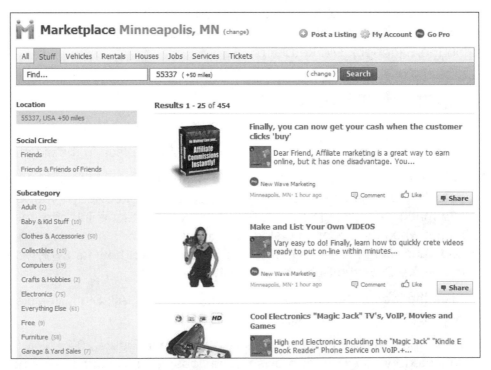

Figure 20.2.   *A main category page.*

5. When the subcategory page appears, use the category-specific controls in the sidebar to further filter the results, if you want. For example, the Clothes & Accessories subcategory, shown in Figure 20.3, lets you filter listings by price range, or to only show those listings with photos.

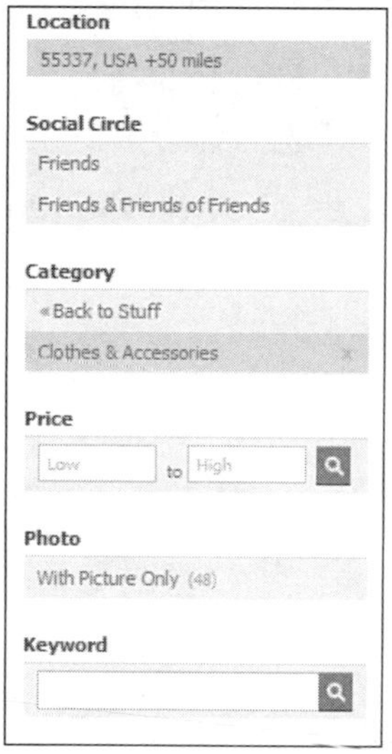

Figure 20.3.   *A subcategory page, with filters for price range and photos.*

6. To view a specific listing, click its title.

Searching the Marketplace

If you have a specific item in mind, it's faster to search for it than try to find it via browsing. Follow these steps:

1. Go to the Facebook Home page and click Marketplace in the sidebar.

2. When the Facebook Marketplace page appears, click the tab for the category you want to search: All, Stuff, Vehicles, Rentals, Houses, Jobs, Services, or Tickets.

3. Enter a short description of what you're looking for into the Find box at the top of the page, as shown in Figure 20.4.

Figure 20.4.   *Searching for items on the Facebook Marketplace.*

4. By default, Facebook searches within 50 miles of the city you specified in your profile information. To change the search range, click the Change link in the Location box (next to the Find box). When the Location dialog box appears, enter a new city name or ZIP code, then pull down the Radius list and select how far away you want to search. Click the Submit button when you're done.

5. To begin your search, click the Search button.

6. Facebook displays listings that match your query, as shown in Figure 20.5. To view a specific listing, click its title.

Figure 20.5. *The results of a Facebook Marketplace search.*

Viewing an Item Listing

Everything you need to know about an item for sale is on the item's listing page. This is the page you see when you click the item's title in the marketplace listings. As you can see in Figure 20.6, there are typically two tabs on this page; the Listing Details tab, which is the one in which you're interested, and the All Listings from *Seller* tab, which lists other items for sale from this Facebook person.

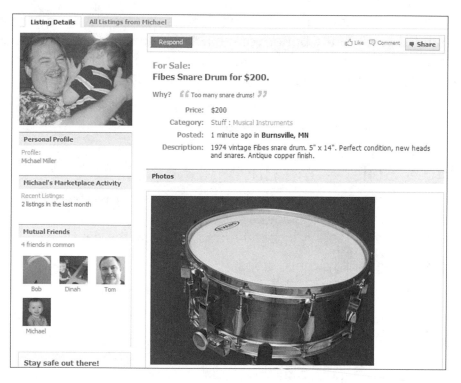

Figure 20.6. *A typical Facebook Marketplace listing.*

The Listing Details tab includes information both about the seller (in the sidebar on the left) and the item for sale. The item information includes details such as why the seller is selling it, a detailed item description, and photos of the item.

Tip

To learn more about the seller, which might or might not increase your confidence level, click the seller's name in the Personal Profile box in the sidebar.

Sharing and Commenting on a Listing

If you think this item is something in which your Facebook friends might be interested, you can share it with them via a status update or private message. Click the Share button to display the Post to Profile dialog box, enter some accompanying text and then click the Share button to post this listing as a status update. To send as a private message, open the Post to Profile dialog box, click the Send as a Message Instead link, and then enter the names of your intended recipients.

You can also comment on a given listing, just as you would comment on a status update. Scroll to the bottom of the listing page and enter your comment into the Comments box, then click the Comment & Share button. Your comment is listed to the bottom of the listing itself.

For that matter, you can "like" a listing just as you can like a status update. Just click the Like icon above the listing.

Contacting a Seller—and Buying Something

The Facebook Marketplace only facilitates the sales of merchandise; you don't involve Facebook in the actual sale. Instead, you contact the seller directly, haggle to your heart's content, and then pay the seller directly.

To contact a seller, follow these steps:

1. Open the item listing page and click the Respond button.

2. When the Respond to *Seller* dialog box appears, as shown in Figure 20.7, enter your email address in the From box.

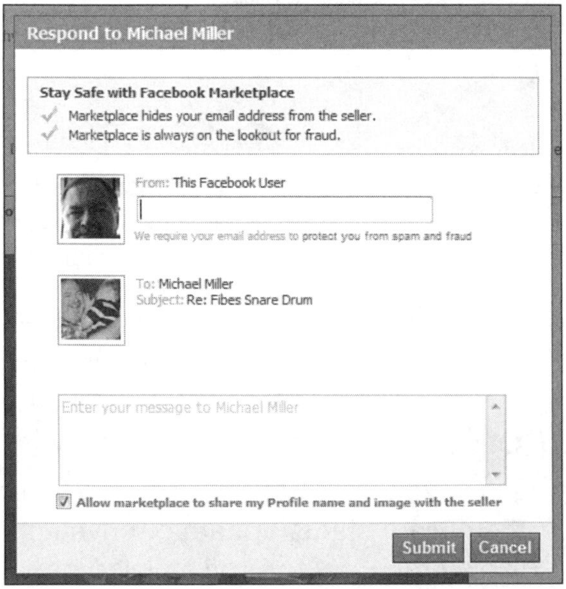

Figure 20.7.   *Responding to an item for sale.*

3. Enter your message into the large text box. This should be something along the lines of "I'm interested in buying this thing. Please contact me so we can discuss."

4. By default, Facebook shares your Profile information with the seller. If you'd rather not, uncheck the Allow Marketplace to Share My Profile Name and Image with the Seller Option. (Know, however, that some sellers might not respond to an anonymous buyer.)

5. Click the Submit button.

Facebook sends your message to the seller. If the seller is interested, he'll get back in touch with you via Facebook. It's up to the two of you to negotiate the final price, arrange payment, and get the thing shipped to you. In other words, it's now out of Facebook's hands.

Tip

Given that Facebook, by default, displays only those listings within 50 miles of your location, you might want to pick up the item rather than have it shipped to you.

Caution

The usual cautions apply when you're purchasing any item through the Facebook Marketplace as they do when purchasing any item found via a classified advertisement. It's always good to see the item before you buy, you should take care when visiting a seller's residence, and, after you get the item, it's pretty much caveat emptor—let the buyer beware.

Selling Your Own Stuff

Where do the listings in the Facebook Marketplace come from? From your fellow Facebook members, of course. Which means that you can also use the marketplace to list items you want to sell.

Listing an Item for Sale

There is no charge for listing items on the Facebook Marketplace. That's right, unlike eBay, all listings are free—the seller doesn't pay, nor does the buyer. So list as many items as you'd like, it won't cost you anything but your time.

To list an item for sale, follow these steps:

1. Go to the Facebook Home page and click Marketplace in the sidebar.

2. When the Facebook Marketplace page appears, click the Post a Listing link at the top of the page.

3. When the Post Listing dialog box appears, as shown in Figure 20.8, enter your Location (country and ZIP code).

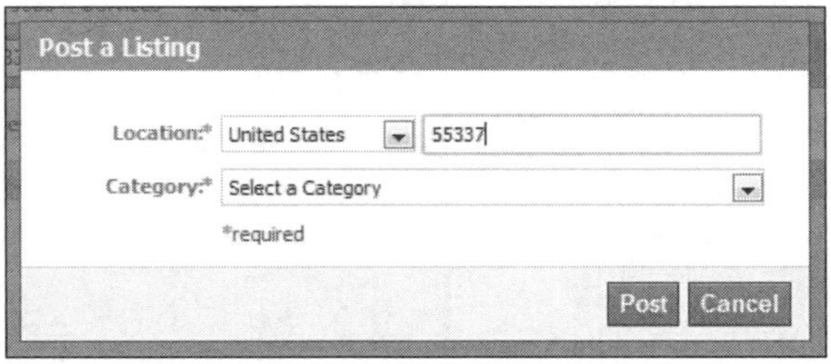

Figure 20.8.   *Getting ready to list an item for sale.*

4. Pull down the Category list and make a selection: Stuff (items for sale), Vehicles, Rentals, Houses, Jobs, Services, or Tickets.

5. After you select a category, the Post Listing dialog box expands with category-specific boxes, as shown in Figure 20.9. Select the relevant Subcategory from the pull-down list.

Figure 20.9.   *The more complete Post Listing dialog box.*

6. Enter the title for your listing into the Title box.

7. If you're selling the item, make sure the For Sale option is checked and then enter your selling price into the Price box.

8. Enter the reason for your sale into the Why Are You Selling It? box.

9. Enter a detailed description of the item into the Description box. Include all relevant details, including age, size, color, condition, and the like.

> **Note**
>
> Facebook also lets you give away items for free (check the Free option) or let people know you're looking to buy a given item (check the Wanted option).

10. Because most items sell faster if they're accompanied by photos, you should take a few digital photos of what you're selling. To upload these photos, click the Choose File button to display the Open dialog box; navigate to and select the file(s) to upload and then click the Open button.

11. If you uploaded one or more photos, check the option that says you have the right to distribute these photos.

12. Click the Post button.

13. You're now prompted to post this listing as a Facebook status update. Click the Publish button to do so, or click Skip to not post it.

That's it; your listing is now live.

Ending Your Listing

If and when a fellow Facebook member is interested in your item, you receive a message from that person, via Facebook, to that effect. You can then reply to that person and answer questions, accept the offer, arrange for shipment or pickup, or whatever. You are under no obligation to sell to any given person. What kind of payment you accept (cash, check, whatever) is totally up to you.

After you sell an item, you need to remove it from the Facebook Marketplace. To do this, follow these steps:

1. Go to the Facebook Home page and click Marketplace in the sidebar.

2. When the Facebook Marketplace page appears, click the My Account link at the top of the page.

3. This displays the listings page, shown in Figure 20.10, with the All Listings tab selected. Go to the listing you want to end and click the Close link for that listing.

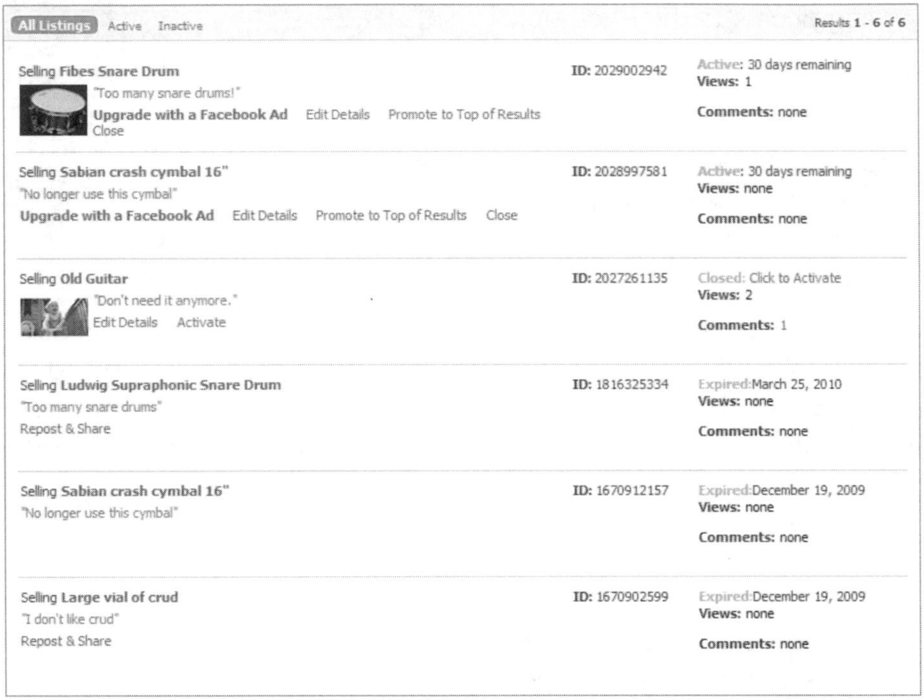

Figure 20.10.   *All of your listings displayed on a single page.*

4. When the Close Listing dialog box appears, as shown in Figure 20.11, check Yes if you sold the item, or No if it didn't sell but you want to close the listing anyway.

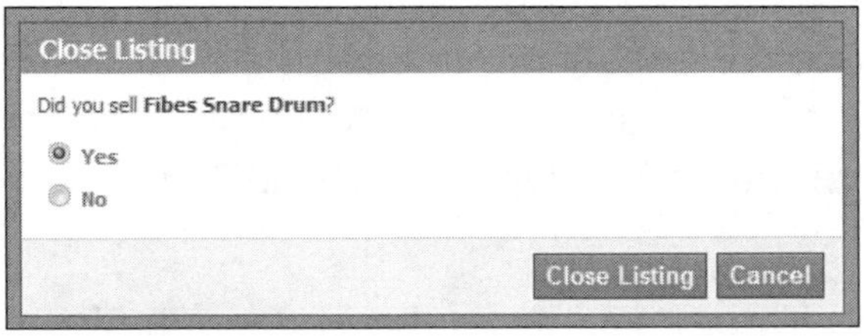

Figure 20.11.   *Closing a Facebook Marketplace listing.*

5. Click the Close Listing button.

6. You're now prompted to publish your closed listing as a Facebook status update. To do so, click the Publish button. To not do so, click Skip.

And that's how the Facebook Marketplace works. Pretty simple, really.

Facebook Marketplace Versus eBay and Craigslist

If you've been around the Internet for any length of time, you're probably familiar with the other, more well-known marketplaces for buying and selling merchandise—eBay and Craigslist. You might be wondering how the Facebook Marketplace compares to both.

Comparing the Facebook Marketplace to eBay is a bit of an apples to oranges sort of proposition. That's because eBay functions as a full-service middleman. eBay not only facilitates item listings, it also handles all contact between buyers and sellers, offers payment services (via PayPal), provides assistance for shipping (via the USPS and others), and offers a buyer protection plan to guard against fraudulent sellers. Facebook does none of these things.

In addition, eBay offers both fixed-price listings and those fun online auctions, where potential buyers bid up the price on items for sale. Facebook offers only fixed-price listings, with no apparatus in place for conducting online auctions.

Craigslist offers a more relevant comparison. Like Craigslist, Facebook is essentially a service for online classified ads. Neither Facebook or Craigslist offer payment services, shipping assistance, or buyer protection plans. Both are purely item listings only, leaving the ultimate sale for the buyers and sellers to arrange between themselves.

The big difference between Craigslist and the Facebook Marketplace is one of size. Craigslist offers many times more items for sale than does Facebook, so you're more likely to find what you want there. If you're a seller, Craigslist offers many more potential buyers than does the Facebook Marketplace; despite Facebook's size, relatively few members actually use the Facebook Marketplace.

So you might want to give the Facebook Marketplace a spin, but know that Craigslist is always there if you can't find what you want—or, if you're selling and you don't get any buyers.

Part VI

Basic Facebook Housekeeping Chores

Chapter 21

Keeping Some Things Private

Facebook is not a paragon of privacy. It's a *social* network, after all, and being social means sharing of oneself. In Facebook's case, it also means sharing all your personal information by default—which is certainly one way to network with others.

Unfortunately, all this sharing poses a problem for those of us who'd prefer to maintain some semblance of a private life. If you share everything with everyone, then all sorts of information can get out—and be seen by people you don't want seeing it. It's a bit of a challenge, and ultimately it involves a degree of compromise to maintain a social profile while protecting your personal privacy.

Understanding Facebook Privacy

Facebook is all about connecting users to one another. That's how the site functions, after all, by encouraging "friends" and all sorts of public sharing of information.

You can understand why Facebook operates in this fashion. The powers that be think they can better connect users with one another, and build a stronger community, by making public all of a user's likes and dislikes. After all, how can you connect to others if you don't know anything about them?

I admit, all this makes some degree of sense in the abstract; the more we know about each other, the more likely we are to find people to interact with. But Facebook might take this openness a tad too far.

That's because Facebook, by default, shares all your information with just about everybody. Not just your friends, or friends of your friends, but the entire membership of the site. And not just with Facebook members, either; Facebook also shares your information with third-party applications and games and with other sites on the Web.

Do you really want your personal information and Facebook status updates shared with millions of strangers and hundreds of thousands of unrelated websites? I think most people would say no, but this is precisely what Facebook now does—unless you specify otherwise.

So, by default, Facebook tries to link all sorts of things together. It shares your Facebook data with partner websites, in the guise of helping those sites "personalize" their content for you. It shares your name with entertainers and companies you say you like, to help them "connect" with you as a fan. And it shares your personal information and the posts you make to everyone on the Facebook site, even if you'd rather keep that information private.

Fortunately, you can configure Facebook to be much less public than it is by default. While this originally was somewhat difficult to do (Facebook didn't put all the settings in the same place—or make them easy to find, for that matter), Facebook has made some changes that make it a trifle easier to control which people and what applications can see your personal information.

Note

This sharing with other websites is part of Facebook's Open Graph technology, which helps other sites link to the Facebook site. This can come in the form of a common sign-in (you log onto the other site using your Facebook ID and password), a Facebook "like" button on the other site, or the wholesale sharing of information about you between the two sites.

Note

Why does Facebook encourage this wholesale sharing of your private information? It's all about Facebook's apparent quest for world domination. Facebook wants to be your gateway to the Internet, your home page on the Web, or, let's be honest, your entire online operating system. Nice for them, less so for you or anyone who values his or her online privacy.

Changing Facebook's Privacy Settings

Most of Facebook's privacy settings can be accessed from a single gateway page. Not all settings are on this page, but you can get to them from here.

To display the Choose Your Privacy Settings page, shown in Figure 21.1, click Account on the Facebook toolbar and select Privacy Settings. The page you now see leads you to everything privacy-related on the site.

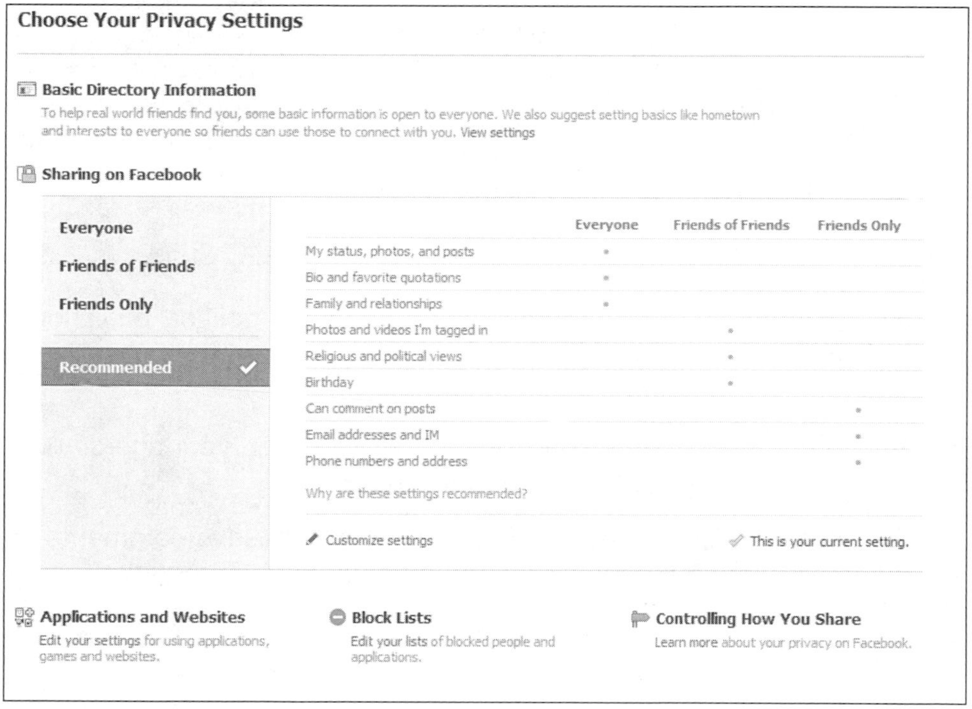

Choose Your Privacy Settings

Basic Directory Information
To help real world friends find you, some basic information is open to everyone. We also suggest setting basics like hometown and interests to everyone so friends can use those to connect with you. View settings

Sharing on Facebook

	Everyone	Friends of Friends	Friends Only
Everyone			
Friends of Friends	My status, photos, and posts	•	
Friends Only	Bio and favorite quotations	•	
	Family and relationships	•	
Recommended ✓	Photos and videos I'm tagged in		•
	Religious and political views		•
	Birthday		•
	Can comment on posts			•
	Email addresses and IM			•
	Phone numbers and address			•
	Why are these settings recommended?			

✎ Customize settings   ✓ This is your current setting.

Applications and Websites
Edit your settings for using applications, games and websites.

Block Lists
Edit your lists of blocked people and applications.

Controlling How You Share
Learn more about your privacy on Facebook.

Figure 21.1. *Facebook's Choose Your Privacy Settings gateway page.*

Sharing Your Personal Information—or Not

You configure most of your important privacy settings directly from the Choose Your Privacy Settings page. It's the Sharing on Facebook section that's key, as this is where you tell Facebook what information you want to share with whom.

There are nine settings included in this section:

- **My status, photos, and posts:** Literally, your status updates, photo uploads, and other Facebook posts.

- **Bio and favorite quotations:** Your detailed biography, as well as your favorite quotations.

- **Family and relationships:** Any family members you've identified, as well as your relationship status—and who you're in a relationship with.

- **Photos and videos I'm tagged in:** These aren't your photos and videos, but rather uploads from your friends and other users in which you're tagged.

> **! Caution**
>
> Pay particular attention to the Photos and Videos I'm Tagged In setting. You want to protect against any "friends" who upload compromising pictures or movies of you. (And they might exist, too!)

- **Religious and political views:** The religious and political affiliations you entered as part of your profile. (Who really needs to know where you go to church—or how you voted in the last election?)

- **Birthday:** Sounds innocuous, but as you get older, your age can work against you. Why publicize how old you are?

- **Can comment on posts:** This controls who can leave comments to your status updates. After all, you might not want any comments.

- **Email addresses and IM:** This is a good one. Do you really want to publicly display your online contact info?

- **Phone number and address:** Ditto with this. It's not necessarily a good idea to have real-world contact information displayed for any weirdo (or ex-boyfriend or -girlfriend) to see.

You can choose to share any of these items with everyone on the Facebook site, your friends on Facebook (that is Friends Only), and your friends and their friends (that is, Friends of Friends).

To apply the same sharing settings across all these items, select Everyone, Friends of Friends, or Friends Only to the left of the list. Even better, select Recommended and Facebook applies the settings as shown in Table 21.1.

Table 21.1 Facebook's Recommended Privacy Settings

Sharing Option	Setting
My status, photos, and posts	Everyone
Bio and favorite quotations	Everyone
Family and relationships	Everyone
Photos and videos I'm tagged in	Friends of Friends
Religious and political views	Friends of Friends
Birthday	Friends of Friends
Can comment on posts	Friends Only
Email addresses and IM	Friends Only
Phone numbers and address	Friends Only

Setting Custom Sharing Options

So far so good. But what if you don't want to share your photos with everyone? Or what if don't want to share your phone number with *anyone*? (Note a lack of "no one" as a sharing option.) Well, now we have to go to Facebook's custom sharing settings.

To set custom settings, go to the Choose Your Privacy Settings page, click the Customize Settings link. This displays the Customize Settings page, shown in Figure 21.2, which has a lot more options than the previous page.

There are three reasons I like this Customize Settings page. First, this page offers a lot more things that you can configure—specific contact information, website info, and the like. Next, you can choose the three primary sharing options (Everyone, Friends of Friends, and Friends Only) for each specific item, not just for groups of items. And, most important, for each item listed, you indicate specific people who either can or cannot see that piece of information. For that matter, you can choose to hide any given item from everyone except yourself.

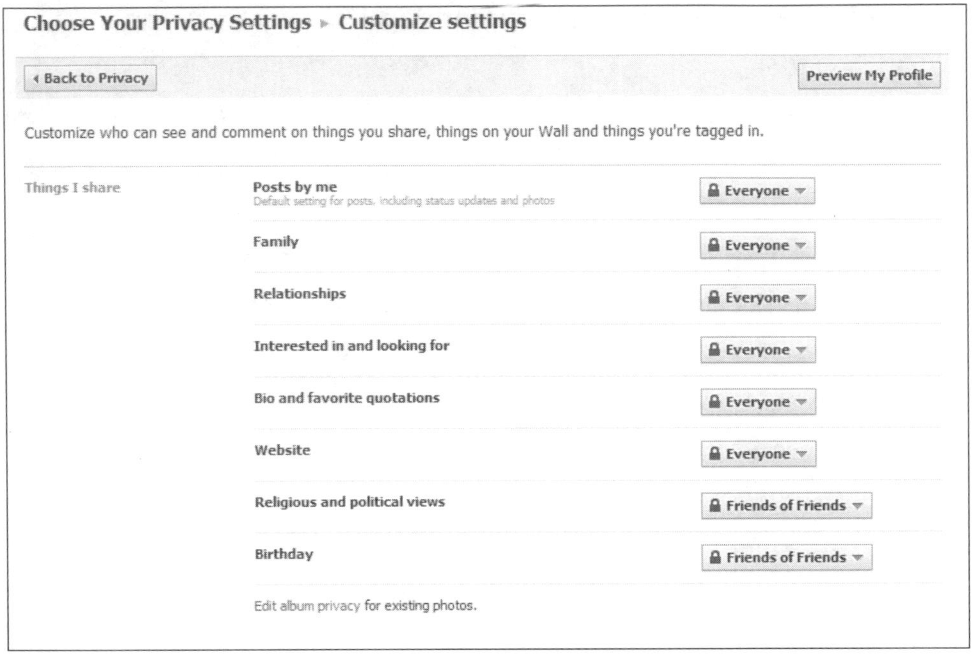

Figure 21.2. *Customizing Facebook's sharing settings.*

How does it work? Follow these steps to customize any given sharing setting:

1. From the Customize Settings page, click the big button to the far right of the item and then click Customize. This displays the Custom Privacy dialog box, shown in Figure 21.3.

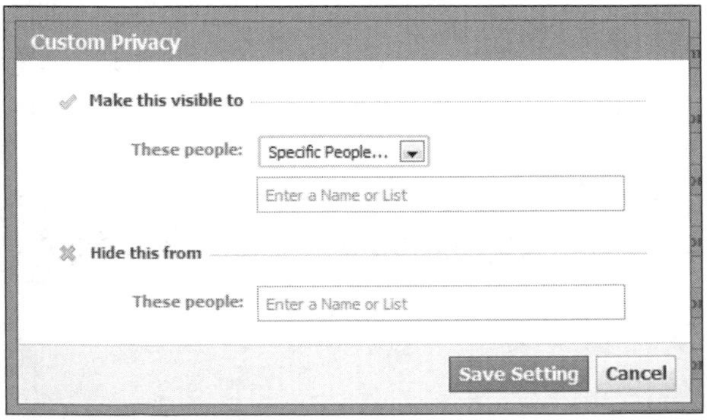

Figure 21.3. *Determining which individuals can or can't view specific information.*

2. To hide an item from everyone, pull down the Make This Visible To list and select Only Me.

3. To make an item visible only to specific people, pull down the Make This Visible To list and select Specific People and then enter the names of those Facebook users you want to see the info.

4. To hide an item only from specific people, enter their names into the Hide This From box. (This is a good way to hide specific info from your boss or spouse—or your kids.)

5. Click the Save Setting button when you're done.

> ☑ Tip
>
> Remember, you can also determine who can view your status updates on a post-by-post basis. When you enter a new status update, you see a lock icon with a down arrow beneath the text box; click this to display the privacy menu of Everyone, Friends of Friends, Only Friends, or Customize. Make your selection and this particular post will only be viewable by the group you select.

Hiding Your Information from Other Websites

One big concern I have with Facebook is how much of my information it shares with other websites. Facebook is on a drive, it seems, to connect everybody with everything, and that means sharing as much information as possible with other sites—which is something not everyone is comfortable with.

So here's a simple way to make sure Facebook doesn't share your information with other websites: Don't log onto these sites with your Facebook profile! That's right, if a website doesn't know you're on Facebook, or who you are on Facebook, it can't link to your Facebook profile. So when you go to a site and you're prompted to use your Facebook ID to log in, just don't do it. Use your normal ID for that site instead—and if you don't yet have an ID, establish one separate from your Facebook ID.

There's more. If, when you visit a website, you see a blue bar at the top of the page informing you that this site is using Facebook "to personalize your experience," you'll also see a "No Thanks" link in the bar. Click "No Thanks" and the site won't use your Facebook data.

In addition, you can configure Facebook to turn off this data-sharing feature. Follow these steps to disable what Facebook calls "instant personalization:"

1. Navigate to the Choose Your Privacy Settings page.

2. Click the Edit Your Settings link in the Applications and Websites section at the bottom of the page.

3. When the next page appears, scroll to the Instant Personalization section and click the Edit Settings button.

4. When the following page appears, as shown in Figure 21.4, *uncheck* the Enable Instant Personalization on Partner Websites option.

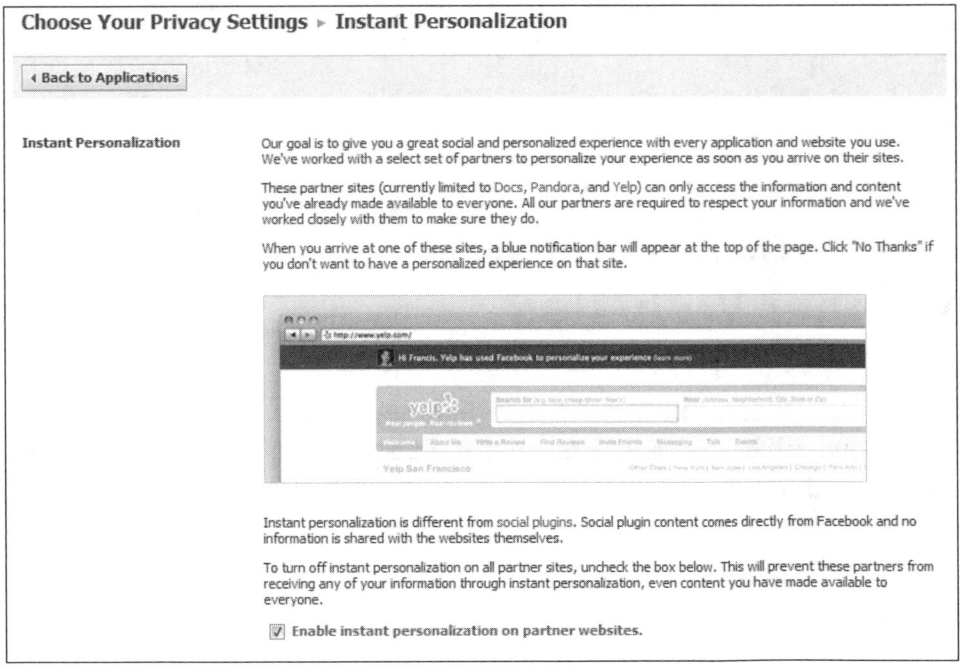

Figure 21.4. *Disabling Facebook's instant personalization feature.*

That's it. By unchecking this one obscure option box, you ensure that Facebook no longer prompts you to nor automatically share your data with other websites.

Removing Unwanted Fan Pages

Something funny happened to me the other day. When I logged onto Facebook and started reading my News Feed, I discovered that Bruce Springsteen had left a message for me. This was a bit of a surprise, as I'm not close pals with the Boss; heck, we're not even Facebook friends, nor had I clicked to become a "fan" of his on the site. But now all of a sudden we *were* friends, and I was seeing all of his status updates in my News Feed.

What's up with this? It's simple, really. Facebook decided to make me a "fan" of all of the musicians I said I liked in my profile. It also decided to make me a "fan" of all the books I mentioned in my profile, and all the movies, and all the actors and actresses and hobbies and activities and everything else that was listed there. Man, I like a lot of stuff!

To be fair, Facebook at one point displayed a window asking my permission to do this, in so many words. Heck, you probably saw a similar notice and did what I did, which was to give blanket approval. Not a good move, as it turns out, but one that can be corrected.

If you want to remove your allegiance to unwanted fan pages, follow these steps:

1. Click Account in the Facebook toolbar and select Edit Friends.
2. When the next page appears, click Pages in the sidebar.
3. Facebook now displays a complete list of all the fan pages to which you're subscribed, as shown in Figure 21.5; there are probably a lot more here than you might have thought. To "unlike" a particular page, click the X on the far right side of the listing.

When you "x"-out a page in this fashion, you're no longer a fan and will no longer receive updates from that person or company or group. Problem solved!

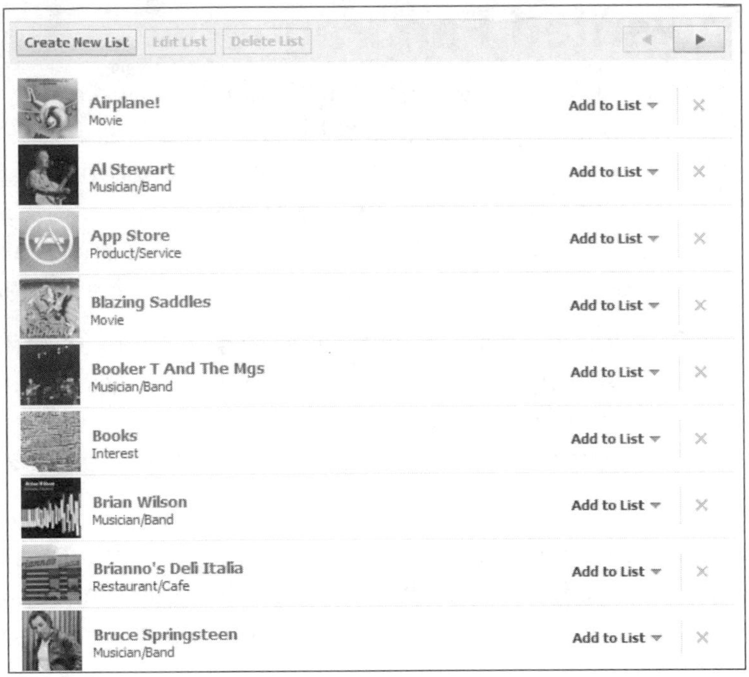

Figure 21.5. Viewing—and removing—Facebook pages. (Hey, I'm friends with the Boss!)

What to Keep Private—and What to Share

All this discussion about configuring Facebook so that it doesn't share everything with everybody begs the question, just what should you share on Facebook? And is there a better way to keep your private details more private?

First question first. What information is best kept private—or at least exposed only to your closest friends? This depends to a degree on your personal comfort level, and your personal life. But in general, you shouldn't share any information that might prove embarrassing to you or your family, or that might compromise your current job or future job prospects.

Naturally, what all this means is going to differ from person to person. If you work for an ultra-conservative boss, for example, you might not want him to know that you're a dyed-in-the-wool liberal. And if all your friends are agnostics, you might not want to publicize that you're a born-again Christian.

But it goes further than that. If you're preaching the "just say no" drug message to your kids, you might not want to list *Cheech & Chong's Up in Smoke* as one of your favorite movies; it might compromise your integrity on the matter just a bit. For that matter, you might want to hide all those photos that show you drinking margaritas on the beach, for both your kids' sake and to ward off any awkward questions from teetotalling employers.

In fact, pictures can be more damaging than words. A picture of you holding a cigarette in your hand could be used by your insurance company to raise your rates. Photos of you partying hardy or just acting goofy can raise doubts about your decision-making abilities. Do you really want your boss or your kids or your ex-husband's lawyer to see you in compromising positions?

The same goes with what you post in status updates. There are stories, some of them true, of careless (and carefree) employees posting about this afternoon's golf game when they were supposed to be home sick from work. Employers can and will keep track of you online, if you're stupid enough to post all your comings and goings.

And it's not just factual stuff. Spouting off your opinions is a common-enough Facebook activity, but some people will disagree with you, or take more serious offense. Do you really want to start an online flame war over something you posted in haste on your Wall?

For that matter, it's a really bad idea to use Facebook to criticize your employer, the people you work with, or just people you associate with in the community. Posting about how much you hate your job will eventually get back to your boss, and then you've got a lot of 'splainin' to do, Lucy.

You see, on Facebook, discretion is definitely the better part of valor. When in doubt, hide it. Or, better still, don't post it or upload it in the first place. It's okay to keep some thoughts to yourself; you don't have to post every little thing you think or that happens to you.

Then there's the issue of your contact information. Here's what I think: You shouldn't make any contact information public. If someone wants to contact you, they can post on your Profile page or send you a Facebook message. They don't have to be able to contact you via regular email, ring you up on the phone, or show up on your doorstep. There are too many nutcases out there. Heck, there's just a lot of people I used to know that I don't want to deal with any more. I don't want to make it easy for these people to get in touch with me. I prefer to keep my distance from them.

Bottom line, then, is this: Be careful about the information you post. It's better to keep most of your personal information private.

Protecting Your Kids—and Grandkids—on Facebook

It's not just your own personal information you have to worry about on Facebook. If you have younger children or grandchildren online, you should be concerned about how they use the site, and what information they share.

Here's the thing with younger folks on Facebook: They tend to be very, very open about their lives, to share just about everything with everyone. While you might have a few dozen friends, your kids will have hundreds of friends. Now, they don't know all these people personally, but they share all their innermost thoughts and personal information with them, anyway. And they think nothing of it.

The problem is, everything that can come back to bite you about Facebook can hurt your kids, too. An ill-advised post about a hated teacher could put your child in hot water in school. A gripe about a boss can cost your child his part-time job. A nasty comment about another kid can result in an online flame war—or something worse.

And, speaking of worse, check out some of the photos your kids and their friends post online. Yes, they're stupid enough to upload pictures of themselves doing all sorts of stupid, unethical, and sometimes illegal stuff. Drinking, smoking, drugs, sex, kids don't think twice about posting all sorts of compromising pictures. Not very smart of them, but then, how smart were you at that age?

The point is, you need to monitor what your kids do online, and steer them away from the most damaging behavior. You probably can't keep them from making dumb posts, but you can discourage them from doing so—and, hopefully, delete offending posts or incriminating photos after the fact. Kids will be kids, after all, and there's only so much monitoring you can do.

But that's not the only thing you need to be concerned about, especially with younger kids. Facebook can be home to dangerous predators, who use the site to befriend victims. There's nothing to say that the 13 year-old girl on your child's friends list is actually a 13 year-old girl; it could a 40 year-old male predator, and you'd never know.

To that point, you should stress to your kids the dangers of meeting up with anonymous "friends" from Facebook. It's okay to share messages online, but when it comes to meeting in the real world, extreme caution is called for. Your kids need to know that people aren't always who they say they are online, and that real dangers exist out in the world. They should never, *ever* arrange for an unescorted real-world meeting with a Facebook friend they've never seen in person before. If they insist on meeting up with an unknown "friend," make sure it's in a public place and be there yourself to supervise the meeting. Your children's safety is paramount, and no amount of social networking should get in the way of that.

Chapter 22

Managing Your Facebook Account

We end our tour of Facebook for grown-ups by looking at all the settings in your Facebook account. We covered Facebook's privacy settings in the previous chapter, and that's a lot of the settings you can configure. But there's more, and you probably need to know how to edit them. After all, you need to let Facebook know if things change in your life.

Changing Account Settings

Your Facebook account contains your basic personal information—your name, email address, password, and the like. What do you do if you change your name after a divorce (or remarriage), get a new email account, or find that your password is compromised? Fortunately, Facebook lets you easily change all of these items.

All you have to do is click Account on the Facebook toolbar and then select Account Settings. When the My Account page appears, click the Settings tab. As you

 Tip

If you're a woman and have been married at least once but you still want your high school friends to find you on Facebook, change your middle name on the Facebook site to include your maiden name—and any other married names you've collected previous to your current one. So, for example, if you were Tammy Smith in high school but are Tammy Borgendorfer now, you should call yourself Tammy Smith Borgendorfer on Facebook. This way anyone searching Facebook for Tammy Smith will still find you.

can see in Figure 22.1, all your basic account information is here, including the following:

Figure 22.1.   *Managing your Facebook account settings.*

- **Name:** You can change your first, middle, and last names, as well as enter an alternate name (like a nickname) you'd rather go by. You can also select how you want your name displayed—first name first or last name first.

- **Username:** This is a little different from a nickname. A Facebook username actually affects the URL, or Web address, of your Facebook Profile page. If you choose to enter a username, that username becomes your Facebook address. For example, if you choose the username "bobbysmith," your Facebook URL is www.facebook.com/bobbysmith. The problem with usernames is that all the good ones are probably already taken. What you have to do is enter your desired username, click the

> **Tip**
>
> If the obvious usernames are taken, try using alternatives such as "bobby.smith," "bobby-smith," "bobbysmith2010," and so forth.

Check Availability button, and see if it's free. If it is, great. If not, Facebook tells you so and you can try again.

- **Email:** This is the email address that Facebook uses to contact you. You can enter more than one address, and specify a given address as the main contact. You can also remove old or unused email addresses. The only thing is, you have to have at least one email address on file with Facebook, so they can contact you if need be. You don't have to display this address, of course; that's determined by your Facebook privacy settings, as discussed in Chapter 21, "Keeping Some Things Private."

- **Password:** You can, at any time, change the password you use to log onto the Facebook site. This is recommended if you think someone has guessed your password. Heck, it's good security to change your password periodically, just to keep the bad guys guessing.

- **Linked Accounts:** Facebook lets you link your Facebook account with other accounts you might have at the following sites and services: Google, MySpace, Yahoo!, Myopenid, Verisign PIP, and OpenID. If you log onto one of these other sites and services, you are automatically logged onto Facebook, as well.

- **Privacy:** Don't be alarmed; this isn't a new set of privacy settings. When you click the Manage link in the Privacy section, you're taken to the Change Your Privacy Settings page we discussed in Chapter 21.

- **Account Security:** If you like, Facebook can notify you if someone tries to access your account from a computer or mobile device you haven't used before. It's a nice security measure, but can also be annoying if it's you who's doing the accessing.

- **Deactivate Account:** Click here if you want to leave Facebook. We discuss this option at the end of this chapter.

> **Note**
>
> Learn more about Facebook's privacy settings in Chapter 21, "Keeping Some Things Private."

> **Note**
>
> By default, you see Facebook in English. If English isn't your first language (and if that's the case, why and how are you reading this book?), Go to the My Account page, click the Language tab, and then select a different language from the pull-down list. At present, you can view Facebook in everything from Afrikaans to Turkish and just about anything in-between.

To change a given setting, click the Change or Manage link to the right of that item. This changes the My Settings page to display the relevant information for that item. For example, when you click Change Your Name, the page changes to that in Figure 22.2, with boxes First Name, Middle Name, Last Name, and Full Alternate Name, as well as a pull-down list to select how you want your name displayed (Display Full Name). Each item on this page has its own unique information boxes for you to work with.

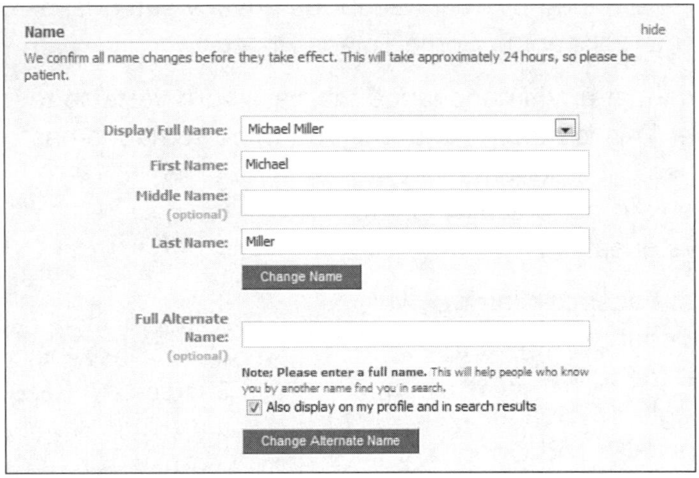

Name   hide

We confirm all name changes before they take effect. This will take approximately 24 hours, so please be patient.

Display Full Name: Michael Miller

First Name: Michael

Middle Name: (optional)

Last Name: Miller

[Change Name]

Full Alternate Name: (optional)

Note: **Please enter a full name.** This will help people who know you by another name find you in search.

☑ Also display on my profile and in search results

[Change Alternate Name]

Figure 22.2. *Changing your name.*

Controlling When and How Facebook Contacts You

Facebook is all about communication. So much so, that the site itself likes to communicate with you—more frequently than you might like, actually.

That's right, Facebook is set up to send you all sorts of messages. By default, Facebook sends you an email when someone sends you a message, adds you as a friend, confirms a friend request, tags you in a post, tags you in a photo, comments on a photo in which you were tagged, invites you to an event, or just updates his or her own Facebook profile. That's a lot of messages—too many for my tastes.

Fortunately, you can control which of these events triggers a message from Facebook—and whether you receive that message via email or on your mobile phone. All you have to do is click Account on the Facebook toolbar and then select Account Settings. When the My Account page appears, click the Notifications tab.

As you can see in Figure 22.3, this page contains a ton of different activities. You can check the option to be notified of this activity via email or SMS (text message on your mobile phone). You can opt to be notified on both devices, on just one, or on neither. That's right, if you don't want to be notified when a particular event happens, just uncheck the boxes for that item. Make sure you click the Save Changes button at the bottom of the page when you're done.

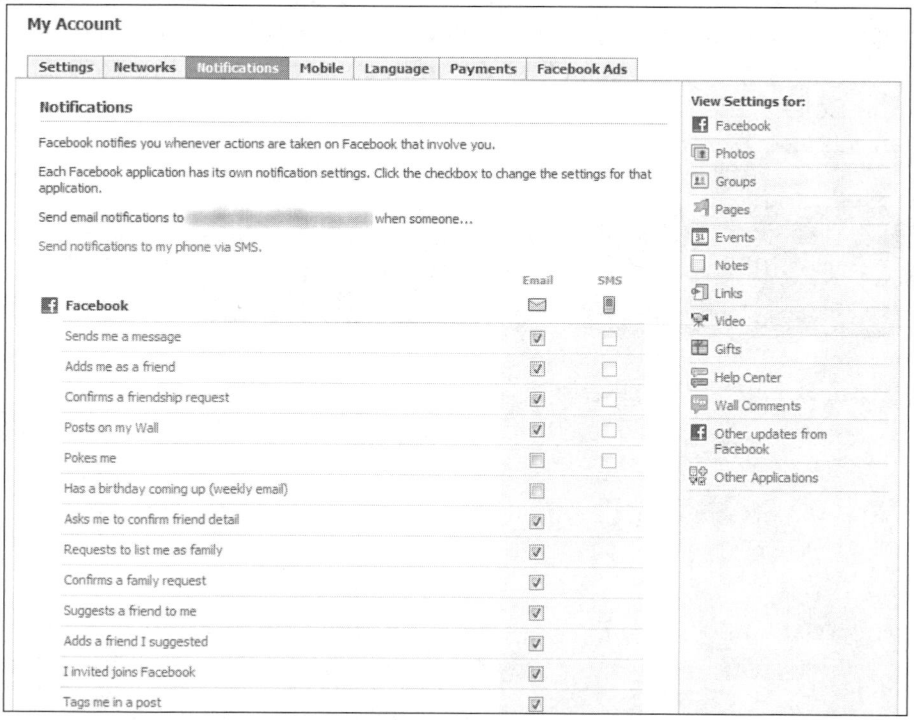

Figure 22.3. *Managing Facebook notifications.*

Leaving Facebook

It happens. You give Facebook a spin but find it's just not for you. Maybe you're just not interested. Maybe you're *too* interested, and find it consuming too much of your time. Maybe you discover that none of your real friends and family members are using the site.

Whatever the case, you can leave Facebook and delete your account. All you have to do is follow these steps:

1. Click Account on the Facebook toolbar and then select Account Settings.

2. When the My Account page appears, click the Settings tab.

3. Scroll to the Deactivate Account section at the bottom of the page.

4. Click the Deactivate link.

5. You now see the Are You Sure You Want to Deactivate Your Account? page, like the one shown in Figure 22.4. (Facebook doesn't make it easy to leave, trust me—look at all the "so and so will miss you" photos along the top!) Select a reason why you're leaving from the list.

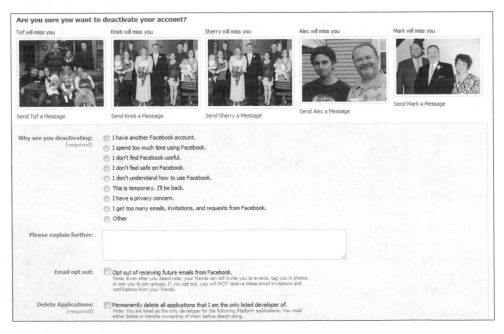

Figure 22.4. *Getting ready to delete your Facebook account.*

6. If you want to explain further, enter your reasons into the Please Explain Further box.

7. If you don't want to receive future emails from Facebook, check the Email Opt Out box.

8. If you want to permanently delete any applications you might have developed (a long shot, to be sure, but required by Facebook), check the Delete Applications box.

9. Click the Deactivate My Account button.

That's it, your Facebook presence is deleted.

> **! Caution**
>
> Know that anything you posted in the past, while it might not be on Facebook anymore, is still out there somewhere on the Web. When it comes to the Internet, nothing is ever erased; if it's out there once, it's out there forever.

Getting the Most Out of Facebook—For Grown-Ups

I've spent this entire book showing you how to use Facebook, with a particular emphasis on those features and approaches of interest to a slightly older audience—grown-ups, for want of a better word. But I'd like to wrap things up by talking about how Facebook works for grown-ups in the real world, just what you can expect to find when you go online and start getting all friendly like.

When you first sign up for Facebook, your first group of friends will be those people with whom you communicate with on a fairly regular basis already. I'm talking co-workers, family members, close friends—anybody who's in in your email contact list. It's easy for Facebook to identify these folks and hook you up, so these will be your first Facebook friends. While talking to these people on Facebook will be unique for a little while, it really doesn't offer a huge improvement over how you're already communicating.

Next up, you'll probably track down and sign up other family members. Expect to add brothers and sisters, aunts and uncles, nephews and nieces, and children and grandchildren to your friends list. In this instance, Facebook ends up being a fairly convenient way to broadcast family information without having to write a lot of individual emails or make a lot of phone calls. If you need to report the latest medical emergency or work promotion or school accomplishment, just post a single status update and the entire family is notified. Easy as pie.

The influx of family members should then inspire you to post a raft of family photos to the Facebook site. Thus inspired, prepare to set aside an evening or two to organize your digital photos and get them uploaded to Facebook. You may even want to upload some home movies, if you have them in a handy digital format. Your family will appreciate the effort.

Of course, while we're thinking about photos, you'll also be looking at the photos that your family members have uploaded. Chances are you haven't seen most of them, so you can spend some time catching up with your relative's activities, visually.

Those of us in the working world will soon add our business associates to the list. I'm talking current and past co-workers, people we work with in other companies, folks we meet at business seminars and conventions, even other local businesspeople we know. Facebook is quite useful for keeping in touch with other professionals with whom we might not otherwise have regular contact. Just remember to keep things fairly professional when you're dealing with this group of friends.

For many adult users, the next logical step is to add your neighbors to your Facebook friends list. This takes a bit more effort, as you actually have to know your neighbors' names (I don't, sorry to say) and then search for them on Facebook. While you're at it, don't forget to add those former neighbors with whom you've always meant to keep in touch, but haven't; they'll appreciate it.

Finally, you're going to start getting curious about your *old* friends. I don't mean those people older than you, but those guys and gals you hung out with in your youth. I'm talking college pals, high school buddies, and the like.

Now, tracking down old friends on Facebook is a bit of a challenge. You can search by name, of course, but good luck finding that one John Brown you used to hang with among the thousands of similarly named Johns on the Facebook site—especially as your Mr. Brown might be living in a different part of the country now.

It's even worse trying to find women who've gotten married and divorced and married again (repeat as necessary). I'm sure you have no idea that the Sally Jones you went to school with in Chicago is now Sally McWhorter of Portland, Oregon.

What you have to do to find these folks is just keep plugging away. Search and search and search some more, and don't forget to look on your friends' friends lists; it's possible that one of your friends has already found this person and done the connection thing.

You should also be prepared to receive a lot of friend requests from people you know, people you think you might know, and people who you either don't remember or never heard of. That's part of participating in the Facebook community. Accept as many requests as you want, but pay particular attention to those who don't necessarily ring a bell; they may be some of your long-lost schoolmates that found you before you found them.

It's also possible that they're people you went to school with but weren't necessarily close to. I can't tell you how many Facebook "friends" I have who know me from high school even though I barely, if at all, remember them. But that's okay; there's no harm connecting with these folks in the virtual manner, at least that I can tell.

When you do connect with old friends, be prepared for some major shocks; there's been a lot of stuff happening since you last talked. People get married, get divorced, move, change jobs, have kids, even change sexual persuasions. I admit to being a little surprised at the handful of formerly straight friends who now say they're gay; I'm equally surprised to find the occasional minister or priest on my old friends list. (None of us were priests back then, I can tell you.)

You might also be surprised—and a little shocked—to see what your old friends look like these days. I admit that I've aged, there's no denying that, but some of my friends... well, the years have not been kind. It's interesting to try to connect the dots between what someone looked like in high school and what they look like today, but I swear, some of these odd-looking ducks are strangers just claiming to be the same people I used to know. There's no resemblance there that I can see.

You also need to be prepared by what your old friends are doing and saying and thinking. When you hang out with a bunch of kids in high school, you all tend to think and act alike. What a shock, then, to find old friends who have become ultra-conservative right-wingers, tree-hugging environmentalists, religious cultists, free love swingers, or whatever. You might think you knew them then, but they're not necessarily the same people today. Life does that to you.

In fact, I guess that's the true lesson we learn from connecting with friends and family on Facebook: Life goes on. And Facebook, fortunately, helps us catch up and stay caught up with the lives of everyone we know. That's what I like about Facebook, and why I use it every day. I think you'll find it useful and interesting, too.

Symbols

W–Z

FREE Online Edition

Your purchase of **Facebook® for Grown-Ups** includes access to a free online edition for 45 days through the Safari Books Online subscription service. Nearly every Que book is available online through Safari Books Online, along with more than 5,000 other technical books and videos from publishers such as Addison-Wesley Professional, Cisco Press, Exam Cram, IBM Press, O'Reilly, Prentice Hall, and Sams.

SAFARI BOOKS ONLINE allows you to search for a specific answer, cut and paste code, download chapters, and stay current with emerging technologies.

Activate your FREE Online Edition at
www.informit.com/safarifree

> **STEP 1:** Enter the coupon code: RIKHTZG.

> **STEP 2:** New Safari users, complete the brief registration form.
> Safari subscribers, just log in.

If you have difficulty registering on Safari or accessing the online edition, please e-mail customer-service@safaribooksonline.com